THE ANSWER
TO ADDICTION

THE ANSWER TO ADDICTION

The Path to Recovery from Alcohol, Drug, Food, and Sexual Dependencies

New Expanded Edition

JOHN BURNS
AND THREE OTHER
RECOVERED ADDICTS

CROSSROAD • NEW YORK

1990

The Crossroad Publishing Company
370 Lexington Avenue, New York, NY 10017

Copyright © 1975, 1990 by The Queen's Work, Inc.

Printed in the United States of America

Library of Congress Cataloging-in-Publication Data

Burns, John, 1910 or 11–
    The answer to addiction : the path to recovery from alcohol, drug, food, and sexual dependencies / John Burns and three other recovered addicts. — New, expanded ed.
    p.   cm.
   Includes bibliographical references (p.) and index.
   ISBN 0-8245-1028-3
    1. Alcoholics—Rehabilitation—Case studies. 2. Twelve-step programs. 3. Dependency (Psychology) I. Title.
HV5275.B87   1990
616.86'1—dc20   90-1933
                                                    CIP

Acknowledgment is made for permission to reprint extracts from some of our Schoolmasters' teachings (see pages 215–251):

The People's Doctor Newsletter, by Robert S. Mendelsohn. Copyright © 1986. Reprinted with the permission of The People's Doctor Newsletter, 1578 Sherman Avenue, Evanston, IL 60201 (annual subscription $24.00).

"Psychological Factors Operating in Alcoholics Anonymous," by Harry M. Tiebout. Copyright © 1946. Reprinted with the permission of Grune & Stratton, Inc., Orlando, Florida.

The Psychological Society, by Martin L. Gross. Copyright © 1978 by Martin L. Gross. Reprinted with the permission of Random House, Inc.

CONTENTS

THE AUTHORS

This book has been planned and researched by the editors of *24 Magazine,* and written by three executive editors of the magazine, John Burns, David Randall, and Robert Calhoun, and one associate editor, Samuel Abrahamson.

All four are recovered addicts. Randall and Calhoun are recovered alcohol addicts, and Burns and Abrahamson are recovered alcohol and drug addicts. Brief stories of their lives, addictions, and recoveries are given beginning on page 14. The names are pseudonyms, enabling the authors to write openly about their membership and experience in Alcoholics Anonymous without breach of the fellowship's tradition of personal anonymity. Note that the authors speak for themselves and are not spokesmen, official or unofficial, for Alcoholics Anonymous.

Freshman author SAMUEL ABRAHAMSON, once addicted to alcohol and cocaine and a heavy user of pot and psychedelics, is twenty-seven years old*and is now in his third year of total and uninterrupted freedom from alcohol and addictive drugs. He is a former landscape gardener and is presently a printer.

Sophomore author ROBERT CALHOUN, once addicted to alcohol, is thirty-five years old and is now in his eleventh year of total and uninterrupted freedom from alcohol. He is a former track coach and professional musician and is presently a school teacher.

Junior author DAVID RANDALL, once addicted to alcohol, is fifty-one years old and is now in his sixteenth year of total and uninterrupted freedom from alcohol. He is a former real estate

*This second edition of *The Answer to Addiction* is directly reprinted from the first edition of 1975. Therefore certain dates throughout the book need to be adjusted by adding fifteen years to make them current. For instance, Abrahamson is now forty-two years old and has been alcohol-and-drug-free for eighteen years. Make similar adjustments for figures given on pages vii, 20, 31, 33, ff.

broker, advertising agency account executive, trade magazine editor, and city desk man and is presently an editorial director.

Senior author JOHN BURNS, once addicted to alcohol, codeine, barbiturates, and amphetamines, is sixty-three years old and now in his twenty-eighth year of total and uninterrupted freedom from alcohol and addictive drugs. He is a former Madison Avenue advertising man and is presently a publisher.

The authors represent a total of fifty-eight years of true recovery: complete abstinence from addictive substances and full return to responsible life. In their recovered years they have worked closely with, and helped in the recoveries of, thousands of other alcohol and drug addicts.

Note: In the matters under consideration in this book, your authors have been taught chiefly by four or five dozen basic schoolmasters—not gurus or rabbis but simply competent and highly respected teachers. The following are some of them:

In religion—
C. S. Lewis
George MacDonald
J. R. R. Tolkien
J. P. de Caussade
Malachi Martin
Jacques Ellul
The Pilgrim (and the Philokalia Fathers)
M. K. Gandhi
Frithjof Schuon (and the Sufi Saints)
Israel ben Eliezer (the Baal Shem Tov)
Ko Hung (and the Taoist masters)
In philosophy—
Lev Shestov
Martin Buber
Irving Kristol
Robert Novak

Fyodor Dostoevsky
Jacob Boehme
St. Thomas Aquinas
Plotinus
Hermes Trismegistus
In natural science—
Ernst Lehrs
Guenther Wachsmuth
In history—
Will and Ariel Durant
Bruce Catton
William Manchester
Anne Catherine Emmerich
Mary of Agreda
In medicine—
Robert Mendelsohn
Norman Cousins
Berton Roueché
David F. Musto
Samuel Hahnemann
Paracelsus
Hippocrates
In psychiatry—
Harry M. Tiebout
O. Hobart Mowrer
Thomas Szasz
C. G. Jung
In psychology—
Maurice Nicoll
Martin Gross
In magic (black and white)—
Arthur Machen
A. E. Waite
C. S. Lewis
George MacDonald

There is an Appendix in the back of the book called "A Sampler of Some of Our Schoolmasters' Teachings in the Lifesavers Way of Life," beginning on page 215, where you can get briefly acquainted with some of these people and their teachings if you wish.

Theme

The theme of this book can be stated in seven propositions:

1.

Western culture, followed recently by the whole world, has abandoned God.

2.

But God is real after all, and men cannot live without him without going out of their minds.

3.

Men who are going out of their minds urgently need relief from their pain, and alcohol and drugs provide such relief.

4.

Therefore we have a lot of drinking and drugging, and a lot of addiction.

5.

There is only one real solution to the problem: spiritual conversion, return to God. This is a demonstrated fact. God historically has proved indeed to be the Answer to addiction. All other resources have failed.

6.

The whole medical-professional-governmental attempt to deal with addiction is failing, and must continue to fail, because it is indentured to the modern materialistic view of man and cannot conceive of spiritual reality, let alone deal with it.

7.

This is not primarily a religious or philosophical problem but an ontological problem, concerning (a) what men believe to be real and (b) what actually *is* real.

SECTION I

The Reality of the Answer and the
Hindrances That Surround It

We don't know how much you already know about addiction. If you get your ideas of it mainly from run-of-the-mill publicity, you will see it as a terrible unsolved problem. But maybe you already know enough to know better than that.

Whatever addiction is, it is not an unsolved problem. Over quite a period of years now there has been a clear-cut, widely available, free, and not-too-difficult way out of this sickness. The problem has been solved, but the solution has been only partially applied. Indeed, any particular addict who is looking for the solution can get in touch with it only by finding his way through a maze of hindrances and difficulties. That is the situation to which we will be addressing ourselves.

This book is in three sections, of which section 1 is an account of what an addict needs *to know* and *to do* in order to recover. Further details of the subjects briefly mentioned in this first section —movements which are the bearers of the Answer to addiction, problems an addict will encounter in dealing with medicine, psychotherapy, and the addiction "field"—are covered more extensively in following sections.

We will be referring often to the two main groups of people who deal with the addiction problem—the professionals and the amateurs. In this context a professional is anyone who helps addicts for money or for pay; an amateur is anyone who helps addicts for love or on an unpaid basis. Of course many professionals and professional organizations at times help addicts for love and without pay, and certain amateurs and amateur organizations at times work for pay in their helping activities. But the lines are sufficiently clear. Main professional and amateur groups are as follows:

PROFESSIONALS

American Medical Association
American Psychiatric Association
National Association for Mental Health
American Psychological Association
U.S. Department of Health, Education, and Welfare, including
  the Alcohol, Drug Abuse and Mental Health Administration,
  which consists of the National Institute on Alcohol Abuse and
  Alcoholism, the National Institute of Mental Health, and the
  National Institute on Drug Abuse.
World Health Organization
Center of Alcohol Studies, Rutgers University
National Council on Alcoholism
Alcohol and Drug Problems Association of North America
North Conway Institute

AMATEURS

Washingtonian Movement*
Oxford Group*
  and its offshoot
Alcoholics Anonymous
  and its offshoots, chief of which is
Synanon
  and its offshoots, including

*No longer in existence. Included for historical reference

Daytop, Phoenix House, Renaissance,
Odyssey House, Gateway House, and many others
Teen Challenge and other evangelical groups

The orientation of the authors, in assessing the activities of the professionals and the amateurs, is pragmatic. We have no prejudices as to the relative merits of love or money as motives for helping alcholics. We are concerned with what works. If money works better than love, hurray for money. And vice versa. If you are an addict and have reached the hurting stage of the game and are looking for help, you do not scan the motivational background of your helper. All you want to know is, can he indeed help.

CHAPTER 1

Good News for Addicts:
There IS an Answer

What is addiction? There is an Answer. But there are also obstacles. How to find the Answer without getting hung up in the obstacles. The Common Denominators. Note to genteel addicts. The movements in which the Answer has appeared. In one word, what the Answer is. Don't gag on the God problem. Not a matter of philosophical outlook but a matter of fact.

For openers, we will postpone the grim details and the statistics about addiction. If you know anything about it at all, you know well enough that it is a mess and that a lot of people are mixed up in it. If you are personally involved—if you know you are an addict or suspect you may be—you do not need a lot of fill-in on the ramifications of the mess or the dimensions of it.

A very simple definition will tell you what addiction is: *If you are using alcohol or drugs harmfully, and if you can't stop and stay stopped even when you seriously want to, you are addicted.* And you are condemned by your addiction to a radical disintegration of your life and to an early, ugly death—unless you find the Answer to the problem.

Very fortunately there is an Answer. Whether or not you will be able to find it and apply it is another question. But there *is* an Answer to addiction. That is to say, there is a cure[1n]* of the disease, a complete deliverance from the affliction, and a total and perma-

---

*All footnotes followed by "n" are found in the Notes section (p. 321). All footnotes without "n" are in the References section (p. 330).

nent solution of the problem. In honor of the great thing that it is, we spell it with a capital A.

The authors of this book are former alcohol and drug addicts who have found the Answer, and who are alive, sane, and free from addiction today as a result. If there were only the four of us, or only a few hundred of us, it would not be so big a thing. But actually we four are members of a huge army of recovered addicts, whose very existence, year after year and decade after decade, is living proof that there is indeed an Answer to the problem of addiction, that the Answer is widely available, and that it is fully effective wherever it is seriously accepted and sincerely used.

This great event of our times—this blessed healing for one of the worst of our ghastly modern plagues—has not appeared in a corner, and its light is not hidden. Hundreds of thousands of alcohol addicts and drug addicts know it from immediate experience. Literally millions of families of addicts and friends of addicts know it from having seen their loved ones restored to life and sanity by it.

But there are difficulties. The Answer is well known, but not nearly *well enough* known. And in recent years there have been remarkable and indeed fantastic confusions on this scene. The result is that an addicted man or woman, searching for the Answer, is apt to encounter obstacles of so serious a nature as to make the difference between life and death. And that, briefly, is what this book is about: how to find and apply the Answer without getting hung up in the obstacles. Since the confusions loom as threats to the survival and the sanity of addicts everywhere, we shall be taking a hard look at them later on. But first we want to talk about the few things an addict needs to know in order to find the way out of the addiction nightmare.

The Answer to addiction has appeared at different times over the past 134 years. It has appeared in various circumstances under several different names. But it is not several different answers; *it is one and the same answer.*

The essential signs by which the Answer may be known, the

hallmarks by which it may be recognized under its various names, are these: (1) surrender to God and to the truth, (2) cleansing and amendment of life, and (3) helping others. These are the Common Denominators. To a jaded modern ear, these things will sound naive, platitudinous, moralistic, and (ugh!) religious. But whether you like the sound of them or not, the fact is that these three principles have enabled countless addicts to break out of the trap, to stay out, and to become fully reestablished in useful life. An equally striking fact is this: where these principles are *not* used, the problem of addiction is back where it was before the Answer appeared: nowhere. The recoveries by any and all other means are few indeed. So if you are an addict,[2n] or if you have any addicts among your family or friends, go back, take another look at these Common Denominators of the Answer, and make a mental note of them. They are bigger than anybody's mere likes or dislikes. They may save your life or the life of somebody you love.

By the early part of the nineteenth century, addiction had already become a world-wide sickness of extraordinary proportions, one of the greatest scourges of all times, just as deadly, even more degrading, and far more widespread than such horrors as leprosy and the Black Death.

As if in response to the need, the Answer appeared for the first time in 1840. It emerged in an outburst of spiritual energy and activity called the Washingtonian Movement.

The first recovered-addict society of which we have any record appeared, flourished, and disappeared meteorically in the middle of the nineteenth century. It bore a powerful resemblance to Alcoholics Anonymous, and during the period of its existence it was spectacularly successful. The Washingtonian movement was launched in Baltimore, Maryland, in April, 1840, by six drunks who signed, and kept, pledges of total abstinence. The original members were a tailor, a silversmith, a coachmaker, two blacksmiths, and a carpenter. The group met regularly, witnessing to their recoveries, and they were soon joined by others; within a year they had a sober membership of 1,000, and subsequent development was explosive; by 1844 the Washingtonians included 100,000 "reformed common drunkards" plus some 300,000 "common tipplers" who became total abstainers. And the growth continued from there. There are of course no reliable statistics, but it is clear that the numbers of recoveries involved was very large.

The movement was based on six principles: (1) drunkards helping one another, (2) weekly meetings, (3) sharing of experience in the cleansing and amendment of life, (4) constant availability of fellowship with the group and its members, (5) reliance upon God and the truth, and (6) total abstinence from alcohol.

Before 1840 there had been very few recoveries from alcohol addiction. The malady was destructive of body and soul, and the two or three out of a hundred who recovered did so by means which nobody, including the recoverees, well understood or could apply to the desperate needs of the ninety-seven or ninety-eight out of a hundred who floundered to their miserable deaths in the grip of the affliction.

Therefore the event of 1840 marked a crucial turning point in human affairs. It was historic in a sense which even continental discoveries and world wars are not. The Washingtonian movement itself did not long survive, but the Answer to which it bore witness *did* endure and, after a period of latency, has reappeared among us in greater power than ever before.

The Washingtonian society fell apart as dramatically as it had come together. Torn by religious squabbles, involvement with the temperance movement, political divisions, and the professionalization of some of the members, the movement by 1848 had ceased to exist, except for some declining activity around Boston. It would be many years, until the appearance of Alcoholics Anonymous, before the power of "one recovering drunk talking to another" would again be widely available to alcoholics in their attempts to achieve recovery.

The Answer reappeared in the early twentieth century in the

Oxford Group, passing by direct communication in 1935 to a world-wide influence in Alcoholics Anonymous, and thence in 1957 to its unprecedented healing of drug addiction in Synanon and the therapeutic communities. The same power has shown itself, working the same wonder of recovery, in Teen Challenge.

The chances are you never heard of the Washingtonians. And probably you have heard little if anything about the Oxford Group. Alcoholics Anonymous of course you do know about, and probably also Synanon, the therapeutic communities, and Teen Challenge. But these things are of remarkable significance for modern man. There is more here than meets the eye of a casual observer. This sequence of movements is a phenomenon of extraordinary importance, because it is the trace in history of the definitive solution of one of the worst problems of this present era. The solution works wherever it is sincerely applied. It has worked no further than it has in our society because it has been no further applied.

Please notice what the chroniclers of our age have ignored but what is nevertheless clearly a fact: These various movements all have been marked by the great Common Denominators. These several societies all are the vehicles of *one and the same influence,* operating under *the same set of principles.* And this influence and these principles are actually, demonstrably, provably, historically, and obviously the Answer to addiction.

The Answer has shown itself in our times, but it is not a product of our times or of our culture. Indeed the Answer has had to do its life-saving work in the teeth of a culture which despises and rejects its very essentials. The current culture is atheistic, materialistic, cynical, sophisticated, sensate, and self-centered. The Answer to addiction is God-centered, truth-centered, spiritual, simple, altruistic, and self-sacrificing.

Let there be no ambiguity as to what is being said here. The Answer to addiction—that which cures the disease and releases the prisoner where nothing else can—is the grace of God. It is the truth of God, the power of God, the Spirit of God. If you want a one-word equivalent, the Answer *is* God.

The recovery movements are vehicles, more or less faithful. The Answer is God. Not, however, the God of arguments and debates, not the God of the sectarians and the bigots, not the God of the academically certified, not the God of the philosophers or of the wise but the God of Abraham, the God of Isaac, the God of Jacob —very God of very God pouring himself unmistakably into human affairs, God as living, communicable, holy power, intervening in a specific manner, with specific principles and a specific teaching, to provide a specific way of life as a solution of a specific human problem which was going beyond all bounds, e.g., the problem of addiction.*

Now—how does all this talk about God sit with you? Not so good, eh? If you are an unbeliever, it probably merely gripes you in the ordinary way. If you are a believer, you are probably nervous that we will be getting outside the canons of your belief. Alas, this is a box we simply cannot get out of, so we will have to rattle around in it. In this book we are right up against the problem of God, and there is no way of escape. Usually, today, people just decently avoid the subject, which has become an embarrassment to everybody, believers as well as nonbelievers. But we cannot avoid the subject, because we are dealing with addiction, and God is related to addiction as food is related to hunger. God is not merely an answer to addiction; he is *the* Answer. It is impossible to talk intelligently, or even rationally, about addiction without talking about God.

So please stay with us. Even though you may be constitutionally somewhat repelled by the direction this discussion is taking, you must respect facts, and it is on a factual basis that we will be considering the matter. We will be looking at God as a living power —who either exists or doesn't. We ask merely that you keep your mind open to the possibility that he does.

Whatever your beliefs or disbeliefs about God, your thoughts and emotions, your inclinations and aversions, it will help if you will keep all that in suspense and let the facts speak for themselves. The fact is that, on the record, for the past 134 years God has

*See Harry M. Tiebout, M.D., on the Answer as it comes through Alcoholics Anonymous (p. 220).

played, and to this day continues to play, the outstanding role in actual, visible, tangible, proved recoveries from addiction. The very great majority of recoveries have come from God-centered and truth-centered movements. Recoveries attributable to other sources, strictly exclusive of the God-centered and truth-centered movements, are so few that they are practically inconsiderable.

Recoveries among addicts who sincerely involve themselves in the God-centered and truth-centered movements run around six to seven out of ten. If these movements were eliminated, it seems likely that the recovery rate would drop to what it was before they appeared on the scene—one to three out of a hundred. The overwhelmingly dominant influence of God and truth in producing recoveries from addiction is a fact which no one who impartially examines the history of our times can escape. However you theorize or rationalize it, the fact of the influence must be taken into account in any practical survey of the alcohol and drug scene. The question is not whether anyone likes or dislikes religion or likes or dislikes God or thinks God is real or unreal. Leave the matter of God's reality or unreality out of it for the moment. The question then becomes: has the mere *idea* of God played a central and critical helping part in recovery from addiction in recent years? And the answer is simply and obviously yes.

CHAPTER 2

The First Thing You Need to Know

It works. Beware stupid believing and disbelieving. Faith goes beyond belief. Trusting, relying, hanging on. Who convinces whom. Samuel Abrahamson's story. Robert Calhoun's story. David Randall's story. John Burns's story. Your life hangs on the principles. The Three Common Denominators. The Four Absolutes. The Twelve Steps. The Ten Practical Points.

The first thing you need to know about the Answer is that it works. And the only way you can know that is to listen to people for whom it actually *has* worked—people who used to be hooked on alcohol or drugs and who are now clear and staying clear and living a sane and joyful life.

You have to hear *and you have to believe* what these people say. Of course you are utterly free not to believe, but if you do not believe the truth when you hear it, that is simply your very hard luck. If you are careless about what you believe and don't believe, you can really put yourself out in the cold. If you have ten thousand dollars in the bank, but if for some reason you don't believe it, the money is no good to you.

Belief plays a critical part in recovery from addiction. Not blind belief, but belief in the evidence of your own eyes and ears, belief in the undeniable experience of the people who have already found the Answer you are looking for.

Then comes faith. Go slowly here. Something big is meant, and your life and sanity hang on it. Faith goes beyond belief. *And the*

Answer will work for you only if you have faith in it. Faith is a technical term in the life of the spirit. It means (1) that you *trust* the Answer, (2) that you *rely* on the Answer, and (3) that you *hang on* to the Answer.

Now you can't have faith unless you are convinced. And nobody has the job of convincing you. It is *your* job to convince yourself. And there is no way on earth to accomplish that except to listen to the people who have already done what you are hoping to do.

The Answer always and everywhere has been communicated by witness—by recovered addicts telling their stories. When you connect with the recovered addict society that fits your situation, you can begin to listen to all the recovery stories you need to hear, and you can begin telling your own story, for that is an essential part of it. But for something to start with right now, here are the stories of the recoveries of your present authors. There are only four, so they do not begin to cover the waterfront of addictive experience, but they are true stories of real addiction and real recovery, and no addict whose ears are even slightly open to the truth can hear the story of a recovered addict without being touched by the reality and the power of the Answer.

SAMUEL ABRAHAMSON'S STORY

After a modest beginning with port wine, he graduated to beer, then to liquor, then to pills, then to pot and acid, and finally to a steady running mixture of booze and cocaine. Geographical and all other cures failed, until at last a friend's example opened the door to freedom.

I came to the end of the road when I was twenty-five years old. I had spent nine weird, crazy, miserable years drinking and taking all kinds of drugs—narcotics, barbiturates, amphetamines, psychedelics, anything I could get my hands on.

I guess nobody starts out to be an alcoholic and a drug addict. Certainly that was the last thing I expected to have happen to me. I was too smart, too talented, too intelligent. I had too many good things going for me. My parents were both doctors, so our family was pretty well off financially. I got along well with my brothers and sisters, made friends easily, had no trouble with schoolwork, and was good at athletics.

The only cloud on the horizon was that although I was mightily attracted to girls, I was shy. One night I discovered the remedy for the shyness—a bottle of port wine. My girl and I both got sick after drinking it, and I didn't drink again for a year, but I never forgot how the shyness, the uncertainty, and my feelings of morality dropped away when I started drinking. I never forgot how useful alcohol had been. I was just sixteen when I learned that lesson.

I went off to college in downtown Manhattan. For a little while I was enthusiastic and interested in the schoolwork. I had notions of becoming a lawyer, or an economist, or an architect—a profession in which I would make big money in a hurry. By the end of my first year, however, I was more interested in good times and girls than I was in making big money at some time in the future. I began drinking and running around to one party after another every weekend. Drinking still made me sick, so it took a couple of days every week just to recover from all the "fun" I had had on Friday and Saturday nights.

My second year of college was like the first, and by the third year I was in real trouble. I rented a sixth-floor walk-up apartment in the Chelsea district of Manhattan. There were eighteen bars between me and the college. Within a few weeks I had stopped going to classes altogether. There was a lot of booze in my life, a lot of sex, and a diet that consisted mostly of cigarettes and canned spaghetti. At the end of the semester, I showed "incomplete" in all my subjects except one, and I failed that one.

I got scared enough by the report to make it back the next semester for another try, but that didn't work any better than the earlier attempts had. Liquor replaced beer, and by midterm I was washed up. I had a sustained case of the shakes and was given a medical leave of absence for emotional and alcohol-related problems. I was sent to a psychiatrist, the first of many, who loaded me up with tranquilizers and shipped me off to Scotland for a geographical cure in the company of my parents. The trip seemed to help, and after we got home I got a good job in an oceanographic institute. All was well for a few months. I did not seem to need to drink or take drugs any more. I thought my problems were behind me and that I would be able to return to school before long.

But then, after a ferocious argument with my father, I moved out of our home and into a nearby boardinghouse. It was a pretty bad move. The "boardinghouse" turned out to be a sanctuary for nearly all the potheads and acid freaks in the area. For the next ten months while I stayed there I was stoned all the time. I got very sick physically, and I also began to have crippling depressions and frequent thoughts of suicide.

The spring of 1968 was the time of the assassination of Martin Luther King and Bobby Kennedy, the Poor People's Campaign, and the Columbia University riots. I was quickly caught up in the revolutionary politics that were so much in the air. I deeply believed that revolution was close, and I committed all my energies, such as they were, to that end. I was drunk or stoned on drugs most of the time and living with a fifteen-year-old girl, but I still thought I could solve the nation's problems.

The reality of my situation began to hit me in early June of that year. I was cut off from my family and from most of my friends. I was broke and out of work. I had burned my draft card and was faced with the alternative of leaving the country or going to jail. And I was beginning to see that no real revolution was about to take place.

One Saturday afternoon a friend offered me some STP, a superpsychedelic. Two hours after I had taken it, I was having convulsive shakes. I could not face the possibility of twelve to forty-eight more hours of the agony. I wound up in a private hospital in the city, where I stayed for four months. After being released, I hung around Manhattan, working and drinking, but laying off drugs. I met and set up housekeeping with the girl I eventually married. We were both working, and the next few months were better, more peaceful than any time I had known in years. But I was still depressed, living without much sense of meaning or direction, and looking to booze to provide the excitement I felt I needed.

The following year I discovered a new way to fill the spaces: I began stealing diet pills from my father's office. Then I ran onto something even better. A friend got me started on cocaine. I thought I had finally found the answer. It was the perfect high. I could work, think, relate freely, all without a letdown. Provided I didn't overdo the cocaine, I had it made. . . .

After eight months of snorting cocaine and drinking, my life was a total chaos. I was so ill and so depressed I did not have any idea of what to do next. Finally I went off to England for another geographical cure. Again the trip seemed to help. I returned determined to set my life straight. I would not drink again. I would not use drugs of any kind. And I would get married and settle down. Everything would be all right. I was full of hope.

But it was another disaster. Within two months after I came home, I was drinking and using cocaine as much as ever before. By winter of that year I was sleeping fourteen to sixteen hours a day. I could not bear to see anybody except my girl. Depression and paranoia followed every attempt to get high on drugs or booze, so I stopped trying. I was completely spaced out.

At that point I got a break.

A close friend gave me a copy of the Twelve Steps of Alcoholics Anonymous. She was not an alcoholic, and I do not think she thought I was an alcoholic, but she had got relief from crippling anxiety by working with these Steps, and she thought they might help me. I had seen spots on television about AA, but had not thought much about it otherwise. I had never considered myself a drunk. I knew that I drank too much too often, but I thought I was a different kind of animal—not an alcoholic, just a product of the wild and crazy sixties, a member of the drug culture, a revolutionary, a guy destined for very great things who had somehow gotten untracked. But no drunk. I liked drinking. In fact I had a romantic attachment to it that I was certainly not about to give up.

If matters had stayed there, I would be insane today or possibly dead. But my thinking began to change. My friend Susan had started a process in me that was to turn my life upside down. I acknowledged that I was really miserable and had to get relief. And Susan was living proof of what she was saying: you do not have to be an alcoholic to work these AA Steps and get a complete recovery. She had been a living ghost only a few months before, in continuous terror, so stricken with anxiety that it was hard to believe she had ever been the intelligent, sensitive girl I had once known. Hospitals, drugs, doctors, family—nothing and no one had been able to help. In desperation, her husband got her into a recovery community which based its way of life on the Twelve Steps of AA but was not limited to alcoholics. Many members of the community had themselves recovered from alcoholism, but others were ex-drug addicts or had been suicidally depressed or in other major life troubles.

After five months in this community, Susan was a new person. She was in radiant good physical health and had regained all her old zest for being alive. What is more, she had a new kind of inner strength that seemed to completely quiet the craving for the wild living and excitement all of us used to think we had to have. She said her new life was a gift of God and that it was hers as long as she consented to let her life be guided by him and as long as she tried to help others. She made a flat promise that I could change, too, if I would just make an open-minded experiment with prayer and if I would start getting honest about where I had been wrong. I had been an atheist most of my life, but was no longer sure what I believed. I did know that I wanted relief, and I did not know where else to get it. So I went to the community.

I made a connection right away. The people were different. The ideas were new. Something inside me said, this is it. I think what happened was that I no longer had to feel like such a freak, forced to maintain a front but in agony behind it. These people knew what it was like to be miserable. They also knew that they had not been able to do anything about it by themselves. Most of them had shared my experience of exhausting the usual sources of help—psychiatry, drug therapy, hospitals, traveling, and endless personal resolutions to do things differently. In desperation they had turned to a Power greater than themselves, and found real help at last.

I did the same. I was self-conscious about trying to pray; my whole background rose up against it; but I kept at it, and I got the strength to stay away from booze and drugs. I also got the courage and wisdom to open up to other human beings and get honest about what I had been doing.

There was a great big new idea here: *I am responsible for my troubles.* It is *I* who have been messing everything up. Suddenly I felt hope. As long as I thought that my misery was caused by my genes, my upbringing, schooling, or whatever, there was nothing I could do. But if the trouble was my fault, if I caused it and was responsible for it, then with God's help I could get out of it. I couldn't change the world, but with the help of experienced friends I could change myself.

I made a list of all the things I could remember doing wrong. And though plenty nervous about doing it, I sat down with one of the senior community members and admitted everything. When I left that session, I went up to my room and got down on my knees to thank God. Then the tears came. The terrific burden of guilt and unaccepted responsibility for all those years of rotten, selfish behavior was lifted. In that moment, I surrendered deep down in some very basic place in myself. The surrender needs daily renewal; the ego is far from dead; but the power to live a new life is unmistakably there each day.

After that, I started coming out of myself. I became an active member of Alcoholics Anonymous. I began taking an interest in and helping people who had come into AA after me. It was a tremendous feeling to be able to give something to someone else. I found that my ability to think and to work was improved.

That was three years ago. I have not had a drink or any drugs since. I have married; we have a child; I have started a new job. I originally came to the community and to AA in order to get my old life straightened out. Now my focus is on maintaining and strengthening an entirely new one. It is a life that is already higher than anything I ever dreamed of in the old drugging days, and it is moving into more beautiful country with every twenty-four hour period that passes.

ROBERT CALHOUN'S STORY

You can't just quit the army, so this soldier eased his suffering with terpinhydrate and codeine, then with a lot of other plain and fancy pain killers. Depression, violence, stealing, uncontrollable drinking, and the crazy notion that death was at hand finally brought him to ask for help—of which he got a lot more than he bargained for.

In December of 1961 I was drafted into the army, and my life started to fall apart. I was twenty-two at the time and not cut out to be a soldier. I was no good at taking orders, and I was in poor physical condition. Tent dwelling in midwinter disagreed with my weak constitution. I soon ended up in the post hospital. Being sick was no fun, but the real bitter pill was having to do something I devoutly did not want to—not just for a month or so, but for two long years.

Up until now, when I got into situations I did not like, I always had the same ready solution: I quit. I had quit Boy Scouts, high school chorus, college (twice), ministerial training, my one serious girl friend, and a good job at the post office. But it is not so easy to quit the army. I tried every device I could think of to finagle a medical discharge, going on sick call day after day through the spring and summer of 1962. When it became apparent that this was getting me nowhere, I sank into the deepest, longest depression of my life.

I had suffered from periodic fits of despondency since my early teen-age years, the worst lasting all of the fall semester of my junior year at Yale and ending in my leaving school in January of 1960.

In high school I had had something to drink on only two occasions. This was unusual behavior in my crowd, most of whom drank often and many of whom got drunk regularly. My father is an alcoholic, recovered in Alcoholics Anonymous. His experience impressed me early in life with the potential dangers of alcohol addiction. I had a sincere religious streak which ran deep. But my depressive streak ran deep, too, and as my depressions worsened in college, I sought release in alcohol—and found it. Moderate drinking never did a thing for me, but drunkenness broke through the walls of my gloom. It also led to frightening, uncontrolled actions: emotional excesses, sexual excesses, and later, violence. So I became an alcohol abuser with a long-term periodic pattern. Remorse and fear kept me dry for considerable stretches, but sooner or later boredom and hopelessness drove me back to drink.

During my first weeks in the army I got on cough medicine, terpinhydrate and codeine. I got on it quite by accident (I really did have a bad cough), and it made me pretty crazy. Then for over a year I did not drink at all. I knew myself well enough to know that drinking would only make my bad situation worse. Staying dry that whole year in the face of intense psychic misery was the hardest thing I had ever done in my life. But it came to nothing. In July of 1963 I started drinking again.

My deterioration assumed a speed and unpredictability which, even in my confused and befogged condition, stunned me. No longer could I keep away from alcohol for any length of time. I repeatedly made solemn vows, to myself and to God, to quit—a device which had always worked before. Now it did not help. I began to steal. I became more violent. My moral conduct shocked and disgusted me when I was sober. And my mind, which had hitherto been my trusted ally, began slipping out of control. I became obsessed with the notion that I was about to die. Nothing I could think or do had power to shake that conviction. No amount of liquor could wipe it out.

This whole mess took just six months to engulf me. During that time I was discharged from the army and returned to college, but that change afforded me no relief. My drinking got steadily worse. By February of 1964 I was at the end of my string. I was scared of dying, scared of breaking down and getting sent away. I knew that help was available to me through Alcoholics Anonymous, but I couldn't, or wouldn't, reach out for it.

For three months I teetered on the edge of the precipice. Then I contacted a man in AA and asked him for help. I cannot explain to this day what it was that changed my mind, why one day I became ready where before I was not. I know "grace of God" is not an expression which satisfies the skeptical (I know because I myself am a skeptic by nature), but that is all the explanation I have ever had, and it has satisfied me better and better as years of happy sober living in AA have built up.

At first I had reservations about AA. I did not want to give up all the pleasures of life at the tender age of twenty-four, and I was not at all certain that I was a full-fledged alcoholic. Sure, I had had my troubles. I had behaved badly, and booze had been prominently involved through it all. But I had never been a daily drinker; never had blackouts, DT's, or convulsions; never been jailed or hospitalized; never even lost a job through drinking.

I stayed dry for three months on conversations with this one AA member, kept my resolve to stop lying and stealing, and made some sporadic attempts at prayer. But in August I drank again. I hadn't planned to drink, didn't want to drink, stood only to lose from drinking—and yet I drank. Really frightened, I admitted my lapse to my AA sponsor and asked his advice. He repeated a suggestion which he had made a month earlier and which I had quietly ignored at the time. He recommended that I take the Fourth and Fifth Steps of the AA Program. These Steps involve making a thorough moral self-inventory and admitting to God, to oneself, and to another person the exact nature of one's wrongs.

That whole business was fine right up to the point about telling someone else all my dirty little secrets. I was not proud of the things I had done wrong. My own memory of them was hard enough to bear, and I was not about to intensify that anguish by telling them to someone else.

But by now my faith in my own notions of how to get straightened out was exhausted. I was ready to try doing things my sponsor's way. I made an appointment to see a young Methodist minister. We sat in his study late one Saturday afternoon, and I told him every wrong thing I could remember doing, from earliest childhood right up to that week. When it was over, he looked at me, obviously moved, and said, "I've had something like this happen by accident from time to time. A person comes in to talk about a quite ordinary matter and suddenly finds himself, almost against his will, blurting out some terribly personal incident. But this is the first time anyone has ever come to me with the expressed intention of putting his whole life on the record."

My minister friend had been touched, but I had been transformed. An immense load, which had been there so long I had almost got used to it, had fallen away in that hour's time. In its place was—not excitement or euphoria—but a quiet, calm feeling of peace. All these years I had been thrashing around tortured by injustice in the world and weakness in myself, and it had been to no purpose; and it was over now—maybe not forever, but surely and blessedly for the present.

That was over ten years ago. I have not had a drink since. One of the early Christian fathers said, "Would you know God? First, know yourself." I experienced the truth of that saying in my own life when I took the Fourth and Fifth Steps of the AA Program. I had always before believed in God, but somehow that was not good enough. I did not start to straighten out until I faced my shortcomings, objectively, almost as if they were someone else's, not overreacting to them, but asking God's help to do what I could, to put them right and conform to his will.

Soon afterward I accepted the fact that I was an alcoholic simply on the basis that my drinking had reached the point where I was powerless to stop and stay stopped without the help of God and Alcoholics Anonymous. With that, my reservations evaporated, and I plunged wholeheartedly into the AA way of life. I worked some part of the Twelve Steps—AA's recovery program—every day. I went to AA meetings several times a week. Here I met and made friends with all kinds of people I would never before have mixed with. By the time I got to AA, my horizons had narrowed to a point where I could not easily relate to anybody whose likes were not pretty much the same as mine. But once I got off booze, all my old drinking friends and I did a sort of mutual fade-out. Drinking, it turned out, was really about all we had had going together.

My new AA friendships were different. What we had in common was gratitude to God for getting us straight, a desire to help each other stay straight, and an eagerness to carry the message to other sufferers. Working this way with other people was, for me, a whole new high. Every Wednesday three or four of us would go to an AA meeting held in a state hospital for the criminally insane. The guys in that place had the bleakest imaginable futures. Many of them had been locked up for fifteen years or more. Still, they looked forward to the AA meeting as the high point of their week. It certainly was a high point in mine. Often on the drive over there (it was forty-one miles one way) I would be dead tired from the day's work. But after an hour and a half of talking AA, I always felt like a new man. Part of it was the magic in witnessing to others about the healing power of God and the AA Program; part was seeing how insignificant my own troubles looked beside theirs.

The AA principles helped me on the job front. I had been a quitter before, but now I found myself able to hang on even when things got very tough. A favorite saying in AA is, "one day at a time." When I first heard it, I thought it was simple to the point of being pretty silly, but I began to use it anyhow, and time and again it has been the difference between my making it and not making it at work. When everything goes wrong, when problems pile up to the place where I can see no way to handle them, I still do what they taught me when I first came into AA: I ask myself if there is anything I cannot bear for just this one day, with God's help. The answer is always no. With God's help I can put up with *anything* for one day. I don't have to drink, and I don't have to quit. This thought reminds me that it is a mistake to act as if I had no one to call on for support. I start praying to God to help me. As soon as possible, I get in touch with an AA member or some spiritually minded friend to talk over my situation. With this approach I have found that there is always a way through. In all my years in AA I have never been fired and I have never just up and quit. On the few occasions when I have changed jobs, it has always been after prayer and careful discussion with sane, responsible friends.

God's help has bailed me out in another old area of weakness. From childhood I have had a great fear of physical pain. I have never been a brave or patient sufferer, and that made me a sitting duck for liquor. Life was full of suffering, and booze had the power to block some of it out temporarily. A few years ago I had heart trouble. The doctors said it was serious and recommended that I have a coronary angiogram. In this procedure a wire is run up through a vein in your arm and dye shot into the heart to get a picture of how the coronary blood vessels are functioning. A general anesthetic cannot be used because you have to cooperate with the process by breathing in a certain way when they are shooting the dye.

When they explained all this to me, there was no way I wanted to go through it. I refused as long as I reasonably could. When it was clear that it would be foolish, irresponsible, and cowardly to keep saying no, I consented. But it still seemed beyond my strength. In the old, pre-AA days I am sure I would have found some way to cop out. In this case I started praying and kept praying. I took each day as it came, doing my best not to dwell on the operation ahead of the day it was to take place. When that day came, I got quietly on the table and went to the operating room, praying all the way. I made it through the operation, and the results contradicted the original pessimistic diagnosis, so it was a good thing to have done. At the time my performance didn't look so great. In spite of my prayers, I was scared stiff, and the doctors and nurses all knew it. But the whole point is, I was able to do the necessary, and it was God's help that made that possible.

Over these past ten years I have had my troubles just like anyone else, and I have repeatedly fallen far short of being the kind of man God wants me to be. But I am committed in principle to doing things his way—I really am. And God's grace has never once failed to give me enough strength to do what had to be done, a day at a time. I am an extraordinarily fortunate person. I am so much happier than I used to be and so much happier than most folks I know who are just trying to get by in life that I am still lifted up in grateful amazement when I think about it. My joy doesn't come from a trouble-free life, and it doesn't come from my being a heroic or even a good fellow. It comes simply from trusting God, from depending on him and leaning on him just exactly the way I used to lean on booze.

It is said that one should be independent, that one should not have to rely on a support or "crutch." But nothing could be farther from the truth. *Everyone* relies on "crutches." Take air for instance. We are utterly dependent on it. Remove our supply for five minutes and we die. Booze was bad for me, not because it was a crutch, but because it was a crutch that did not work. It promised freedom but produced craziness, misery, and slavery. For me the

AA crutch and, above all, the God crutch, have worked. They have made me sane and happy.

Every day that I submit my life and will to the will of God is a day in which I am bound to a sane power from which nothing on earth can alienate me. I cannot be separated from it by personal suffering, or life difficulty, or a bad government, or an unfair boss. In short, no person, no group of people, and no set of circumstances can cut me off from my strength and my joy. That is real invulnerability. That is true freedom.

DAVID RANDALL'S STORY

A Harvard graduate can't become a bum or a fool—or can he? This one just eased his way into addictive drinking early in life, was shocked into two years of sobriety by a doctor's warning, shocked into Alcoholics Anonymous by a relapse into drinking, and shocked back into AA by an "ancient mariner" in an Atlantic City bar.

I felt that life owed me a good deal because I was a college graduate. The uninspected idea that I was somehow made safe by my Harvard degree was one of the main reasons I could not see my own alcoholism for so many years. The difficulty any alcoholic has accepting the idea that booze is his primary trouble was intensified by my feeling that as a college man I simply never could become a *bum* or a *fool*.

I got out of the navy in 1946, tried a bit of secondary-school teaching, and went back to graduate school at Columbia in 1947. I thought I would get a master's degree and teach, perhaps in a high school, perhaps in a college. The motivation was weak. Going to school seemed preferable to working. But what, really, should I do with my life?

I had a thousand ideas, which was the same as having no ideas at all. My mind was clouded, my emotions were unstable, and my will was weak. Something was very wrong—but what? Despite great internal misery, I was unwilling to ask anyone for help. Instead I worked out an evasive life-style. I slept mornings, drank afternoons and evenings, and studied very little. I was a hooked drinker, an alcoholic, by the time I drifted away from Columbia after a year or so. Then came a series of aimless jobs in merchandising, after which I wound up selling real estate on Cape Cod from 1950 until 1956.

That year a doctor told me I was an alcoholic. Somehow he got by my defenses, and I believed him. The shock sobered me up for two and a half years. He also told me to join Alcoholics Anonymous, but that was an unacceptable prescription. I would take care of the matter myself.

I decided that now I had to make something of myself. I was thirty-three, and time was running out. No more fooling around. I went back to New York City to get a career going and make some money. I went into advertising by a back door that one of my older brothers was able to open for me. I thought that all I had to do was to stop drinking, and it would be simple to solve all the other problems. (The invincible arrogance again.) This attitude left entirely out of account that something had been terribly wrong before I ever slid into alcoholism, that it was still wrong, and that unless I somehow changed at depth it was bound to lead me right back to drinking or some other equally serious trouble.

And indeed I did resume drinking in 1958. The drinking and its aftermath in hangovers and missed time at work were worse by far than ever before. After about a year of bad trouble, I gave up and joined Alcoholics Anonymous. I had married by now and had a young child. My wife provided the steam for this move; I just pulled the lever. Specifically, I dialed an AA number she gave me. They sent a man around who suggested I give the Fellowship a try. He was so reasonable and personable that my hopes immediately started to rise. Maybe this Holy-Roller show would not be too bad after all. I went off willingly to my first AA meeting that Friday.

When it was over I told the people that I would come back the next Friday. Meanwhile I had a business trip to make to Atlantic City, so I went down there, and without much thinking about it, started in to do a little drinking. It was all that casual.

I look back now and I can see in myself a sad sack who had no idea what was happening to him. He was cheerful enough up front, but he was in the grip of murderous psychic forces that regularly turned him to self-destructive drinking. Somewhere beneath the surface amiability the forces of pride and resentment were ruling his behavior; but he did not even see that, much less know what to do about it. He had no idea that he was responsible for those inner psychic forces, that he had unleashed them, and was being forced to pay for what they made him do. His whole pose was: "Don't look at me; I'm not to blame. I just drink a little, but I don't mean to bother anybody." He had learned to assume this self-deprecating stance as a defense mechanism, but he was completely taken in by his own act, and so he could not see that it concealed its opposite: overweening self-conceit.

And then this poor fool was lucky enough to get to an AA meeting, and somehow managed enough perceptiveness to react to it by saying: "Great. These people aren't so bad. In fact they are kind of fun. They are real, and honest. I like sitting here gabbing about booze. And their ideas make sense: it's the first drink that does it, so stay away from the *first* drink, one day at a time. Put the AA Program first in your life; if you don't, you won't have any life anyway. If you feel like taking a drink, get in touch with an AA right away. Yes, these people really do know something about drinking, and how to stop it."

I left my first AA meeting, thinking how wonderful it was, went down to Atlantic City and in a couple of days forgot the whole thing. I quite routinely went out to drink, and got half potted, and only quit and went back to my hotel when I had the hair-raising experience of meeting in a bar a kind of authentic crazy man, a manic fellow who said he was an AA who had just resumed drinking, and walked out on his wife and kids, and taken all the money, and planned to get drunk and stay drunk.

In the seventeen years since I had had my first drink I had never met anybody in a bar who made a long speech about AA, or any kind of speech about AA. But four days after I went to my first AA meeting, I met this chap, and he singled me out to hear his whole story. He was my ancient mariner; his story chilled me to the bone. I was not up to doing anything about saving him; I just thought about getting myself back into line. I left him and the bar, went back to the hotel, left for home the next afternoon, and left drinking permanently behind me.

The result of my contact with the Atlantic City wild man between my first and second AA meetings was that I went to that second meeting in a different frame of mind. I was considerably less slap-happy, and very considerably less inclined to condescend to AA. I was spooked. The old arrogance was penetrated. I was saying to myself that there was something precious in this AA thing, and that I wanted it. I now knew that it was possible to get it and lose it. I had a sense of the importance of sitting up on the edge of my chair and listening and participating and taking the advice of the old hands, so that I might not end up. the way my ancient mariner had, drinking in some God-forsaken Atlantic City strip house with a determination to commit suicide by drowning in ethyl alcohol.

It is clear enough in hindsight that I was way over my head in those first weeks of AA. I had fallen into a network of spiritual energy whose very existence I had never suspected. Here it was, saving my life, but I had no mental or spiritual equipment to enable me to appreciate it properly. I now see those two weeks in October 1959 as the fulcrum of my entire adult life, but I had no idea then how important that first exposure to AA was, no idea how easily I might have thrown away an irreplaceable chance for sober, sane, and productive life.

The really alcoholic part of my drinking career lasted from 1946 to 1959—thirteen years. I have been sober now about the same length of time, actually a little longer. So what I see when I look back is a miserable, sick stretch of drunken living reaching back thirteen years from those two weeks when I first encountered AA, and a little better than fourteen years of sober, progressively happier, more meaningful life coming forward into the future from that same crucial two-week period. It diagrams like this:

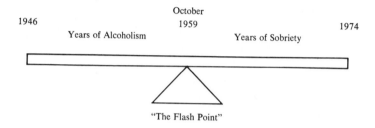

"The Flash Point"

In those first AA meetings, my sanity—my ability to live as other than a *bum* and a *fool*—hung in the balance. Here I was, suddenly, for the first time in my adult life, able to live contentedly without alcohol. (During my self-imposed dry stretch I was far from contented.) Alcohol had been killing me, and now it no longer was. It was almost too much to take in. What had happened? What was this total reversal of field? It is only recently that I have begun to see at all objectively what happened to me.

By the time I came to AA I had tried every way that I could think of to straighten out my life. I had drawn on all the wisdom that I had, and I had checked my wisdom against all the wisdom I knew anything about. I spent some time trying to find out what modern psychological science had to say about such cases as mine. For two and a half years after I knew that I was an alcoholic I avoided AA, because I thought it was revivalistic and cultish; and *my* wisdom told me that that sort of thing could not help my sort of person. For the two and a half years that I stayed sober, I thought that *my* wisdom had at last proved sufficient. I was on top of this thing. I had won. Then unaccountably I was drinking again, and, hard as I tried, I could not get back the old immunity. I kept on drinking. So *my* wisdom had brought me to total bankruptcy.

Then at that flash point in October 1959 I met AA, and it said, "Here is something you have not bumped into before. This is not common sense, and it is not your sort of standard-educated book-sense. This is *uncommon* sense. Let go of your old ideas, and try it. As long as you depend on your own wisdom, count on it, you will fail. So give up all hope. You are licked."

This was AA's First Step: the admission of powerlessness. At that point, when the idea of the true hopelessness of the situation got past the barrier of my querulous, assertive, rational mind and connected with the starved and lacerated soul, a great door opened, and there was a kind of rush of ease and quiet: the fight was over. Suddenly I could tap the most extraordinary resources of strength to keep away from drinking. AA said that this strength came from a Power greater than myself. I came quite quickly to believe that that was true. In the Third Step of AA, this higher power is identified as *God, as we understood Him.* Years ago I had abandoned all effort to deal with God. It seemed to me that whoever or whatever had set up the universe had left men alone to work out their destinies for themselves.

How was I to handle this? I decided that, with respect to alcohol, Alcoholics Anonymous was my higher power, and that I would surrender my will in all that affected drinking to its Program. For the rest of it, I would try to keep an open mind on the question of God.

About five years after I joined AA I resumed membership in a Christian church. A few years after that, I joined a community of men and women committed to a more inclusive and intensive application of AA principles to all aspects of life than is usual in most AA groups. Just in recent years—indeed months—I think that I am at last beginning to understand how profound the AA Program is, that it is nothing less than an articulation of the challenge that Christ gives men and women. (At the same time I am beginning to get a real look at how far I am from meeting that challenge.)

Where AA had at first seemed to me to be wholly about stopping drinking, I am coming to see that it is about learning to live an entirely new way. The whole ship of one's life is to come round and head in the opposite direction—God's way, not my way. If you take the AA Program at all seriously, you see that it really does not compartmentalize life; it calls for living *all* of it, not just the drinking part, in this new way.

In my own case, I have found that money, and sex, and jobs, and ambition, and the vanity that is connected with all of these, have been places where I have repeatedly hung onto my own way. Whenever I have, the old inner misery has returned and stayed, until I came back, with whatever difficulty and reluctance, to taking that critical First Step—the admission of powerlessness. Amid much inner strife and rebelliousness, when there is the willingness at last to accept the truth, the door in the soul once again swings open, and God's help can enter. It is always just as it was that first time, with alcohol. Only when all my wisdom has failed and I give up hope in it, only then does the light and power flood in, bringing the real solution. This indeed is no ordinary wisdom; all ordinary wisdom opposes it.

The result of that first opening of my soul's door to God's help back in 1959 was that I became a willing student and worker in AA. I became an eager friend and fellow of anyone else who really wanted to get sober. AA became the most important thing in my life. I went to meetings regularly; they were my happiest times. They were the times when I was out of myself, and into God's work.

The process since then has been one of enlarging the area of what is God's work, of applying the AA principles of rigorous honesty and responsibility in more and more of my life. Fourteen years ago it was a giant breakthrough to get sober and stay sober. A few years later I saw that my ideas and behavior in the area of money and debts needed drastic overhauling. A few years after that it became plain that sexual behavior I had defended until then was out of line and ought to go. I used the Twelve-Step Program in this as I had for drinking, and had the same result: release from old patterns of thought and behavior I had supposed could never be changed. I stopped smoking (three packs a day) six years ago; and I no longer eat like a pig as I did in the period after I first stopped drinking. All the result of the application of the Program.

None of this goes forward without difficulty, but the great thing is that it goes forward. Everything depends on remembering the first principle: when things are out of sorts, and I am down, and my behavior is not what I know it should be, the return to AA's First Step—the admission of powerlessness—is the open sesame. When that door in the soul swings wide once again to God's help, everything changes. Life is once more back on track and going somewhere.

JOHN BURNS'S STORY

Drinking wasn't a problem, it was the solution of life's problems—until two trips to the bughouse complicated things. Thereafter the alcohol got mixed with barbiturates, amphetamines, paraldehyde, codeine, and a few other chemical answers. And five years of failure in Alcoholics Anonymous led to the remarkable insight that the Program is true.

It never occurred to me that I was heading for big trouble in life. I had an ordinary childhood. I was one of two children, and although I was mixed up now and then and alternately scared and aggressive as most kids are, I had a good time and got along. In high school I was a "success." I played football and did a lot of activities—you know, the personality act—which I enjoyed and felt satisfied and self-assured about.

During high school I got rid of my religion. It seemed the thing to do. The smart crowd were doing it, and you could tell that the teachers were on that side. It felt advanced, and modern, and sort of scientific. It seemed right to me. I had no notion that I was setting myself up for trouble later on.

In college, all of a sudden I was nowhere. Things didn't make sense. I couldn't understand why, but nothing added up, and nothing went anywhere or even pointed anywhere. I struggled around at the University of Illinois and finally went over to the University of Michigan, and there, after quite a bit of flaking around, I got it together again. I became the editor of the humor magazine, and began to do the same sort of "success" act that I had done in high school. I made the junior and senior honor societies, became involved in the boy and girl scene, and began to drink.

Drinking for me, right from the start and for many years afterward, was not a problem; it was the answer to a problem—actually, the answer to a number of problems. I had always been shy and uneasy with people and had had to work hard to overcome this trait; my popularity had been built on top of it and in spite of it. But with a few drinks in me, I was not uneasy with anybody; I felt good, without having to work at it. I always worried a lot about a lot of things. With a few drinks, I didn't worry. At times I used to be really fearful about where I was going in life and what was going to happen to me. I was seriously bugged by it. With a few drinks, I wasn't afraid, and I wasn't bugged.

After I got out of school, got married, and went to work, booze became a prominent part of my life. I drank every day, and I drank quite a bit, but there was no problem—rather, it was now, as it had been from the start, the answer to my problems. I hated to work, but I had to work in order to get money. The drinking, which started at noon, made the working life tolerable. I was in the advertising business, and many of my colleagues drank. I just fell into a way of life that involved a lot of drinking daily. My wife liked to drink. We did plenty of private drinking, and we also did the usual things, parties and socializing, with a lot of drinking mixed in with it all. But if anybody had said I had a problem, I would have laughed. At that point I guess I *didn't* have a problem. Exactly when I went over the line I couldn't say. It was some time about the fourth year after my marriage.

The amount I drank every day increased slowly but steadily. Occasionally it occurred to me that I was drinking too much, and I would slow down for a few days. I began to be sick in the mornings, but I got used to that. I began to make more and more money, and again I seemed to be a sort of "success." Life seemed good to me.

We moved from Chicago to Detroit to Cleveland and finally down to New York where the big money was, and by the time we arrived in the East I was drinking about a fifth of liquor a day. Not to get drunk on. I got drunk weekends. During the week it took a fifth a day just to keep me functioning. I worked very hard in New York. I loved the work; it made me feel important. And I loved the money. The amount of booze I was running on did seem quite a bit out of line, but I didn't know what to do about it. The idea of quitting, or even cutting down very much, seemed simply fantastic. I couldn't imagine living any other way; life without booze, without a *lot* of booze, seemed a mere impossibility. I was working ten and twelve hours a day, six or seven days a week.

And then suddenly, on the twenty-ninth day after my twenty-ninth birthday, the whole show blew right up in my face. I had some convulsions out in my home on the Fourth of July weekend. When I came out of the convulsions, I was off my rocker. They rushed me off to a mental institution, where I stayed for ten weeks, with a diagnosis of manic-depressive syndrome. I returned home and to work with instructions not to work such long hours and not to drink at all, ever.

I guess I stayed sober for two weeks after I got out of the bughouse, and then I very carefully had one drink every day for six weeks. That proved to me (and to my wife) that overwork and not booze had made me crazy, so I went back to drinking on a modified schedule, which quickly developed into an unmodified schedule, that is, the old fifth-a-day routine.

A year later I was back in the bughouse. This time I got metrazol shock treatments, and this time I took it seriously that I was in big trouble. After the period of treatment, the doctor I was working with sent me to Alcoholics Anonymous, where I got sober and began to stay sober. This was in 1941.

I liked the AA Program. I liked helping other people. I liked everything about it except the God business. I couldn't buy that. I figured no intelligent man could, but I thought I could get along on the friendships and the meetings and the activity.

For one year I didn't drink. But then I did drink. I thought I would have myself a little "slip"—and if that didn't work (and I was prepared to believe it might not), I figured I would return to AA and be a "success" again on the Program like I had been before.

My slip lasted longer than I had planned, but at the end of six weeks I was ready for some more AA, and I went back to the meetings and began trying to work it the way I had worked it before. But it didn't work. I went into a pattern of being sober in AA for a few weeks and then drunk for a few weeks. That went on and on. Somewhere along the line I began taking barbiturates, amphetamines, codeine, and a little paraldehyde when I couldn't get anything else.

The years went by; I couldn't do my work. I was writing radio shows and doing well at it, but I couldn't stay on the job and kept getting fired. At last there was a period of almost unrelieved drinking and drugging, with a lot of very batty mental phenomena and a lot of almost totally irresponsible behavior. I kept going to AA meetings all this while, because I did see that those people had the answer, even though I didn't seem to be able to connect with it.

And then, I don't know how it happened, but sometime in the fall of 1946 something turned over in me. I didn't see any lights flashing and I didn't have any emotional experience, but very quietly the AA thing began to make sense to me. *The God thing began to make sense.* On October 10, 1946, I had my last drink, and I have been sober and free from drugs ever since.

The power of the AA spirit just wore down my insanity and my self-will. I reached a point where I couldn't argue against it anymore, because I didn't believe my own arguments anymore. I had heard too many people, too often, say that God was the answer. I began to believe it. And that was my salvation.

I had been around AA and falling on my face all those years, and people kept saying to me, "You are too arrogant. You have got to *surrender.*" I didn't know what in the hell they were talking about. I thought, "What is this surrender business? I am as beat up as most people in AA and more beat up than some that are doing all this smart talking about surrendering. What am I supposed to do, sign a treaty, or hand over my sword like Lee at Appomattox, or what?" Finally after months and months of repeated failure and disaster, I did begin to see that there was something in me that wouldn't give up, but I didn't know what to do about it.

I still don't know exactly what happened when the turn came. I just quit fighting, and at the same time, without any great excitement but quite clearly, I began to see that the Program was *true.* I don't know how, but I began to value the truth. I began to hope and believe in it. I saw that the truth and my sanity were somehow related to each other, and that without the truth I would stay crazy. It is a very practical thing. I don't know why I didn't see it for so long a time.

I began to live by the Program in a new way. Before, I accepted as much of it as I could understand and as made sense to me. I left out big chunks which seemed to be not my style, and what I did take I took as a necessity, as a trip laid on me. Now I began to work the whole Program, not because I had to but because I saw it was true—and good for me. The fighting phase and the split-bet phase were over. I accepted the whole thing at last. I certainly do not mean that I did it all or did it well, but I got my back under the whole load. Where before I snarled over split hairs and quarreled with myself and everybody I could induce to quarrel with me over large issues and small, now I accepted the whole package and everything it implied—and lo and behold, it was sweet and good in a way I would never have dreamed possible. At last I did see a little bit of what surrender means. It has something to do with *not fighting the truth.* It is a secret of admitting defeat.

Trying to live by the truth, trying to be honest, began to be the biggest thing in my life. It still is. Everything—absolutely everything—turns on it.

I began to try to be honest in my relationships with myself, honest in business, honest in my marriage—with revolutionary and transforming results. It was not easy; sometimes it was like a series of surgical operations, with a shock level that terrified me. There were periods when I wondered whether I could endure it. But a strong, steady, unwavering power began to grow up in me and to prevail through smooth times and rough. It was the power not to break down, sell out, or do unworthy things under pressure. It was the power—how precious it is! how dearly bought!—to weather the storms. Not to look good or to shine or to cut any kind of a figure, but to stand fast in rough weather, without lying to myself or others, without running, without drinking or drugging, without betraying the Truth which is my life.

I was sick—mentally sick for a while, pathologically anxious and depressed—and physically sick for a very long time, about five years after I stopped drinking and drugging. And I had a hard time earning a living. But the turn had come, and no amount of misfortune or suffering or sickness could alter the fact. My physical and mental recovery progressed very, very slowly, but at last the time came when the anxiety and the depression flickered out and disappeared, never more to return. The physical sickness—mostly allergies and illness coming from a damaged liver—began to subside.

And I returned to the land of the living, bearing with me a priceless treasure from my long sojourn in the land of the living dead. I brought with me not just the belief but the sure knowledge that God indeed does help those who help themselves, but more important, he helps those who are so sick and so beat up that they can't help themselves.

All you have to do is ask.

And the one thing that puzzles me most now is this: Why did I—why would any human being—have to go through that whole long agony, over all those years, in order to get around to something so simple as just asking? I think that this is not only the mystery of my own life, but the mystery of our whole race. We do seem to be willing to endure almost any kind of suffering, rather than ask a favor of the Power who created us.

The beginning of recovery for many an addict has been in listening to stories such as these. Better to hear them than to read them, but reading will do until you get in direct touch with the people.

Maybe you won't like the first story you hear; maybe you won't agree with it; maybe you won't believe it. And the same with the second and the third and the fourth. But sooner or later you are going to hear a story that you've got to believe, because it is so much like your own. And then you will hear another one, and another, and another. And then the time comes when you begin telling your own story. It takes a huge load off your chest, but more important you see other people getting strength and hope from it. And after a while, gradually, by this process you realize that you *belong*—to a society of people who are saving each others' lives and helping each other to stand on their own feet and become human beings again. And whoever you are, you have got to realize that you are involved in some rare and beautiful thing.

The people you will meet and live with and work with and receive help from and give help to, are basically and desperately important to you. But even more important than the people are the *principles* by which they and you live. Without the principles all these beautiful people would be just a bunch of hopeless, degenerating, and dying addicts.

The following are brief statements of these principles as they have been practiced in the successful Answer-bearing recovered-addict societies:

The Three Common Denominators: Core principles which are common to all of the recovery societies. Very simple but very fundamental, very deep, and very powerful:

1. Surrender to God and to the truth
2. Cleansing and amendment of life
3. Helping others

The Four Absolutes: Used in the Oxford Group and in the pioneering years of Alcoholics Anonymous, these life-transforming principles in one form or another have been the foundation of the spiritual life in all ages and all cultures. They were the bases, for example, upon which Gandhi's ashram operated; they are among the essentials of the first of the traditional eight limbs of yoga (the *yamas*); and they are clearly the principles to which a life in Christ requires allegiance:

1. Absolute honesty
2. Absolute purity
3. Absolute unselfishness
4. Absolute love

The Twelve Steps: The most effective and most widely applied statement of the Answer to addiction in modern times, and one of the greatest working statements of the spiritual life of all times, this fundamental version of the Program of Alcoholics Anonymous was in general use throughout the Fellowship even before the publication of the AA Big Book in April 1939. The shorter statements which had preceded it are now forgotten, and the Twelve

Steps have become the universally accepted and only generally known version of the Program. These steps are literally a lifeline for alcohol addicts, many of whom, lacking opportunity to contact an AA group, have recovered by the mere knowledge and application of these twelve principles. From the standpoint of the whole world of recovery from addiction, it is impossible to exaggerate the importance of the Twelve Steps of Alcoholics Anonymous. If an addict who is sincerely seeking the Answer had no other tool than a working knowledge of these steps, he would have a very good chance of recovery. Do not let the simple language in which they are stated fool you. They are a spiritual powerhouse to which many thousands of alcoholics now walking the streets as free men owe their lives and their liberty:

1. We admitted we were powerless over alcohol—that our lives had become unmanageable.
2. Came to believe that a Power greater than ourselves could restore us to sanity.
3. Made a decision to turn our will and our lives over to the care of God *as we understood Him.*
4. Made a searching and fearless moral inventory of ourselves.
5. Admitted to God, to ourselves, and to another human being the exact nature of our wrongs.
6. Were entirely ready to have God remove all these defects of character.
7. Humbly asked Him to remove our shortcomings.
8. Made a list of all persons we had harmed, and became willing to make amends to them all.
9. Made direct amends to such people wherever possible, except when to do so would injure them or others.
10. Continued to take personal inventory and when we were wrong promptly admitted it.
11. Sought through prayer and meditation to improve our conscious contact with God *as we understood Him,* pray-

ing only for knowledge of His will for us and the power to carry that out.

12. Having had a spiritual awakening* as the result of these steps, we tried to carry this message to alcoholics, and to practice these principles in all our affairs.

The Ten Practical Points: Chapter 5 of the book *Alcoholics Anonymous†* has always been a faithful guide for people who want to practice the Program. The following Ten Points represent an epitome of the life-saving directions given in chapter 5, as boiled down and practiced by one group which bases its way of life on the steps. The Ten Points include wisdom of the most practical kind, much of it not found in statements of the Program outside of chapter 5.

We commit ourselves to work toward recovery and spiritual awakening by sincerely and responsibly trying to do what the AA Big Book suggests:

1. by *completely giving ourselves* to this simple Program;
2. by practicing *rigorous honesty;*
3. by being *willing to go to any lengths* to recover;
4. by being *fearless and thorough* in our practice of the AA principles;
5. by realizing that for us there is *no easier, softer way;*
6. by *letting go of our old ideas* absolutely;
7. by recognizing that *half measures will not work;*
8. by *asking God's protection and care* with complete abondon;
9. by being *willing to grow* along spiritual lines;
10. by accepting the following pertinent ideas as proved by AA experience:
    (a) that *we cannot manage our own lives;*

*The only word in the Twelve Steps that has been changed since their first publication in 1939. "Awakening" was originally "experience."

†The basic text of the Fellowship, the so-called Big Book, is *Alcoholics Anonymous* (New York: Alcoholics Anonymous World Services, Inc., 1955.)

(b)   that probably *no human power can restore us to sanity;*

(c)   that *God can and will,* if sought.

Altogether (leaving aside the commentaries) there is not a lot of material here. And it is pretty simple stuff. *But it embodies the very power of life over death.* It is a thoroughly tested and proven expression of the Answer to addiction. And its healing power extends even beyond the problem of addiction. Our experience proves that *anyone*—drunk, drug addict, pillhead, sex compulsive, suicidal, resenter, smoker, anxiety-freak, overeater, depressive, or just ordinary citizen—can attain spiritual awakening, self-control, sanity, peace, and joy if he will go to sufficient lengths in adopting these principles as a way of life.*

One other point: we leave it to your imagination what would happen if large sections of the general population were to adopt these principles as a way of life. It probably will not happen in our times, *but if it did,* can you picture what life on this earth would be like?

*See "The Lifesavers Way of Life," page 253.

CHAPTER 3

How to Make It Work for You

First things first. Hang on to God. Hang on to the truth. Hang on to total abstinence. Hang on to your recovering brothers and sisters. A group is necessary. Use related help wisely. How to field free advice. The question of psychotherapy. What to look for from the doctors. The problem of the professionals. Where the real power is. Whether or not to start a new group.

If you are addicted to alcohol or drugs; if you want to recover; and if you are willing to accept and act on suggestions from people who themselves have recovered—the outlook for you is good. Do not let anybody tell you that recovery from addiction is impossible, or unusual. Hundreds of thousands of addicts have recovered—fully, beautifully, and permanently.

The people who clutter up the addictive scene and make it seem like a big deal are the addicts (all of us, at one stage of the game) who do not really want to recover and who are still horsing around with the situation and mainly playing games. When you reach the point of wanting to recover and becoming willing to do what recovered addicts tell you to do, the battle is more than half won.

In the beginning of your recovery you are so weak physically and so bombed out mentally that you are easily confused and easily put off. Therefore you have to make "first things first" a rule and stick to it.

The first thing you do is to learn the *first principles of recovery* from someone who knows them and practices them, and to begin to practice them yourself. If you approach them with a little humility, they are not hard to understand, and it is not an impossible task to follow them. These principles (and the company of the people who practice them) are your lifeline. You simply cannot afford to argue about them. You merely have to *do* them, one day at a time.

The way to recovery begins with a few simple, uncomplicated first principles, which come to you as suggestions. Maybe you will not like some of these recommendations, but the thing to remember is that they work, and none of them should be left out. The whole problem is to *hang on* while you are coming out of the woods, and these suggestions tell you what (and what not) to hang on to.

HANG ON TO GOD

The first source of help to which an addict needs to turn—first in the order of time and first in the order of importance—is God. This is not a matter of religion or philosophy but simply a matter of fact. It is the power of God which enables addicts to recover. Without that power, there are very few recoveries.

Now there are a lot of different opinions about God, but we are not talking about God as an opinion but as a living power. You have to remember that you are an addict, not a professor. Do not waste time theorizing about God. What you do is *get in touch* with God by the simple and direct means of talking to God, that is, by plain old ordinary prayer. Every nitwit knows how to pray; the knack here is to *do it.* No preliminary ducking or bobbing is necessary. Just do it.

Do not waste energy debating about God. Take God as a *possibility*—a working hypothesis. Make the experiment of getting in touch. This comes ahead of everything else, and anybody can do it. *You* can do it. Hundreds of thousands of alcoholics and drug addicts (many of them atheists) have made this experiment and proved to themselves that there *is* a Power greater than themselves who responds and gives real, practical, effective help when called on. All real recovery begins here. It makes no difference whether you are a believer or not. If you are not, start by praying to the God you don't believe in. Just park your objections for a while, and *do it* as an experiment.

HANG ON TO THE TRUTH

You connect with God by means of the truth. And you connect with the truth by stopping lying. All addicts are liars. Please do not resent this. It is just a statement of fact. Some of us lie in gross ways, some in subtle ways; but all of us addicts are ferocious liars.

As a starter, stop lying to yourself about your addicted condition. Stop pretending it is better than it is. You are in the grip of a disease which is a vicious killer, and you cannot do anything about it—not by yourself and not with the best scientific, psychiatric, or medical help in the world. Addiction is usually incurable except through spiritual conversion. Face that fact, and your chances for recovery are good. Ignore it, and your chances are practically nil.

Next, stop lying to get out of jams or to smooth off the rough edges of life. Don't lie for the sake of peace; don't lie when common sense invites you to do so; don't lie to cover up your past; don't lie on job applications, expense accounts, or tax returns; don't lie to your boss; don't lie to your husband or wife. Just don't lie. When you fail in this resolve (as you will), admit it promptly. And don't indulge failure; that is, don't fail any oftener than you have to.

This policy of nonlying takes real courage if you have a messy past, as most of us do. It feels like it is going to cause problems for you, rather than solve them. But in actual practice it is a life-saver and a life-transformer. Try it, and you will find that nonlying simplifies life and makes it easier to deal with. And it does something else of greatest importance: When you take truth telling seriously, you put yourself in direct touch with God. God *is* truth, and throughout the day every decision you make to be honest opens you up to the healing light of his presence. This is not just a pretty thought; it is something real, like electricity, only alive. Work for the truth, as best you can, and the living Truth—God— will work for you. He will give you the strength which you yourself lack, the strength to take the next step.

HANG ON TO TOTAL ABSTINENCE

One day at a time, stay away from alcohol or drugs. *Total* abstinence is the key. That means *none*—not even a little bit, not even one or two, under any circumstances, for any reason, ever. One day at a time, with the help of God and the truth, *you can do it.* It is the first drink or pill or shot to which you must say no. One day at a time, stay away from the first one, and you will never have to worry about all those disastrous ones that follow. "One day at a time" is not a trick with words; it is a thoroughly practical, well-proven formula for success. No addict can face the prospect of a whole lifetime of total abstinence. It is too big an order. But any of us, with God's help, can stay away from the first drink or pill or shot for twenty-four hours. Do not underestimate the power of this principle.

HANG ON TO YOUR RECOVERING
BROTHERS AND SISTERS

You cannot recover alone. It is a deadly mistake to think that you can. In our times God has chosen to speak to addicts through brother and sister addicts who are ahead of them on the road to freedom. These are the people who can show you how to recover. Find them. Learn from them. Work with them. If you are an alcoholic, get in touch with Alcoholics Anonymous. If you are a drug addict, look up Synanon or one of the therapeutic communities or Teen Challenge. If you cannot locate a group, do what the pioneers in this field did: dig up a couple of people who are also looking for recovery, and start your own group.

A group is necessary; you cannot sustain a recovery without it. But the group is not God; it is only a vehicle through which he works. Alcoholics Anonymous, Teen Challenge, and Synanon and the recovery communities are great, but none of them has a monopoly on recovery. It is the principles that communicate the power. Recovery begins with getting in touch with God. *He* gives us the courage to get honest; *he* gives us the strength to stay away from the first drink or pill or shot, one day at a time; and *he* puts us in touch with the people we need to work with. At the same time, do not use trust in God as an excuse to avoid people or to try to get around any of the other factors in the basic equation. God, honesty, staying away from alcohol or drugs, and working with your recovering brothers and sisters—these constitute the formula for recovery, and they go together. You cannot work successfully with any of them unless you are working with all of them.

There is an enormous amount of fill-in—physical, psychical, and spiritual know-how—necessary for recovery, but all that comes in due course from working with your recovering brother and sister addicts.

USE RELATED HELP WISELY

There are other kinds of help which may apply to you. Some kinds of "help" turn out to be simply dangerous nonsense. But certain helping resources may be of life-or-death importance to you; for example, medical help in the physical crises of your addiction and your recovery. You should be cautious how you use these latter resources, however, because they can harm you as well as help you. Be on the alert for these various kinds of help. Use them wisely when they apply, and avoid them carefully when they are pitfalls. Watch out for these things:

Advice from ignorant well-wishers: When you are in the kind of deep trouble that addiction causes, you will never lack for people who want to tell you how to straighten out your life. Their intentions are often admirable, but most of them do not know the first thing about recovery from addiction. These are the friends and relatives who often feel downright obligated to impart some words of advice and comfort. Their theme is usually something like this: "Cheer up. Things are bound to get better. You just have to pull yourself together."

Counsels of optimism for addicts are always dangerous. Mere sentimental talk reinforces the lying self-will, the "I'll-take-care-of-it-myself" mentality which wants to push doggedly on through endless personal tragedies and wrecked relationships on its road to insanity and death.

Real recovery, when it comes, is born out of a very different view of the situation, a view which searches out, not the pleasant or the cheerful, but the *true* state of affairs. And in this view, things are even worse than you thought they were. You and your life are out of control. Your position is indeed hopeless—unless you can bring about a radical turning away from self-will to the higher power of God for help. If you do not see the actual, terrible hopelessness with unblinking vision, you will never have the heart to turn to God with the necessary sincerity. The unvarnished truth is not a threat or a burden but a priceless aid; it is the only bridge across the chasm.

Psychotherapy: At some point in your addictive career, one or another form of psychotherapy may be recommended to you as a way that can solve your problem. The evidence is against it. The record is clear: an addict is as well off without psychotherapy as with it. This is the conclusion of repeated scientific studies within the field itself. (See page 112.) Psychotherapy is not among the more successful recovery resources for addicts, and it is a dangerous thing for any addict to get involved in even after he is well on the road to recovery, because it can lead to relapses in those who try to use it as a substitute for the real recovery resources. Conventional religion, philosophy, various kinds of pop psychology, mystical and metaphysical kicks—all of these things likewise can be relapse producers when used as substitutes for the real recovery resources.

Doctors: Medical help is a problem.* It may save your life. At the same time, wrong medical attention has harmed many addicts, and it may harm you. It is a foolish addict who forgets this. Get the medical help you need, *but get it from a doctor who knows enough about addiction to know the following:* (a) that he, as a doctor of physical medicine, cannot supply special help for your spiritual illness of addiction but only for its physical complications, and (b) that addicts should not be given mood-changing medicines (central nervous system depressants or stimulants, hypnotics, anodynes, or narcotics) except under strictly emergency conditions, and then only with the utmost care and really responsible follow-up to insure that the drugs are properly limited and properly withdrawn and that they do not cause readdiction. *Any time you take these drugs, you are risking readdiction.* As a matter of fact, some doctors *do* give mood-changing drugs to both active addicts and recovered addicts without anything like proper care. You have to be alert to this problem any time you see a doctor. It is your right *and your responsibility* to insist that, as an addict, you are not dangerously or harmfully medicated.

Run—do not walk—away from any doctor who wants to "man-

*Doctors and modern medicine have played a critical part—both to help and to hinder—in your authors' recoveries from addiction. Our chief teacher in modern medicine has been a very stern but very fair schoolmaster, Robert Mendelsohn, M.D. See page 216.

age" you by putting you on methadone, Thorazine, Librium, Elavil, Valium, or any other mood-altering drug, for an extended period of time. Some of these drugs are sometimes useful during the first few days of acute withdrawal. All of them absolutely bar you from sane, sober, responsible membership in the human race when used continually as tension relievers, depression relievers, anxiety relievers, or props for daily living.

Do not expect too much from doctors, even very good doctors. Doctors can treat physical problems accompanying addiction, but they and their art can do nothing for addiction itself, the uncontrollable urge to return to the addictive substance. On the record, only one thing can overcome that urge: a new relationship with the truth and with God.

The doctor is not ultimately responsible for your health. *You are.* You are not a child or an animal but an adult human being, and both you and your doctor ought to remember that. Cooperate with your doctor, and in every way possible help him to help you. At the same time, remember that he is not your father, your mother, your keeper, or your priest; and he is not God. A confused and authority-starved society has thrust these roles upon mere medical men, but you should take care to stay out of that act. As an addict, you cannot afford to get involved in any such games, because you cannot stand the wrong directions and disillusionment that come of it. When you go to a doctor you must have faith in him, but it should be a reasonable faith. Faith that is erected upon pseudo-scientific illusions and deceptions will not stand the shock of reality and eventually is worse than no faith at all.

One of the chief obstacles—perhaps *the* chief obstacle—to real recovery from addiction today is the increasing muscle of the professionals. (See section 2.) These folks often mean well and sometimes do well, but they are burdened by the most serious kind of factual and conceptual errors, and they are full of a recently acquired and largely unwarranted self-confidence. As an addict, you should try to remember this obvious truth: the professionals do not have the keys to recovery, and they often do not know or will not admit where the keys really are. The professionals may help you in certain ways, or they may harm you. You may need professional help, but in using it be on your guard. Never forget where the real power is. It is your life and your sanity that are at stake.*

The real power for recovery from addiction lies in the *principles* which alone produce recovery, the principles of surrender to God and to the truth, cleansing and amendment of life, and helping others. These principles are the Answer you must find if you want to live. The various amateur movements which work with these principles are where you will find real recovery help, and they are normally indispensable. In a really abnormal situation—that is, if for some serious and valid reason you cannot relate to one of the movements—it is possible to recover by working directly with the principles. That is the position that the founders of the recovery movements were in. And others have done it too, at need. Thousands of alcoholics, for example —the so-called "loners" who live in remote places or on ships at sea or in like circumstances—have recovered merely by reading the book *Alcoholics Anonymous* and putting its principles into practice. It is possible by starting with a knowledge of the principles and the company of two or three fellow addicts who also are seeking real help to start a group which will lead not only to your own recovery but perhaps also to the formation of other successful recovery groups.

The Answer is greater than the movements; the principles are greater than the personalities—but still, you cannot do an end run around the movements. Many a "smart" addict has tried this maneuver and ended up on his butt. If you *can* get in touch with one of the existing Answer-bearing movements, and you choose to

*See Martin Gross on "The Psychological Society," page 242.

avoid it out of laziness, self-centeredness, timidity, or some mere prejudice, you probably will spoil your chances for recovery. A new group of your own is a good resource only if you really cannot make contact with the presently working groups. Recovery is usually easier and safer in an established, proven group than in a new and untried group. Nevertheless, when they are necessary, the new groups work.

The Answer is available. It is up to you to relate to it.

CHAPTER 4

The Greeks Had a Word
for the Kind of Trouble You May Have

Why don't more addicts recover? The problem of scandal. Christ's warnings about it. Occasions of scandal, amateur and professional. The trouble can be avoided. The spiritual movements all have their faults. Some of which are really bad. But the amateur movements are indispensable. You cannot afford to be offended. A different kind of scandal in dealing with professional help.

If the Answer is real (and it is); if it really works (and it does); and if it is free and widely available (which it is), why do not more addicts recover? Hundreds of thousands do, but why don't millions? Why hasn't the whole addiction problem already been *wiped out* by this famous Answer?

Herein lies one of the hardest facts of the whole problem. The Answer works for a very high percentage (60 to 75 percent) of addicts who want to recover. (See page 183ff.) *But only about one addict in ten does want to recover.* And in order to change *that* situation, our whole society would have to change—a possibility which is well beyond the limited range of the present discussion, but which nevertheless bears on the problem unavoidably. This is such a crusher of a problem that we carry it over for later examination. (See page 142.)

In addition to this difficulty, the Answer works under a further handicap, the name of which may surprise you. It is properly called scandal.

The Greek word *skandalon* is a technical term of prime importance in the main spiritual teachings of mankind. Christ makes a critical thing of it, and he pronounces the strictest kind of warning against it. To be "scandalized" is to be "offended," not merely in the sense of being miffed or feeling resentful but of being *effectively put off.* It means that you lose your chance at the Answer. To be scandalized in this sense means to be practically turned away and disconnected from the possibility of rescue. It is the gravest misfortune that can happen to an addicted man or woman.

If you never hear of the Answer, if you just never come across it, then of course you will sink into your addiction, into your insanity, and into your grave without ever having had a chance of recovery. But this is unlikely, the Answer being now as well known as it is. Probably at some time you will hear about it.

At this very point there arises the lethal possibility of scandal. Having heard of the Answer, or having contacted it, having it actually within your reach, you may be *offended* by some real or fancied fault in the movement or the people with whom you are dealing. You may be *put off,* and thus fail to receive the indispensable life-saving help which was so close to you.

Christ drives the point home in strong terms: "It is impossible but that offenses *(skandala)* will come, but woe unto him through whom they come. It were better for him that a millstone were hanged about his neck, and he cast into the sea, than that he should offend one of these little ones" (Luke 17:1–2).* "And if thy hand offend *(skandalizē)* thee, cut if off: it is better for thee to enter into life maimed, than having two hands to go into hell, into the fire that never shall be quenched: where their worm dieth not, and the fire is not quenched. And if thy foot offend thee, cut if off: it is better for thee to enter halt into life, than having two feet to be cast into hell, into the fire that never shall be quenched: where their worm dieth not, and the fire is not quenched. And if thine eye offend thee,

---

*A "little one" is someone who is small or frail in understanding, i.e., a newcomer or beginner in the new life.

pluck it out: it is better for thee to enter into the kingdom of God with one eye, than having two eyes to be cast into hell fire: where their worm dieth not, and the fire is not quenched" (Mark 9: 43–48).

Don't let the old language soften it up for you. He is talking about a very hard matter. He says you are better off to be maimed or half blinded or drowned than to offend or be offended in this way. And you can see that—at least in the case of an addict—it is just as tough a piece of business as he says it is.

So then there is the intensely practical problem of dealing with it. A modern addict who is looking for help may be scandalized— offended, put off, turned away—by one of two things: the first is the imperfections of the Answer-bearing recovery movements, all of which are in the charge of highly fallible amateurs. And the second is the confusion caused by the recent professional eruption onto the scene. Whether his turning away is occasioned by the defects of the amateurs or of the professionals, the scandalized addict suffers the same fate in either case: he miserably dies. (This is not to say that it is ultimately somebody else's fault; it is certainly the addict's fault; he digs his own grave. But the people and the movements who give occasion for scandal bear a fearful load of responsibility nevertheless.) The problem is of the utmost gravity, and hence a major portion of this book is devoted to it.

If you are an addict looking for help, we say this to you: *do not let yourself be scandalized.* You don't have to be. You can be forewarned and so forearmed. We will be pointing out difficulties in both the amateur and the professional areas *with one purpose in mind and one only:* so that these difficulties will not come as a surprise or an offense to you, and so that you can find your way through them to the recovery that is there waiting for you if you will do your part, which is to hang on and go after it.

The good news is as good as it could possibly be: there is an Answer to addiction, and you can find it and make it your own, whoever you are. And the bad news is not so bad: the Answer is surrounded by difficulties which may tend to offend you, but you do not have to be put off if you choose not to be.

The difficulties, the possibilities for scandal, on the professional scene are examined later on. The difficulties among the Answer-bearing amateur recovery movements are looked at briefly below, and more fully in section 3.

The Answer is one thing. The movements which have been its vehicles are something else. These movements have done their job presumably in the best way they knew how, and it is a poor show to criticize them carelessly. At the same time, in sheer self-defense against the failings and shortcomings of these movements, you must be aware of the following.

Criticism of sacred institutions sometimes is regarded within the institutions themselves as disloyalty, but that can't be right. There are circumstances in which criticism is not only permissable but, under the highest of all obligations, necessary. A man who owes his life and his sanity, for example, to Alcoholics Anonymous and to the Christian church will himself take no joy in criticizing them, and he will be pained to hear them criticized by anyone else. At the same time, he is false to the first principles which they have taught him if he pretends that AA and the Church are inerrant or if he lies to himself or others about their faults. To put any organization ahead of the Truth which it exists to serve is a classic error which tends to destroy the very structure it wants to defend.

It is a common characteristic of all movements which are the bearers of authentic spiritual power—and this is true of the greatest as well as the smallest of them—that although they bear the very Spirit and Life of God, they themselves are human and subject to error. In spite of their holy inspiration and divine commission, they make mistakes. Along with the good they do, they also do wrong. It is a striking fact that the presence of so great a thing as the power of God within them does not make the spiritual movements infallible. They have their faults.

There is no use getting mad about this state of affairs, or making it the occasion for dumping on religion in general or any spiritual movement in particular. The fact is, *we cannot do without these movements.* A "humanist" may tell you that men would be all right if left to themselves without these agonizingly intermixed influxes of divine grace, but it is simply not so. Men left to themselves invariably degenerate. All cultures and all progress originate in great spiritual movements. "Humanism" is a regularly occurring late phase in the spiritual movement itself, a phase of loss of spiritual insight and consequent dissolution and decay, accompanied by an increase in prolixity and verbosity.

All authentic spiritual movements without exception go through the same cycle. They all begin small; some of them remain small; some, the great ones, go through periods of mighty expansion and efflorescence; but inevitably there comes a period of loss or betrayal of original principles, followed by a final stage of fragmentation and confusion which may involve actual inversions and reversals of the original values. Small or great, all of these authentic movements are eventually more or less unfaithful to their trust.

Consider for example so beautiful a movement as the Friars Minor. Holy poverty was a first and basic principle upon which the order was established; yet within the lifetime of the founder, to his great grief, the principle was widely compromised or actually abandoned throughout the brotherhood. The following account is given by Brother Leo:*

One of Blessed Francis's companions once said to him: "Father, forgive me, but I want to say something to you which several of us have already discussed. You know how in times gone by the entire Order strove to attain the purity of perfection, how all the brethren with great fervour and solicitude observed the rule of holy poverty in everything . . . and how

*Karrer, Otto (ed.), *St. Francis of Assisi: The Legends and Lauds.* (New York: Sheed, 1948).

they were unanimous in loving God and our neighbours, like truly apostolic and evangelical men.

"But now, since some little time, this purity and perfection has begun to diminish, and some say that this is because such a great multitude of friars cannot observe it. But many of the brethren are so stricken with blindness . . . that it would seem they despised the way of holy simplicity and poverty and set it at naught, although it is the beginning and foundation of our Order. And we, considering all this, are convinced that it displeases you, but we are greatly astonished, if it does displease you, that you endure it and do not correct them."

Blessed Francis answered, and said to him: ". . . As long as I was in a position to direct them, the friars were true to their vocation and profession, and although I have always been ailing since the beginning of my conversion, with my small efforts I satisfied them by my example and my preaching; but later I saw that the Lord multiplied the numbers of my brethren, and they, through tepidity and poverty of spirit, began to slide back from the straight and sure way along which they used to walk. . . . But as I cannot correct and improve them by preaching, admonition and example, I will not play the part of the executioner with punishments and castigations, like the authorities of the world. . . .

"Nevertheless I will at least continue until the day of my death, by good example and acts, to teach the brothers to progress on the way which God has shown me, and which I have shown and taught them by words and by my example. They have no excuse before the Lord, and I will not be called upon in the end to answer for them before God."

Another example: Alcoholics Anonymous is a movement which received as a source of primal power from its spiritual fathers the magnificent legacy of the Four Absolutes: the principles of absolute honesty, absolute purity, absolute unselfishness, and absolute love. After some years of brilliant success in curing hopeless alcoholics with the aid of these thundering–and–lightning battle cries, the movement took advantage of its prosperity to gradually and quietly drop the principles. The key word "absolute" was simply let slide.

Love and unselfish service continued to be practiced and to be wellsprings of AA's great power to rescue addicts and transform lives. But the fervor and inflaming power which arose from the absolute commitment largely disappeared. In the interests of the growth of the movement (which indeed *were* served by this device), the original great trust was watered down and, in its true form, ignored. Absolute purity, by which the fathers had meant first of all sexual purity, was simply let go of; purity, whether absolute or relative, in the love between the sexes or in any other aspect of the human economy, soon became no longer a serious concern of the movement. Absolute honesty was moderated to "rigorous" honesty, which still had some bite to it, but a tendency developed to soft-pedal even that. In the preamble which is read before many AA meetings, the requirement of "an honest desire" to stop drinking became simply "a desire" to stop drinking. And finally in recent years, at least at the level of official AA, the requirements of the truth seem to be assigned second place to a mere policy of staying out of controversy. (See further, page 190).

Still another example: Synanon is a movement whose founder was cured of his addiction to alcohol in Alcoholics Anonymous. In establishing Synanon, the first successful application of the Answer to narcotics addiction, he brought forward some of AA's basic principles, notably the principle of honesty. But the principle of surrender to God was abandoned in Synanon and thus largely ignored throughout the therapeutic community movement which stemmed from Synanon. These communities gained great power by their honoring of the truth, and indeed their restoring it to the place it had in early AA. But the therapeutic communities have suffered grievous weakness by their disregard of the prime principle of the Answer, surrender to God. Thus they lost touch with man's only refuge from his isolated individuality, the one and only real corrective of egotism, the only defense against the tendency of success to degenerate into arrogance. *

But the most arresting examples of all; the most terrifying jetti-

*See Note, page 214.

soning of principles; the most deadly scandals of all have occurred in the most sacred body of all: The Christian church itself.

Christianity begins as a movement which has received from the mouth of God incarnate the solemn and unmistakable commandment that Christians are to love one another. Several hundred years later Christians are burning other Christians at the stake for differences of opinion on doctrinal matters. This grisly development was foreseen. The Master had said, "Yea, the time cometh, that whosoever killeth you will think that he doeth God service." But even in so unmistakable a prophecy the worst truth was veiled; the apostles could hardly have imagined that it would be "Christians" who would do the killing. It was an observer in the Far East who made the definitive statement on this murderous tendency of the followers tỏ bury the Founder's principles, and the Founder along with them. "The sect," said Kabir, "is the mausoleum of the guru."

It is no part of the job of this book to expand on these things or to dwell on them. But let no one say that we ignore this aspect of the problem, or that we ask you to ignore it. The Answer to addiction is the Truth, and when the Truth is abandoned the Answer is lost. There is no way around the faults of the people and the institutions, but there *is* a way *through* them which gives access to the treasure of which the spiritual movements are the guardians.

The fact remains that these movements, with whatever faults, are indispensable. There are no substitutes. Ersatz or invented spiritual movements, or purely "humanistic" movements, simply do not work; they do not have the power. And when new authentic spiritual movements appear, which overlap or replace the older ones, these new movements follow the same cycle: they are human; they make mistakes.

As you value your life, please do see the point here. *You cannot afford to be put off by the faults of the spiritual movements.* You dare not indulge the luxury of being offended. Recognize the faults, yes. Be on your guard, yes. But don't go away mad. There is nowhere to go. If you are an addict, you cannot get along without the God-centered and truth-centered recovery movements. If you are an alcohol addict, for example, you cannot get along without contact with Alcoholics Anonymous. Your chances of finding the Answer outside of Alcoholics Anonymous are practically nil. For any addict there is room for maneuver as to how and where you will relate to these movements. But it is a simple fact that—barring a thousand-to-one fluke—you cannot recover without them.

It is impossible to give any kind of account of these fellowships without referring to their faults. The Washingtonian movement, for example, after doing magnificent work among alcoholics for a period of years, put itself right out of business as a result of internal dissensions and ill-advised excursions into politics. While not ignoring these faults, you must be able to profit from the experience of this great movement, to see how it was indeed the bearer of the Answer for its time, and to recognize how mightily the great Common Denominators worked in it—the identical basic principles which characterize every movement which has real power to change human life and to deliver men from hopeless illnesses of body and mind.

The same kind of forbearance is needed—if possible it is even more rigorously required—when the problem is brought up to date and you are relating, with your very life hanging in the balance, to one of the contemporary Answer-bearing movements. Alcoholics Anonymous, for example, has got a lot more wrong with it than the few faults we have mentioned. And you may dream up some obstacles in your imagination. Anyhow, you will find things in any given group or in the movement as a whole which you don't like. In any given case, maybe you are mistaken, or maybe there really *is* something wrong. Either way, find your way through it; do not withdraw; stick with the fellowship—for the simple reason that for an alcoholic it is the only show in town. It *does* have the keys to recovery.

There have been innumerable earnest attempts by both amateurs and professionals to find a substitute for Alcoholics Anonymous, for the benefit of those tender-souled alcoholics who do not like God, or who are "not joiners," or who are too busy to go to meetings. But it never works. It is like trying to find a substitute for air. There isn't any.

There are two good reasons why you should not demand perfection, or even an agreeable odor, from the movement or from the people upon whose help you are dependent. First, you won't find it. And second, if you did find it, the thing would be so far above your head that you couldn't relate to it. Just ask yourself, "Have these people demonstrated and proved in their own lives that they have the Answer I am looking for?" If so, you have found the pearl of great price. Never mind the mud it is set in.

We don't say that you should never see the flaws in the movement and the people who are your life-savers. But is *is* a good idea, at least for the first year or two, to work with your newfound brothers and sisters with a minimum of criticism of anyone but your own sweet self. A rather strict moratorium on complaining, bitching, bellyaching, fault-finding, and mountain-top surveys of the situation would be one of the greatest of all possible practical aids to your recovery.

An addict without help—*an addict on his own*—has practically no chance for recovery. Therefore, if you have any hope at all of staying alive, you must find the right kind of help, accept it, hang on to it, and work with it. If in seeking help you are put off, offended, scandalized—you then *are* back on your own, with a very low survival and sanity expectation. The moral of this story cannot be sufficiently emphasized; it cannot be overly drummed up, nailed down, reiterated, rubbed in, or roared out. If you love someone who is about to die, and you can save him by shouting, you naturally shout yourself hoarse. Are you listening, dear brother or sister addict? The moral is: *be aware* of the deadly possibility of scandal, and even if somebody spits in your eye, *do not permit yourself to be scandalized.*

We have mentioned the sort of occasion where you might be offended in dealing with your primary helping resources—the Answer-bearing, God-centered, truth-centered recovery movements, all of them in the hands of amateurs.

The possibilities of being scandalized in dealing with professional help are of quite a different nature. They are not so much an offense as a stumbling block. They are so complicated and so difficult, and at the same time such a serious threat to your chances for recovery, that it will be worth our while and yours to examine them in detail. There are a number of things in the ramified and burgeoning professional picture which are not generally known but which you ought to know if you value your life. Section 2 immediately following is devoted to this inquiry.

In relating to professional aid, the addict runs the risk not so much of being put off as of being taken in; that is, of being led into illusory hopes and misplaced confidence in "resources" which do not really help, in "treatments" which do not really cure, or, worst of all, in programs of endless medical "management" which are founded in frank despair of recovery.

SECTION II

The Strange Miscasting and Consequent
Confusion of the Professionals

Over a period of about twenty-five years, there has been a large effort on the part of doctors, psychiatrists, medical and social researchers, and other professionals—backed by the United States government—to find a solution to the problem of alcohol and drug addiction. This effort has been a failure. That is to say, no medical or psychiatric solution has been found, and none is in sight. The physical complications of addiction are treated successfully by medical means; the disease itself, the inability to stop drinking or drugging and stay stopped, is not.

"In the fifteen years I've been working in alcoholism, there have been no dramatic breakthroughs in understanding the disease." (Dr. Benjamin Kissen, director of the Alcoholism Program at Downstate Medical Center, Brooklyn. *New York Times,* July 18, 1972.)

"The search for an effective medical cure for [narcotics] addiction has so far failed. The occasional cure that has gained brief professional endorsement and popularity has later proved to be the result of wishful thinking, financial investment, or poorly designed

69

evaluative methods." (David F. Musto, M.D. *The American Disease*. New Haven: Yale University Press, 1973.)

To point out this failure is no dishonor to doctors. Their profession has embraced the spirit-denying world outlook of the present age, and that outlook radically disqualified its professors from certain activities. It would be no disgrace to farmers if they were required to produce locomotives, and failed. So it is with our doctors. Our society has thrust upon them a basically spiritual problem, the essential realities of which lie outside the modern medical purview and hence outside the field of the doctors' competence.

Massive confusions, however, arise from the fact that the professionals are not enlightened by repeated failure and continue, at great expense and diversion of precious resources, to seek answers from a materialistic outlook and discipline which, in the very nature of things, cannot provide the answers.

The prospects for an improvement in this picture are not good. It is not some kind of conspiracy among the professionals which keeps their failure covered up. What really keeps the professional record obscured are some of the deepest assumptions of our entire cultural world-view. The prevailing professional outlook is disdainful of morals, oblivious of God, and deeply concerned with money as a prime goal in life. The whole contemporary world outlook absolutely agrees, approves of, and indeed is the culturing medium for, this theoretical and practical approach of the professionals.

Therefore the great majority of the people at large are apt to believe that the professionals can do no wrong. If the pros haven't got an answer, well, there just isn't any answer, or one will be found very soon. And when the amateurs come on talking about moral rigor, submission to the truth and to God, and selfless and nonpaying service to your fellow man, you can see, given the present world outlook, that the general public *must* believe that the amateurs are nuts, *even though they are producing hundreds of thousands of recoveries from addiction* while the professionals are producing very few.

The problem we are talking about is involved in the sickness of an entire civilization, arising from deepseated, long-standing mistakes as to basic principles of the most elementary kind. In the face of this profound aberration, your authors certainly do not have answers which we think people in large numbers anywhere are about to believe. The answers are evident and simple enough, but the difficulties in a widespread change of belief are formidable. Important change is unlikely to occur as a result of any such efforts of which we are capable.

We do think that there may be some help in a fresh look at the problem from a standpoint which, whatever its defects, is *not* merely another rinse out of the current brainwashing machine to the effect that the professionals, if they haven't turned the trick yet, are nevertheless just about to turn the trick. We start from what appears really to be the fact, namely, that where the addiction problem is concerned the professionals have not gone anywhere and are not likely to go anywhere—an impasse resulting from their immersion in a spiritually blind outlook.

In dealing with addiction there are two basic approaches being practiced today and known by their results—the materialist approach and the spiritual approach. Both can be messed up when applied by corrupt or inept people. But note: The materialist approach produces *very little* results, even when applied by people with resources, skill, intelligence, and competence. And the spiritual approach produces *very large* results, even when applied by people who are broke, clumsy, stupid, and nearly or actually insane.

There are very practical reasons for all of us to put aside our philosophical prejudices and to take a new and unbiased look at the spiritual approach. But nobody can do that unless he has first seen the extent of the failure, in the hands of our professionals, of the materialist approach.

Chapter 5

The Worm's-Eye View of Man—
Spawning-Ground of Addiction

The modern world outlook. The flight from the past. The new view of reality. The universal view. The two views contrasted. Which is true? Intolerable conditions. Nature's answer to the problem: a popular anesthetic. Addiction is born. How do you like your suicide, slow or quick? A change of view has already taken place.

There is a general impression that alcohol addiction, if not drug addiction, is an ancient problem. As a matter of fact, alcohol and drug addiction are modern phenomena. They were unknown until comparatively recent times. The ancients had all kinds of troubles, but not this kind.

The sin of gluttony and the condition of drunkenness are as old as history, but the *compulsion* to drink or take drugs, the *inability to stop* drinking or drugging, are of relatively recent occurrence. Trying to find examples of true addiction, you will search the history and literature of early times in vain. Instances may have occurred, but if so they were exceedingly rare. To confuse drunkenness and alcoholism is a common and capital mistake. A person may have a lot of drunkenness in his life, even very bad drunkenness, and have a serious problem with drunkenness, and yet not be an alcoholic or anywhere near to being an alcoholic. Alcohol or drug addiction is *compulsion,* inability to stop drinking or drugging. The various studies of alcohol use among the ancients (Loeb, 1943,[17] McKinlay, 1953,[19] Keller, 1970,[13] for example) invariably turn out to be studies of drinking and drunkenness, *not* alcoholism, among the ancients. Dr. Ravi Varma's 1950 study, "Alcoholism in Ayurveda,"[21] is obviously mistitled; it is concerned throughout with descriptions of drunkenness and hangovers in the Vedic text, with no reference anywhere to compulsion, no mention of anyone's trying to stop drinking, let alone trying and failing to stop, no mention, that is, of alcohol *addiction,* of alcoholism properly so-called.

The story of addiction begins about four hundred years ago, and it begins not at first with addiction but with a radical shift in *world outlook.* Just offhand you might not think that world outlook had anything to do with addiction, but it turns out to have a great deal to do with it. How much, we shall see.

It is of course well known that human life proceeds in such a way that every so often there is a major change in the way people look at things. Not everything changes at such a time; some things endure; but some pretty big ideas change, with powerful effects on people and on the whole scene.

In the fifteenth and sixteenth centuries one of these big changes began to take place, and the *modern world-view* began to emerge. It was several hundred years in taking shape and gathering power, and at the present time it has extended from thinkers, philosophers, scientists, and teachers to the people at large and now reigns supreme over all the earth. With the growth of modern education and mass media, there is hardly a human being anywhere who is not deeply indoctrinated.

The modern world-view is something like a tent over all mankind. We are all under it from infancy, and most men regard modern ideas, if not exactly as the only ideas that ever existed, certainly as the only scientific and sensible ideas that ever existed. That some of our modern ideas may be wrong and some other ideas may be right is a possibility not often entertained in the modern world.

The modern change in view was different from any previous

change in certain basic ways. No other change had ever become the outlook of all cultures in both hemispheres as has the modern. And the modern view is marked by another highly peculiar feature, namely, a mania to repudiate, reject, discredit, and ignore the things of the past. It is as if modern humanity had some terrible need to get rid of its own roots, to stamp out its own history, to kill its own memory. It is as if an individual man wished to forget everything that happened in his life up until two or three hours ago. Such an effort, to the extent in which it succeeded, would mentally cripple the individual, and our society's flight from the past no doubt has much to do with the world-wide modern increase in insanity.

Another peculiarity is the revealing name which we have chosen for the outlook of our age. No other world-view would have deigned to call itself *modern,* a word which means "of the mode," a mere style or manner or fashion, and inevitably suggesting disinterest in the whole scope of human reality and incompetence in dealing with it.

Well, so there has been this radical shift in outlook, and we were saying that it has something to do with addiction. We will come to that in a moment, but first—

What *was* the big change? It was a change basically in what men took to be real. In all previous world outlooks, the primary reality in man and in the universe was considered to be spirit. This view of spirit at the core of things and as the source and support of things was one of the elements that had never changed but remained constant in all times and in all cultures, primitive and civilized, all over the earth. The *emphasis* among world outlooks has shifted from ideational and spiritual to sensate and materialistic and back to spiritual again many times throughout history, a development which Sorokin has documented in a key book, *The Crisis of Our Age.*[26] But there never has been a time until the present when *a radical repudiation of all spiritual reality* has become the philosophy of practically the whole world. The view of spirit as essential reality was held so widely, over so many millennia, and consistently through so many changes in world outlook that it may properly be called the *universal world-view* of reality.

Now we come to a critical point: In the modern world-view, not just a modification took place but a reversal. Men began to think that *matter* might be the basic reality in the universe. And then, rather quickly as such things go, it became the modern belief that matter is the *only* reality.

Somewhere along the line it was discovered that you cannot really get a fix on matter at all but that energy is what is involved. This was a considerable jolt to the "we've-got-hold-of-something-solid-at-last" mood of the times, but it caused hardly a philosophical ripple. The thinkers just said that matter-energy is the only reality, and the whole modern thought structure and scientific enterprise continued to be based on the gross materialist assumption.

The logical and practical result of all this was that the moderns began to look at *man* in a new way. In the modern view, spirit has come to be regarded as nil, soul as nil, and mind as a kind of bodily emanation. The universal view of man had seen him as consisting of spirit, soul, and body. The modern view began to see him as body only, with a little room left for mind as a kind of effluvium or "epiphenomenon" of matter—something arising out of matter more or less as fogs arise out of swamps.

The universal view is a true *theoria*—a God's-eye or bird's-eye view of man—taking in his whole nature, including his lowest, middle, and highest aspects. The modern view is a worm's-eye view, concentrating as it does upon man's lowest parts and not only minimizing but amputating his higher elements. Soul and spirit have become for modern man not merely nebulous and unimportant but unreal, nonexistent, and, even as mere concepts, stupid and superstitious. The two world-views, the universal and the modern, are contrasted thus:

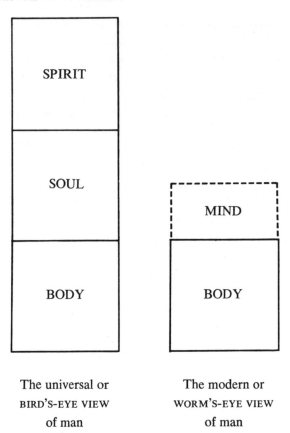

The universal or
BIRD'S-EYE VIEW
of man

The modern or
WORM'S-EYE VIEW
of man

Which view is true?

To anyone who is really sold on the modern world-view—and that means practically everyone—this is a foolish question. The modern view is right, unquestionably.

How come? How did people get to feeling this way? How is it that we will not even consider other views, and particularly we will not consider older views? It is because modern men feel themselves to be the wisest men who ever lived. In spite of appalling contradictions, we maintain a childlike confidence in the modern outlook, and we deeply distrust and despise anything which our ancestors thought. If, for example, you want to put an idea down, you can give it the kiss of death by saying that it "harks back to the Middle Ages."

Now the universal view of man as spirit, soul, and body not only harks back to the Middle Ages, it harks back to the Flood and beyond. The universal view most certainly is *outmoded* by the modern, but we are not dealing here with a mere matter of modes, styles, or fashions of thought. We are dealing with a serious question of basic reality, with practical and urgent consequences hanging upon the answer. The question is: "May not the universal view be *true* after all?"

Could we at least keep the possibility open? Really, the notion of modern men's infallibility is not an honorable part of the modern outlook but something more like a paranoid excrescence. In fact there *are* some things about which we moderns have been seriously mistaken. We once thought that atoms were little solid pellets. And we once thought that we could solve our alcohol problem by passing a law. And we once thought that cigarette smoking was harmless.

You may say that modern experience and modern research have cleared all that up. Well, yes, *but modern men once believed all that and were wrong.* Could we admit, as a working fact, that modern men can be wrong and modern views can be wrong? If we are able to do this, the door to major solutions to major problems stands open. We do not ask you, the reader, abruptly to change your view of man but merely to entertain the possibility that the modern view is mistaken—that the universal view was and is right—that man indeed is not merely body but *body, soul, and spirit.*

If this *is* the truth, it explains a lot of things. It penetrates certain stubborn modern "mysteries." It goes a long way, for example, toward untying the knot of addiction.

Remember what we said at the outset: addiction is a modern phenomenon. Since prehistoric times there have been gluttonous eating and drinking among humans and plenty of drunkenness, but alcohol or drug addiction as we know it—as compulsion and inability to stop—was practically unknown until three or four hundred years ago. Alcoholism, the first and still champion of the drug addictions, appeared in the seventeenth and eighteenth centuries, *precisely at the time when modern man on a wide scale was rejecting the soul of man, the spirit of man, and the Spirit of the universe.*

Addiction made its appearance in exactly the period when man was in the process of being dehumanized and alienated from God. Could it be that there was a profound reciprocal relationship between these two events? It seems more than likely. To have your spirit and soul amputated, to be so brainwashed that you go into hypnotically effective disbelief in your own higher members and higher possibilities—this is a critical and agonizing operation. Perhaps the pain of it had something to do with the sudden, widespread need for a readily available, popular, powerful anesthetic and for the sudden widespread, addictive dependence upon the anesthetic.

Nature seems to make remarkably apposite responses to strong and extensive human need, whether the need be for something good, bad, or neutral. The modern world of automobiles would be impossible without a tough, flexible, air tight, grippy substance to hold the cars on the road. Nature's answer was rubber—brought to light exactly at the time it was needed. The modern world of spiritual vacuum, crazy pressures, and corrupt environment would have been unendurable without the availability of cheap, effective, portable, and pleasant anesthetics. Nature's answer was distilled spirits[3n] and narcotic drugs—brought to light exactly at the time they were needed.

Somewhere around 800 A.D. "human ingenuity evolved the process of distillation. . . . An Arabian alchemist named Jabir ibn Hayyān and known to the West as Geber is generally credited with this resounding feat"[23] but he evidently saw no practical use for the stuff. In the thirteenth century Arnold de Villanova and Raymond

Lully, both also alchemists, described medicinal properties of "aqua vitae." But distilled spirits remained for the most part a mere oddity of the pharmacology of earlier times.[4n] Then suddenly, in the seventeenth century, as if by a revelation, they became generally available and went into popular use in a number of European countries almost simultaneously, soon spreading from there all over the world. Narcotic herbs and drugs have been used for millennia in therapeutic, social, and religious contexts, but the vicious use of these materials, *narcotics addiction,* first appeared in the Orient at exactly the same time that alcohol addiction was emerging in the West.[5n]

Well, so men thought to get rid of spirit, soul, and God, but it was a bungled operation which left the patient in agonizing pain and set up in him a desperate need for anodynes. And it solved no problems. It was, after all, a head trip. You cannot get rid of ontological realities by thinking them away. You produce some effect on yourself, but the realities remain. You may think that the Atlantic Ocean does not exist, but that does not change the ocean or make it go away. It just changes your relationship to the ocean for the worse and creates certain stubborn difficulties in your dealing with reality.

Spirit, soul, and God never actually were altered by the modern outlook; they remained just what they always were. But man was *effectively robbed of his knowledge and faith* in these realities, and this loss hit him in his vitals. It was as if—indeed it was worse than if—a man were to lose knowledge and use of his own legs and bowels.

Spirit is the source and the principle of meaning (from *intellectus*), of strength (from *voluntas*), and of joy (from *caritas*). When man began to lose conscious touch with spirit, his life and his surroundings were progressively drained of meaning, strength, and joy. It is possible to trace this actual development historically in great detail. It is sufficient here to note that the worm's-eye view of man on a world-wide scale began to produce conditions of mind and conditions of environment which are literally intolerable to very large numbers of people. The need for a popular anesthetic became imperative. And since the need was so desperate, the development of dependence, and finally unbreakable dependence, was inevitable. Thus addiction was born.

Before we go on to consider compulsive drinking and drugging as a chief disease and burden of modern man, let us give the devil his due. Let us consider the possible good that addiction has done.

When faced with really intolerable pain—particularly spiritual, psychical, or mental pain over months and years—men are powerfully inclined to kill themselves. It is possible that alcohol and drug addiction, coming in when it did, has forestalled widespread epidemics of suicide. We kill ourselves at a pretty lively rate as it is, but booze and drugs may have taken the edge off the ferocious pain of modern life sufficiently to slow the disaster down somewhat.

Granted, addiction itself is slow suicide. Nevertheless, we may have distilled spirits and mood-altering drugs to thank for postponing the death crisis in many men and in the whole culture itself. The postponement may turn out to be a bitter deception in many cases, and it may yet prove so in the culture; the final ruin may be as bad as outright self-murder would have been. But where there is life there is hope, and we cannot do other than hang on to that hope and to the promise that with a change of view, a change in the whole addiction situation is possible.

Now, as we have seen, a change of view has already taken place. The recovered-addict societies—rejecting the worm's-eye view and reembracing the universal view of man—have found the Answer to addiction. In large numbers, they have found the way through to total freedom from alcohol and drugs *and from the spiritual nightmare that leads to their use.* This discovery appears to be potentially unlimited in its application, but it is actually greatly hindered by the still-dominant influence of the worm's-eye view on the modern scene.

CHAPTER 6

Let George Do It

We are oblivious of the obvious. The three-point proposition. The amazing vitality of failing scientific enterprises. The three Georges. The preacher has a go at it. The cops are called. The painful sequel. Enter George the Third. Back to the drawing board. Why George is unable to do it. The problem cannot be solved by force, or from the outside. Why the medical impasse is being covered up.

We've got a very tough problem with alcohol and drug addiction. It keeps getting tougher. And we keep making the same mistake in trying to solve it. We do not see the obvious.

Obviously addiction is the addicts' problem. Nobody but the addicts themselves can solve it. Nobody else can solve it for them. But we keep expecting that somebody else *will* solve it for them; we keep insisting that somebody else *must* solve it for them. For a hundred and fifty years, right up to the present day, our approach has been one of straight paternalism, and since addicts are a dependent sort of folk, they are apt to play right along. The addicts themselves are not expected to deal with the difficulty. And the public is not expected to deal with it. Somebody else is.

Our attitude is to let George do it.

Over the years, there have been several Georges. The one we have at the present time is George the Third. Right now George wears a stethoscope. Our current white hope is the doctor. We have spent about twenty-five years setting him up for this role. A considerable publicity apparatus has worked hard to sell both the doctors and the public on a simple three-part proposition: (1) addiction is a disease; (2) doctors successfully treat disease; (3) doctors can and will successfully treat the disease of addiction. The seeming logic of this proposition has proved irresistible. It has swept all before it. Practically everybody now believes it.

But it has one defect. It happens to be wrong. It is a *non sequitur.* The first and second parts of the propostion clearly are true. The third part simply is not true. On the record, doctors cannot successfully treat addiction. The physical complications of addiction, yes. The addiction itself—the inability to stop drinking or drugging —no. The proposition is a false syllogism. The ineffectiveness of any and all medical methods in dealing with the spiritual disease of addiction has been clear for a long time. The failure is recognized in the highest places. But at the same time there are no signs of admitting defeat, and no interest at all in other solutions.

Failing scientific enterprises have amazing momentum. People just cannot believe that the race is lost. The horse comes thundering down the stretch, going the wrong way, on the wrong track, and instead of kind and decent attempts to stop the poor beast, there are cries of, "Fetch a whip!" and, "More oats!" Bucked up by demands for more money and for more research, a very large medical effort continues, in the expectation that there will yet be a breakthrough, somehow. There is something magnificent in this plowing ahead in the teeth of contrary evidence and repeated failure. There is something dangerous in it, too, because it encourages false hopes in people to whom false hopes may be fatal, and it drains off resources that could be better used otherwise.

Our romance with George the doctor is the last in a series. Fifty years ago it was George the policeman. And before that it was George the preacher.

Serious attempts to do something about addiction got going in this country early in the nineteenth century. Alcohol, then as now, was the big addiction substance; indeed, drug addiction was at that time hardly a factor. But booze trouble was widespread, and it was big trouble by anybody's accounting. Even the most ardent boozers sheepishly had to admit that there was a national mess. So what did we, the people, do? Then as now, we called in the experts. Then as now, we did not want to dirty our own hands with the mess. Then as now, it did not occur to anybody that the addicts themselves should or could do anything about it. So, then as now, the cry was, "Let George do it."

In those days George wore a halo. George the preacher, George the religious expert, really didn't need to be called in but, like his kind from time immemorial, was ready to rush in unbidden. Women's lib, without the label yet but very much alive, was a big factor in this campaign, and George was not only assisted but surpassed by Georgette. Lady religious experts flooded the scene; the excitement and the energies were immense; and altogether it was rather a terrific time. There really were high expectations for a solution.

But all the while there was this fatal flaw in the operation: it was somebody else who was going to fix the victims. The drunks themselves were patients, not agents. And by the turn of the century it was evident that George and Georgette were not making it. With all the work and all the hope—and there was a lot of both—the alcoholic mess was clearly getting worse.

And now a rather dazzling thing happened. As in a critical relay race, George the preacher passed the baton to—of all people— George the cop. It was an astonishing maneuver, but strictly logical, too. After all, when religion fails, what *do* you do? You call in the cops, of course. Laws were hurriedly pasted together and rammed through the Congress, the legal plaster was laid on the whole country, and we were off to the races once more with hopes higher than ever.

Let us here spare ourselves even the briefest review of the career of George the cop as an alcohol problem-solver. Let us draw the veil over the noble experiment. The Prohibition story is too well known and too painful to bear another look. We learned nothing from it, and we are in no mood to learn anything from it now. Everybody by this time recognizes that George the Second—George the cop—is not to be blamed. The burden was foisted on him with a vengeance. It never really was his trip at all. Half the time he was a drinking man himself. The way it was set up, the police and the law never had a chance. It was a total bummer, attributable not to the personnel but to a crashing mistake in principle.

All right, time marches on, and the relentless logic of the problem marches with it. When there is bad trouble, and you call in the preacher, and he can't handle the situation, and you call in the cops, and they can't handle it, either—what do you do now? The answer of course is perfectly obvious: you call the doctor.

If the patient is morally intractable and physically unrestrainable, one thing at least is clear: he must be sick. And the doctor is the man for that. George the Third comes on the scene.

And there are great sighs of relief all around. Why was this solution not thought of long ago? The whole problem now emerges into beautiful country. The poor addict was *sick* all along. Not a moral leper. Not even a naughty boy. In fact, he was never wrong at all. Nobody is to blame. It isn't anybody's fault. All that time he was just diseased—and the doctor can handle that.

What a relief! How many agonies ended at last! The whole moral problem solved at a single stroke! The legal, enforcement, and custodial problems all lined up for neat, medically oriented solutions! And the worst one of all, the responsibility problem, now finally off the preacher's back, off the cop's back, off the public's back, off the addict's back and into competent hands at last! Dear doctor, *do* take over! The problem is all yours!

The whole professional field went up in a balloon over the sickness idea as soon as they saw it—except the doctors themselves. They were not so quick on the uptake. By training and experience they were cagey, and they knew the history of the problem. Lacking the preacher's fervor, and not under public authority like the cops, the doctors were in no hurry to accept the assignment. But the pressure was very heavy. Special groups came into existence, like the National Council on Alcoholism,[6n] whose chief mission was to hammer the "it's-a-disease" concept and subtly and by every means to insinuate its presumed corollary: "The doctor can handle it."

At last—somewhere in the fifties—the public, the government, and the doctors themselves were persuaded. The doctors took on the job. "Yes," they said, "it *is* a disease. And yes, we can handle it. Not right away, and not very effectively at first, but with more research . . ." Ah, yes. With more research . . .

A long time has now gone by, longer than all of Prohibition time, with the problem in the doctors' hands. And they are still nowhere with it, as nowhere as the preachers were and the cops were.

But here a very sticky kind of difficulty arises. We are not going to let go so easily this time. We can't, because there are no more experts to turn to. There is no George the Fourth waiting in the wings. We, all of us—the public, the government, the doctors themselves—have a huge rational, emotional, and financial investment in the proposition that there must be a medical solution to addiction. The investment is so vast that it is proving exceedingly resistant to the facts. But the facts are sufficiently clear now, and they add up inexorably to this: The doctors have not done the job, cannot do the job, and show no real promise of ever doing the job.

So, back to the drawing board.

What *is* wrong in all of these cases? It is easy to blame the preachers, the cops, and now the doctors for their inability to solve this problem. But they are not at fault, except insofar as they fall in with and go along with the fundamental error.

What is the mistake?

It is letting George do it. George cannot do it, because it is not his problem. It is not essentially a physical problem, where the cops could use physical force and the doctors could use chemical force.

It is not essentially a psychical or mental problem, where the preachers could use moral pressure or the psychiatrists could use psychological manipulation. Force, pressure, manipulation—these are the only tools George has. And they never work for addiction, because this problem never can be solved by force, no matter how well intentioned and no matter how kindly or skillfully applied. And it cannot be solved from the outside, that is by people who know nothing about it from direct, personal experience.

Addiction is a spiritual disease and a spiritual problem, and it can be solved only by the action of the spiritual free will. It is futile to try to force the addict—religiously, psychically, mechanically, or chemically. And it is equally futile to coddle, wet-nurse, or baby the addict—religiously, psychically, mechanically, or chemically. The job of recovery from addiction cannot be done from the outside by any kind of cleverness, energy, or subterfuge. Outside *help* often is critically and urgently needed, but the *job itself*—breaking the addiction and rebuilding the wreck—can only be done from within, by free consent and in full responsibility, by the persons directly concerned. It is the addicts themselves, individually and in groups, who must solve this problem and do this work, because— how much more proof do we need?—nobody else can.

And already, in large numbers, they *are* doing it. The addicts are solving their own problem. Working under heavy handicaps, they are doing an imperfect job of it, *but they are doing it.* The number of recoveries is large—in the hundreds of thousands—and growing. We have the Answer. We need only to encourage it, support it, and apply it was widely as possible.

The Answer is here—but it has met with a strange reception. The professionals, whose pride and whose pocketbooks are deeply involved, cannot stomach the fact that the addicts have found their own way out. The Answer which is here, the Answer which works, is on the one hand ignored and on the other hand elaborately and cleverly depreciated by the powers that be.

The result is very odd indeed. Even though the Answer is at

hand, and the medical and professional people know it is at hand, the futile medical-professional search for "answers" continues in high gear, at great cost, and with much sound and fury in the public press.

In the nineteenth and early twentieth century we learned our first lesson: that you cannot stop people from drinking *by moral or religious exhortation.* From 1918 to 1931 we learned our second lesson: that you cannot stop people from drinking *by law.* We are late in learning our third lesson: that you cannot stop people from drinking *by medicine.* It is clear to everyone that George the preacher and George the cop have failed. It is by no means as yet clear to everyone that George the doctor has failed. Indeed he *has* failed and must continue to fail, but the professional publicity apparatus keeps the failure covered up.

CHAPTER 7

The Wild-Goose Chase in Search of the Answer that Already Exists

How far should you believe the doctor? The worm's-eye view again. The trouble is with the people. The search for omniscience, omnipotence, and love. The scientific feet of clay. Idolatry is a practical mistake. The professional organizations. No medical cure for addiction. The good news which is ignored, while the goose chase continues.

When this book was being written, a wise and experienced friend said, "Why don't you get a doctor to coauthor it with you?"

We said, "But we will be raising serious questions about medicine, and indeed we are going to have to blow medicine away to some extent."

"Of course," our friend said, "but you still ought to get a doctor as a coauthor. Lots of people will believe the doctor, whereas very few will believe you."

And there you have it, in the famous nutshell. People do believe the doctor, and from that fact great good *and* great trouble arise. To believe the doctor is surely good, up to a point. You cannot get help from anybody unless you believe him and trust him. And in the life-and-death affairs in which you are apt to be involved with the doctor, your belief-and-trust reading ought to be high, and the higher the better, up to a point. But here is the trouble. The point was long ago exceeded. We not only believe and trust the doctor, as doctor. We believe and trust him as priest, as prophet, as God himself. Literally. Look at the modern scene, and you can see plainly that it is so.

The deification of the doctor is not altogether the doctor's fault. It is a result of the worm's-eye view of man. The role of God Almighty has been thrust upon medical men by a culture which, in abandoning spirit, has abandoned the primal Authority and in practical matters is earnestly and indeed frantically seeking effective substitutes.

The doctors, of course, are not wholly innocent in this matter. A considerable section of the profession is human enough to fancy the God role and to play into it somewhat. The medical people are heavily influenced by the worm's-eye view of man and are big believers in it. And every serious worm's-eye man is forced to fill the God-vacuum in himself by deifying his own ego. Doctors are not exempt from this necessity, and so when people all around start bowing down and burning incense, as it were, many doctors are bound to inhale.

The main trouble, however, is not with the doctors but with the people. Led by scientists, philosophers, and educators and aided and abetted by the modern scribes and Pharisees (worm's-eye religious authorities), the people have abandoned God. But they are haunted by the reality they have denied. Their intuitions about the reality are intact and in good working order. The people know perfectly well that the chief practical attributes of deity are omniscience, omnipotence, and inalienable love—*agapē*. The people also know that unless there are omniscience, omnipotence, and *agapē* to lean upon, man must go mad. (Can anyone any longer ignore the rate at which we are going mad?)

When God is banished, and has the dreadful courtesy to accept the ostracism, what is changed? Nothing, really. God is still God, and human nature is still human nature. Nothing is changed, except this: we now seek blindly, irrationally, and madly the reality which in more normal times was sought openly, with reason, and —sick as our race has always been—with some degree of sanity.

So here is our urgent, practical predicament, and here is the history to date of our search for a solution: we are unwittingly but desperately seeking omniscience, omnipotence, and *agapē*. And there is no God. So what *is* there? It is all terribly logical and obvious. There is the scientist.

Yes, there is the scientist. But, steady! don't get rattled. Of course the scientist is not *really* God. Nobody is (yet) so mad as to believe that. But the scientist *does* know a lot. And he *can* do a lot. And he is often very humble about his accomplishments (another attribute of the Most High).

And so for some years, for maybe a century, we tried to make do with the scientist in place of the Deity. This modern mystery play never did quite come off, however, and we began to be nervous again. The scientific feet of clay began to show. Although nobody (except Dostoevski and a few other wild men) ever said so right out loud, we did seem to be going crazy, along with our other achievements. What the scientist knew and could do exceeded our expectations, but it was not enough. And it was not *agapē*. Far from it.

Our next move again was obvious. We found the man who had what was missing. We found *the scientist with a heart.* Who is he? You guessed it. Your doctor.

Who else? Our terrible hope, our desperate faith, our starved and yearning love went out to him, and rested upon him, and still rests upon him. It is so logical and so right, up to a point. The doctor bears the burden of our trust perhaps more nobly (since we no longer recognize saints) than any kind of man in recent history. He deserves our veneration and our trust. But not our supreme veneration and trust. When that line is crossed—and indeed we have crossed it—the fat is in the fire again.

Now here is a curious point: you do not really honor any object when you put it in place of God. Idolatry is no mere theological wrangle and no joke. It is an elementary and devastating mistake. And the more excellent the idolized object, the more devastating the mistake. The better the being, the more revolting is its corruption. The corpse of a man stinks worse than the corpse of a dog. Human beings who idolize their own kind spoil societies and nations; angels who idolize their own kind spoil planets.

Well, come now, you say. After all, is it that bad? The poor old doctor is just down the street there, passing out his prescriptions and doing his best to help people out and to make a buck in the bargain. What is so bad about that?

What is so bad is that this (in most cases) honorable, industrious, and useful citizen really and literally *is* idolized. That is, at the very least, he is estimated far beyond his considerable merits and capacities. And with this result: we individual men, and our whole society, *are* laying an omniscience trip on the doctors, to their great harm and to ours. We really do expect them to be always right, whereas actually they are often wrong. Inevitably.

Now it is a serious thing for the doctor to be wrong. Somebody may get hurt or die as a result of it, and the doctor himself is liable to be injured or ruined as a result of it. Not only the patient but the doctor is vulnerable. Therefore, quite naturally and legitimately, the doctors have taken steps to protect themselves from undue harm as a result of their errors. The outcome has been the growth of powerful professional organizations to protect and foster the welfare of doctors, and these organizations exert very strong influence upon the public through the news media. Furthermore, they bring heavy pressures to bear upon the government, particularly the Food and Drug Administration and the Department of Health, Education, and Welfare, through expensive and efficient lobbying machineries.

The effect of all this is powerfully to reinforce the people's tendency to make God out of the doctor. As a result of the lobbying and publicity activities of the professional organizations, what the doctors do wrong is apt to be concealed or presented in a cleaned-up version, and what the doctors do right is apt to be dramatized or magnified out of relationship to the truth.

Indeed, the professional medical and psychiatric establishment has now reached a position of power in this country in every way comparable to that of the medieval church in Europe. It has practically all of the public credence and trust, and any pockets of heresy are ruthlessly attacked and wiped out. The medical establishment is multiplying hospitals and expanding definitions of disease at such a rate that very soon if somebody says "good morning" to you it will constitute a medical problem and come under medicolegal scrutiny and jurisdiction. This is not a jest. It is a sober fact of our age. We are further along on this road than is generally realized.

The overall result is that instead of having a decent and honorable respect for doctors, for what they really are and what they really can do, we expect them to be what they are not, and we expect things from them that they simply cannot produce.

Recovery from addiction, for instance.

For many years now we have been expecting that the doctors will provide a solution for the addiction problem—that is, a means of recovery for addicts. But the expectations never at any time have been realized, or shown any real promise of being realized. A vast amount of medical research has been done, to no avail so far as recovery is concerned. What has long been known is still the fact: neither alcohol nor drug addiction can be medically cured. There is no medical solution, present or in sight.

Meanwhile, as we have seen, full recovery from addiction is possible and has actually been achieved, over a period of many years, in a large number of cases, by easily understandable, universally available, nonmedical means.

Somehow—it is one of the marvels of the age—the news that full recovery from addiction is in being, in force, and succeeding on a broad front has not reached the medical people. Somehow this magnificent fact of the times has not reached the doctors and their professional and governmental associates. They have *heard* of it of course, but for some reason it has not penetrated, not sunk in, not been recognized. And since the doctors, the professionals, and the government people dominantly influence the news media, the great news of the Answer to addiction has not reached the public, in any form that people can understand or estimate at its real significance.

The news is now well over a quarter of a century old. Each

passing year confirms the reality of it and witnesses the steady growth in the numbers of *fully recovered addicts now spread through all levels of the population.* But the people remain in ignorance of what is really going on; they, too, hear of it, but in such a way that its significance and importance are veiled. It simply is not generally known that full recovery from addiction is widespread and increasing. Yet that *is* the fact, beyond question, beyond doubt, beyond possibility of misunderstanding.

At the very same time, while all these addicts have been recovering over all these years, a whole battalion of doctors—supported by professional co-workers, sustained by the United States government, and encouraged by extensive public sympathy and good will—are pursuing the ever-elusive "answer" to the "insoluble problem" of addiction.

While they are diligently searching the lakes and ponds, the meadows and hedges, the hills and streamsides, the fields and woodlands—the goose is quietly at home in the yard.

The whole picture *is* rather mad.

The present official, governmental, medical, professional effort in dealing with addiction is off on a wrong track. There is important work, in the physical and social *complications* of addiction, to be done by doctors and other professionals. But the present group are off on a wild-goose chase, seeking "answers" to a "mystery" which has in fact already been solved and for which a full working Answer already exists, needing only to be further applied.

If even half of the energy which now goes into the wild-goose chase were put into facilitation and extension of the known Answer, the long-hoped-for "breakthrough" in addiction would quickly come to pass.

CHAPTER 8

The Disease Concept of Addiction—
How It Grew, and the Games that Are
Being Played with It.

*Granted the addict is sick; what is all the shouting about? Tricks
with the word "treatment." Professor Lovibond and his "controlled
drinkers." Scientific whistling in the dark. Smart publicity, dangerous deception. What an addict needs to know. Recovery is possible.
Not treatment but spiritual conversion. The deadly syllogism.*

Hundreds of thousands of dollars have been spent in an effort to
convince the people of America that alcohol addiction is a disease.
In recent years the emphasis of this publicity barrage has been
centered particularly upon the slogan, "Alcoholism is a treatable
disease," or the variant, "Alcoholism is a disease. It can be
treated."

There is something strange in all this. In the first place, why
would all that money have to be spent to convince people of anything so obvious? Anybody who knows anything at all about addiction knows that the addict is sick. Perhaps some public education
on the point would be in order—but a big, continuous, expensive
publicity campaign on this point? What is that all about?

And those claims about treatment. What do they mean? "Alcoholism is treatable." Isn't that an odd thing to say? Any and
every condition is treatable. You can treat everything from warts
to cancer. But what does that prove? Treatment in itself means
nothing, and everybody knows it means nothing. The only possible
point of interest for a suffering man is whether his condition can

be *effectively* treated. Can it be *successfully* treated? That is what he wants to know.

Why, then, do the publicity statements not say that alcoholism can be successfully treated or effectively treated? If this could be said, do you not think it would be? The statement is not made for a very elementary reason: it is untrue.

The fact—to which this remarkable publicity campaign bears striking witness—is this: alcoholism is a disease which *cannot* be successfully or effectively treated in any significant number of cases. If it could be successfully treated, they would say so. Since they do not say so, and are indeed scrupulous to avoid saying so, you can rest assured that it cannot be successfully treated.[7n]

Our files are full of reports out of the medical, professional, and public press of "successful" treatments or therapies for alcoholism. Now if any of these treatments actually *were* successful, you would hear more about it. Any really successful treatment would be bound to cause a sensation and a sustained follow-up, well publicized. But these "successful" treatments, one and all, simply disappear from view and are not heard of again. Sometimes there is a fairly extended flap over a treatment before the inevitable disappointment comes, but more often there is no report of the failure; the obituary takes the form of disappearance and silence.

These will-o'-the-wisps twinkle so luxuriantly in the professional heaven that a whole climate of hope is engendered which is nevertheless quite groundless. Nobody wants to notice that there is not one fixed star in the whole flickering show—that there is no real basis for hope anywhere in this empyrean.

Let's look at just one example out of many: in January 1970, the *Medical Tribune* ran an article under the headline: SHOCK THERAPY FOR ALCOHOLICS ACHIEVES SUCCESS RATE OF 75%. This is such a terrific report you would think they would have run it as a banner across the front page. The editors, however, obviously with tongue in cheek, ran it in small type across one column. They didn't have the heart to say, "Here is just another one of these clinkers." But by giving it minimum space they said in effect, "Don't take this too seriously."

And of course they were right. The text of the article quickly gave the show away. It seems that a certain Professor Lovibond, professor of psychiatry in Sydney, Australia, was administering electric shocks to selected alcoholics in an effort to turn them into "controlled drinkers." Alas, that men calling themselves scientists should waste time on this kind of activity. Here is perhaps the oldest and certainly the dreariest of the alcoholic delusions. Every real alcoholic who ever lived has made the experiment of "controlled drinking." And by this time everybody ought to know the answer: for a real alcoholic there never is, never was, and never can be any such thing as "controlled drinking." Countless thousands of alcoholics, with and without scientific assistance, have died proving this point. How many more sacrifices do we have to make on this gory old altar?

Obit: there have been no further headlines of Professor Lovibond's activities with addicts. Other accounts of the same *kind* of experiment of course continue to appear—and to disappear.

You can make a regular hobby of reading the professional journals and watching these birds-of-a-season come and go. In your first few weeks of bird watching, you will get the impression that the alcohol addiction problem is right on the verge of being solved. After a few months, however, you begin to wonder, since the same birds never return. After a couple of years, the truth becomes painfully apparent: the whole exhibition is just a rather sad form of scientific whistling in the dark.

The next time you hear or read of a "successful" treatment for alcoholism or drug addiction, make a note of it. A year later, inquire around, check the journals, and see where it is. The chances are you can't find out anything about it at all; it will simply have vanished into the night. Occasionally there is a more substantial and protracted pursuit of the illusion, as in the case some years ago of Flagyl as a treatment for alcoholism.

From *Perception* (Greater Boston Council on Alcoholism):

Metronidazole Strikes Out: The general public, made aware that alcoholism is the fourth ranking disease in the United States, has awaited with clove-tinged breath announcement of a one-shot pill to "cure" alcoholism. Three years ago, J.A. Taylor, M.D., announced in the *Bulletin* of the Los Angeles Neurological Society that metronidazole was a new agent for combined somatic and psychic therapy in alcoholism. Dr. Taylor repeated the claim at the meeting of the Federation of American Societies for Experimental Biology at Atlantic City in April, 1966. The Los Angeles announcement had created no great stir, but the Atlantic City hurrah was hailed in the lay press in extravagant and sensational terms. Metronidazole was touted by the press as "blocking alcoholic thirst," "banishing the taste for whiskey," and "making a sober life more palatable."

Metronidazole is marketed by G. D. Searle & Company under the trade name of Flagyl, and is approved by the Federal Drug Administration only for use as a flagellacide to be used in treating trichomoniasis vaginalis, an infection of the female reproductive organs. The story went that an alcoholic in Los Angeles whose wife was being treated with Flagyl for this infection dipped into his wife's pills while drunk and came up with an abhorrence for liquor. Since then, the most extraordinary claims have been made here and there around the country, including an editorial in the Boston *Herald,* hailing Flagyl as the final solution of the dilemma of treating alcoholism.

Then came the April 1967 issue of the *American Journal of Psychiatry* with an article by Dr. Donald W. Goodwin of the Department of Psychiatry of Washington University, St. Louis. In an effort to confirm Dr. Taylor's observations of Flagyl, a controlled double-blind study was carried out in St. Louis. First, 12 alcoholic outpatients, males between the ages of 25 and 50, all in good physical health and with no psychiatric diagnosis other than alcoholism, were chosen. They were selected as good risks in the sense of being of normal intelligence, reliability, cooperativeness, and motivation. They were men most likely to succeed in an alcoholism-treatment program of any kind. They were started on a regimen of Flagyl, supplied by the Searle Company, which also supplied placebos to be used. Three patients were switched to the placebos without their knowledge during the double-blind tests.

Of the 12 who started on Flagyl, 10 spontaneously stopped taking the drug within periods ranging from one to six weeks. Eight promptly resumed drinking, and six of the eight seemed to be drinking more heavily than previously. Of the 12 "good prognosis" alcoholics, eight resumed heavy drinking within six weeks. Two of the remaining four stopped taking the drug because of apparent distressing side effects, and the other two, although abstinent on the drug for four months, remained sober on the placebo and were unable to distinguish the drug from the placebo.

Reactions from taking the drug, when reported, were equivocal, the researchers reported, and in one patient persisted even on the placebo. In short, the double-blind study produced 100 percent failure in 12 patients who had a good prognosis for responding to any kind of treatment. . . . It is commented that it is not unusual for alcholics to maintain sobriety for months at a time after treatment—any kind of treatment—so that without the control data of a double-blind study the purported response to the drug might still seem as sensational as the original sensational report indicated. Metronidazole, anyone?

Methadone is the latest example of such "successful" treatments, in this case for narcotics addiction. The methadone program has already abandoned recovery as a goal (the usual sequence in these failures) and gone over to "maintenance," that is, permanent methadone addiction, as its contribution to human welfare.

As of today, neither alcohol addiction nor drug addiction can be successfully treated, and there is no reasonable basis for expecting that they ever will be successfully treated. The publicity reports continue, however, at full blast to say that "alcoholism is a treatable disease."

Well, but why—out of sheer embarrassment if for no other reason—do the publicity people not cease and desist? Out of mere discretion if out of no nobler motive, why do they not keep silence on this dreadfully revealing point?

What they are doing may seem weird, but it is not stupid. It is a calculated risk, based on the knowledge that people do not reason rigorously at all times and that infrequent unpleasant objections really require no answer but can be ignored. The statement that alcoholism is a treatable disease, without at all saying so, implies *successful* treatment. A lot of people will get the impression that successful treatment is available. It is an old gimmick in the publicity game, and it works. Furthermore, in a good cause, in offering at least hope of success before success is at hand, this subterfuge of the publicity people may be said to do some good. Who is going to blame them?

Well, I guess we are going to blame them. I guess we are going to say that it is a bad show. We are going to say that the alcohol addict who is convinced by publicity that alcoholism can be successfully treated has been deluded on a critical point, and the well-meaning publicity people may have his death to account for as a result.

What the addict needs to know is the simple truth. On that basis, if he really wants to recover he has a very good chance to do so. The truth is now well demonstrated and should be well known: (1) Alcoholism and drug addiction *cannot* be successfully treated; all treatment resources are indeed equally effective; none of them works. The physical complications of addiction can be successfully treated, but the spiritual disease itself—the disease of the intelligence and the will which makes the addict unable to stop drinking or drugging—this cannot be successfully treated. However, (2) *recovery is possible.* Total and sustained freedom from alcohol or drugs with a full return to joyous, responsible life is possible by means of well-established, well-proved, widely available means.

Recovery can be achieved not by treatment (if I went into a meeting of Alcoholics Anonymous and tried to "treat" somebody, they would throw me out), but by spiritual conversion, brotherly love, and the wisdom which arises in a community of recovering addicts.

Spiritual conversion cannot be brought about by any form of

induction, coercion, persuasion, or manipulation—and particularly it cannot be brought about by treatment. It occurs when the addict himself takes responsibility for his situation, turns to God and truth for support, begins to receive and to give help without thought of reward among his recovering brother and sister addicts, and begins to understand and apply the practical wisdom which working with other recovering addicts produces . . . and which nothing else can or does produce.

Spiritual conversion revolutionizes the life. Not by psychological "therapy" or by physiological "treatment" but by a flood of spiritual light—the man is released from the dungeon in which the worm's-eye view of man has imprisoned him. He not only believes but joyously sees and exultantly knows that his tortured body and mind can now be healed because of what he himself essentially and inalienably *is*—an immortal soul, a soaring spirit, a starburst of the eternal life and love which pervade the universe.

These are poor words for what actually happens. It is something very big. But it takes something big to swing the iron doors of addiction. Chemicals and psychological formulae are inadequate to this task. A spiritual lock needs to be opened, and it requires a spiritual key. When the spirit of the addict arouses itself after long sleep and calls upon the Spirit of the universe, everything becomes possible. Without that turning about, without that spiritual conversion, nothing is possible.

The disease concept of addiction is obviously right and good in itself. But it has become the major premise in the formula: "addiction is a disease; doctors can successfully treat disease; therefore doctors can successfully treat addiction." And by this deadly, false syllogism we have mightily deceived ourselves. The disease concept of addiction is a true and humane way of looking at the problem. It engenders a more reasonable, a more charitable, a more humble and helpful, an altogether more sane and practical approach than mere condemnation, coercion, or custody. But this disease concept, this good thing in itself, is being badly abused, and the time has come to ask whether we are not presently doing more harm with it than good.

CHAPTER 9

Abuses of the Disease Concept—
The "Doctor-Will-Fix-It" Fallacy

The doctor can't fix it in himself, let alone others. What he can *do. Treatment of complications is not treatment of the disease itself. The leap that turns out to be a stumble. Not one kind of disease, but three. The rickety annex. Back to the body, and the chemicals. Alterations but no real change. The exact picture of addiction. Effects, consequences, complications. Obedience.*

If by "disease" you mean illness or sickness, addiction certainly is a disease. The addict is sick all the time, miserably dis-eased except when anesthetized by his booze or his drugs and often even then, and out of control as to the course and cause of his illness. Whether the addict's condition can be called a "specific disease entity" is debatable. But then, it is debatable whether the specific-disease-entity concept itself has any validity in fact or is merely a nominalistic peculiarity of the current medical mode.

Let us agree that the addict is diseased. That is not the question. The real question is, then what?

What has followed in the wake of the disease concept of addiction is a series of misconceptions, *non sequiturs,* sly twistings of the term and its implications, and outright fraud. The disease concept has become the hook upon which is hung a chain of disastrous fallacies.

The first of these is the "doctor-can-fix-it" fallacy, which we looked at briefly in the last chapter—the conclusion of the deadly syllogism, "addiction is a disease; the doctor fixes diseases; the doctor can fix addiction."

Now this fallacy is brutally rebuked by the facts. The doctor can't fix it in himself and his colleagues, let alone in other addicts. There are between five and ten thousand alcoholic doctors in this country, and they have a poorer recovery rate in Alcoholics Anonymous than ordinary alcoholics.[8n] There is a staggering number of drug-addicted doctors; and they are in many ways harder to help than street addicts; doctors become addicts at *thirty times* the rate of the general population; narcotics addiction is called "doctors' disease."[9n] Finally, no medical treatment to date, on its own feet and without undergirding by the nonprofessional recovered-addicts societies such as Alcoholics Anonymous—no medical treatment alone has ever produced enough recoveries from addiction to take seriously. The medical enterprise, on its own merits, is a bust.

The doctor simply *can't* fix it the longest day he lives. The quicker we get this extensively proven fact into our heads the better it will be for the doctors, the addicts, the professionals, the government, and everybody else.

But let us grant the solidity of the hook upon which the fallacy has been hung. The doctor certainly can help in the physical complications of addiction.[10n] In such conditions, which accompany the disease of addiction, the doctor may save the addict's life. Obviously, medical help should be sought where it is indicated and needed. It is of the greatest importance, however, to be clear on this point: *treatment of the physical complications of addiction does not constitute treatment of the addictive disease itself, the inability to stop drinking or drugging and stay stopped.*

In dealing with the physical complications of addiction, the doctor is on his own beat and may do a good job. In trying to deal with the spiritual disease itself—the crippling of the spiritual will and intelligence—the doctor is radically off his beat. He is up against a spiritual reality, that is, something for which, as a modern medical doctor, he has no training, no resources, and indeed no conceptual apparatus. Since his whole profession is worm's-eye orientated, he is no more qualified to deal with spiritual disease than is the baker or the plumber, and often very much less so.

The actual record speaks loud and clear. The real-life performance of the doctors themselves tells the painful truth. There are proportionally more addicts *by far* among the doctors than among the general population, and the level of mental health among doctors is lower in important ways than among the general population.[11n] The conclusion is absolutely inescapable: the doctor is not among the first people from whom an addict should seek help for the spiritual disease itself; he is among the last.

The leap from "it's a disease" to "the doctor can fix it" seems so logical that everybody is properly shocked when the leap turns out in fact to be a stumble into a blind alley. What *is* wrong with the logic?

The trouble arises out of a false notion of disease. The medical people, along with almost the whole of our society, think that there is only *one* basic kind of disease, whereas in fact there are three.

If the universal view of man be true, there is not only *physical* disease but also *psychical* disease and *spiritual* disease, and they cannot all be fixed with the same bag of tools. Granted, they overlap and powerfully react upon one another, but each basic kind of sickness requires a very different kind of know-how for its correction.

Ah, you say, perhaps our doctors do not pay much attention to the possibility of spiritual malady, but surely you must agree that they are big, and for many years now have been big, for psychical illness.

Not really.

The medical flirtation with Freud and company was an episode which the best heads in the medical profession are honest enough to be embarrassed about. Not just because it has failed almost totally to fulfill any of the hopes that were placed upon it (see page 112), but because the entire "psychological" annex to modern medicine is in all of its aspects an exceedingly rickety structure from a scientific point of view, and the really good doctors know it and have always known it.

Trying to make a science out of psychology is like trying to make a science out of sexual intercourse. Or it is like explaining jokes. It just doesn't come off.

There is indeed an *art* of dealing with the human soul, but it is something which is seldom aided and often crippled by the introduction of test tubes, chemicals, weights, measures, and "objective" scrutiny. And modern psychology as a term is a glaring misnomer. The modern psychologists do not believe in the very existence of the soul *(hē psuchē);* what they study is not the soul but the mind, and the lower mind at that. Their province is the lower mind *(hē phrēn),* and their science, so far as it has any claim at all to scientific nomenclature, would be properly called phrenology, if the term had not been preempted by the practice of palpating the skull.

So-called psychotherapeutic medical and scientific methods of treating mental illness have been tried aggressively and hopefully over a considerable span of time now, and throughout the entire period of the trial, and more than ever as time goes on, that approach has been found wanting. The psychotherapeutic method has great popular appeal, but the doctors—even while encouraging the public to continue the psychotherapy love affair—have always been aware of its limitations and have been particularly so in recent years. Therefore, in dealing with "mental," "nervous," and "psychological" illness of all kinds, the hopes of the medical profession have tended to be invested more and more heavily in chemotherapy, that is, in drugs.

But the trip from psychotherapy back to chemotherapy is a move from no good to no good. After a long time of trial and plenty of error, the chemicals also have been found wanting. Drugs have effects upon the physical and psychical complications of addiction, not upon the addictive disease itself. In the treatment of complications, drugs may *help* recovery, and they may *hinder* recovery, but they never produce or *cause* recovery. They are a resource of a sort, but they do not in themselves or in any combination constitute an effective treatment, and it is a question whether their extensive use does not do more harm than good.

In dealing with addicts, doctors use two general kinds of drugs: (1) the punishers and conditioners and (2) the comforters.

No kind of threatening or punishment has ever been effective in treating addiction, and chemical threatening and punishment with drugs like disulfiram (Antabuse) is no exception; they may keep an alcoholic in a state of enforced sobriety for a while, but they do not touch the disease itself and therefore cannot properly be called a treatment. And the old-fashioned admonishments, scoldings, denouncings, jailings, beatings, duckings, lashings, and threatenings which are so scandalous to our highly civilized Department of Health, Education, and Welfare[27] seem rather mild when compared to an Antabuse reaction, to which the Department would cheerfully expose an alcoholic as part of his modern, enlightened treatment: flushing, palpitations, heavy and labored breathing, hyperventilation, tachycardia, hypotension, nausea, vomiting, collapse, and death.

The chemical conditioners, such as apomorphine (and including incidentally the physical conditioners such as electric shocks), have never constituted an effective treatment for the disease itself. (See page 148.)

When we come to the provision of chemical ease and relief of addictive suffering, we encounter a much more serious problem. The medical comforters include the psychic-pain-killing drugs and mood-manipulators, consisting of (a) central nervous system depressants: tranquilizers, barbiturates, paraldehyde, chloral hydrate, and other sedatives; (b) central nervous system stimulants and endocrine stimulants: amphetamines and other mood elevators; and (c) narcotics: morphine, codeine, methadone, Demerol, etc.

These agents indeed *do* provide comfort and ease for the addict, but it should be kept in mind—it should be engraved on a bronze plaque and hung on every addict's wall—that COMFORT MAY HELP AND COMFORT MAY KILL. Comfort at the wrong times, comfort too much or too often, may be far worse for the addict than raw suffering.

Remember this: recovery, when it comes, arises out of suffering. If there were no suffering connected with addiction, or if there were little suffering, there would be no recovered addicts. Suffering is not the enemy of recovery but the indispensable helper and handmaid of recovery. God knows, no human being in his right mind would want to *increase* an addict's suffering. But—be warned, you sentimentalizers and easy weepers!—we take upon ourselves an equally terrible responsibility when we presume to *reduce* an addict's suffering or to short-circuit it entirely. Here is a hard problem indeed, to be solved with fear and trembling and prayer for wisdom in each individual case. This much is certain: *it cannot be assumed that the reduction of suffering, physical or psychic, is an aid to recovery.* It may or may not be an aid to recovery. And it may be a death sentence.

But the appeal of drugs to the modern mind, and especially to the modern professional mind, is very powerful. Because with the return of our hopes to the use of drugs as a main resource we are back to where the heart of the worm's-eye man always is, back to the physical body. And back to that stout modern notion which has survived so many onslaughts of contradictory fact and which may indeed be immortal for the duration of our age: the notion that physical reality is the only cosmic reality, that the physical body is the only human reality, and that if the epiphenomenon of mind must be treated, it can only be treated by chemicalizing, cutting and sewing, shocking, and otherwise manipulating the body.

Now the trouble with this approach to the treatment of addiction, with which we really are stuck so long as we hang on to the worm's-eye view of man, is that it simply does not work. You can get all kinds of *alterations* in a man's psychical states by treating his body, but you never get a real change, and hence never a real recovery from psychical illness. Never? Yes, never. You may get what looks like a "remission," and it may last for a few months or, much more rarely, for a few years. But if you follow the case, the man is not changed. The psychical roots of the illness are not touched, and it returns, often worse than before.

> The vast edifice of modern medicine, glittering in the cold sunlight of science, is a machine of incredible complexity, ingenuity, and efficiency. It can examine the lining of your stomach, it can count the corpuscles of your blood, it can measure the oxygen you breathe into your lungs, but it can't tell you why you distrust rocking chairs. For its foundations were laid in the nineteenth century, and that century's one conspicuous medical failure was in psychiatry. The problem seemed simple enough. Until then mankind had been able to devise no better theory of insanity than demoniacal possession. The African witch doctor rattled stones in a gourd to drive out the evil spirit. Christ cast out devils. Orestes was pursued by the Furies. Medieval lunatics were either prayed over or burned as witches. The nineteenth century didn't believe in demons. It believed with all the fervor of its materialistic soul in microscopes and test tubes. Its Pasteurs, its Kochs, its Listers blew the horn of medical science and the walls of many a medical Jericho came tumbling down. But the kingdom of mental diseases was one Jericho whose walls remained unshaken.

That was published in *Fortune* in April, 1935, and it is as true today as it was then. Modern medicine has made thousands of intricate and sophisticated changes in its methods and materials, but it has made not the slightest change in its nineteenth-century-based, materialist, atheist philosophy. And therefore it remains baffled and impotent in the face of disorders of the metaphysical aspects of man, the most obvious and immediate of which is the human mind. In spite of myriads of hopeful medical fads—the barbiturate fad, the shock-treatment fad, the conditioning fad, the psychotherapy fad, the multidisciplinary fad, the amphetamine fad, the tranquilizer fad, the psychic-energizer fad—the modern medical profession endlessly turns in frustrated circles before the mystery and challenge of mental illness. You can see why: it is confronting a reality for which its philosophy makes no room and for which, therefore, it has no resources and indeed no concepts, no ideas, no true words.

And the attempt to affect the *spiritual* nature of the man—the intelligence, the love, and the will—by physical means is even more futile. You can produce negative results by chemical or mechanical means. You can break a man's will, corrupt his love, and blur his intelligence. But even then, the bad result persists only while the physical effects last; there is no permanent change in the soul and the spirit; you have not affected the light, only marred the mirror. And you can do nothing *creative* to the spirit by merely physical means. You cannot increase or rectify a man's intelligence, love, or will by giving him pills or electric shocks. It is some kind of commentary on the intelligence of our age that we ever thought we could.

And this is why worm's-eye medicine and worm's-eye doctors are powerless to deal with the heart of the addict's problem.

Although addiction may spawn dozens of complications in the body and in the soul, its seat and source are in the spirit. We have observed that the chief faculties of the spirit are intelligence, will, and love—and it is exactly here that the addict is essentially sick. His diseased *intelligence* does not know his own good; he sincerely takes a harmful substance as good for him. His diseased *love* has become shrunken to a miserable, infantile egotism, until at last he loves nothing but the fleeting and ever-diminishing time of illusory freedom which the drug gives him. And when suffering finally forces upon him the truth that the addictive substance is indeed harmful, he cannot give it up because his diseased *will* is ineffective. The hallmark of this condition is loss of control, inability to stop drinking or drugging.

This is an exact picture of addiction, and it is an exact picture of *disease of the spiritual elements* of a human being. All the rest of it—the convulsions and the delirium tremens, the hallucinations and the anxiety, the depression and the paranoia, the inflammations and the lesions, the collapses and the comas, the shakes and the leaps, the rams and the horrors, the staggering and stumbling, the weeping and vomiting, the innumerable and indescribable miseries of body and soul which fill out the picture of addiction—all of these things are nothing but physical and psychical *reactions* to the underlying and essential spiritual disease. They are effects, they are consequences, they are complications. They are *not* the disease itself, and they may be "treated" forever, with whatever success or failure, without decisively influencing the basic spiritual illness. Indeed, by ameliorating the complications you may make the spiritual disease worse or delay its healing. Recovery almost never comes until the complications are very uncomfortable. If they are continually ameliorated, the point at which a recovery could begin may be indefinitely postponed. This is not to say that amelioration of complications has no place in the recovery picture. It is only to say that overdoing amelioration of physical and psychical effects may be as harmful as underdoing it.

In every case of addiction, the trouble is in the intelligence and the will, that is, in the realm of the spirit. The physical, psychical, and environmental complications are numerous and grievous, but they are *secondary* factors, and their treatment, in the absence of real spiritual help, never results in recovery from the primary sickness, the spiritual disease, the addiction *per se*.

The medical-professional field, because of its studied ignorance of the very concept, let alone the reality, of spirit, is thereby limited to treating the secondary factors of addiction. That is why the professional field, as long as it remains committed to its present antispiritual outlook, is doomed to go on "managing" and "changing patterns" and "improving" and "maintaining" without ever daring to talk straight out about *recovery*—because recovery is forever outside its scope.

And that is why the doctor, as doctor, cannot cure addiction, in himself or in anybody else. His techniques and resources are simply not relevant to the essence of the problem. Indeed, if pressed too far, his materials and methods may constitute a dangerous mixing of levels, an intrusion, quite literally a profanation and a harmful rather than a helpful influence.

In order to produce a recovery, spirit must speak to Spirit, and spirit must obey Spirit. If the word "obey" gives you a twinge, you can tell from that how modern you are. A primer of recovery can be stated only in the language of the spirit, and in that language, whether we moderns like it or not, obedience is a key word. In the universal view, every being has its natural superiors, its natural equals, and its natural subordinates. All disorder, and all disease, arise when natural superiors fail to rule and natural subordinates fail to obey. Thus:

A man's body should obey his soul, and when it doesn't, physical disease results.

A man's soul should obey his spirit, and when it doesn't, psychical disease results.

A man's spirit should obey God (the Way, the Truth, the Law, the Rita, the Tao, the Dharma), and when it doesn't, spiritual disease results.

Now it is a fact that every attempt to correct the spiritual disease of addiction by manipulating man's lower principles results only in an endless circle of inconclusive results, never in recovery. It is also a fact, of the greatest practical import, that movements which have indeed produced recoveries from addiction everywhere and always have been movements which have shown addicts how to reestablish contact with their primary natural Superior—God (the Way, the Truth, the Dharma)—and to obey him.

CHAPTER 10

Abuses of the Disease Concept—
The "Psychotherapy-Will-Fix-It" Fallacy

The dead man who cannot expire. Other means ignored. John Burns's experience is almost everybody's experience. HEW's astonishing statement. What is this "available evidence?" The Eysenck problem. The emperor's clothes. The frantic confabulation. Reappraisal eight years after the first big blow. Scandal within the profession. After 15 years: "Controlled studies have been unable to invalidate Eysenck's conclusion." The latest words from the horses' mouths: the null hypothesis stands. Neurotics and alcoholics.

How hard a death dies the notion that, since addiction is a disease, somehow the doctors can deal with it! As a matter of fact, the notion does not die but lingers on pervasively in an atmosphere devoid of any real truth which might support it. It is the horrible case of a practically dead man who cannot expire. The "psychotherapy-will-fix-it" fallacy is a peculiar extension of the "doctor-will-fix-it" fallacy. It constitutes a desperate refusal to give up on the doctors as a base of hope for recovery from addiction.

The hope is stubborn. In recent years, more and more reliance has been placed on one or another form of psychotherapy as the answer to problems which are epidemic in the nation—alcoholism, drug addiction, and all the varieties of mental illness. More than half the beds in hospitals across the country are occupied by people suffering from mental and emotional disorders. One person out of every thirty-five will be certified mentally ill at some point in his life. Hundreds of thousands of patients are being treated every year by some kind of psychotherapy, and thousands more are on waiting lists. Each year the total amount of government funding for psychotherapeutic rehabilitation programs for alcoholics and drug addicts increases by millions of dollars. Other means of help often are ignored or put down.

As H. J. Eysenck[9] (1966) observes:

> In the United States at least, and to a somewhat lesser degree in many other countries as well, psychoanalysis and psychoanalytically orientated psychotherapy have achieved a position of unrivaled dominance. The claim is made in the majority of psychiatric textbooks, psychoanalytic writings, and lectures by leading psychiatrists to their students that (1) psychoanalysis can cure all types of neurotic disorders, and (2) that *only* psychoanalysis can effect a cure. This message has been rammed home to the man in the street very thoroughly by novels, film makers, cartoonists, social workers, teachers, and others, to such an extent that for the average person psychology and psychiatry do not exist other than in the image of the psychoanalyst and his couch. This has led to the serious position in which alternative approaches and methods are not even mentioned in textbooks, these alternative approaches are not taught to trainee psychiatrists, and criticisms of the existing orthodoxy are suppressed and withheld from students and practitioners alike.
>
> The effects of such a policy are of course very clear. Professional advancement, the obtaining of research grants, and the very earning of a livelihood are to a large extent dependent on the young psychiatrist's acceptance of this premature crystallization of spurious orthodoxy. All experimentation which takes inspiration from sources other than Freud, or which uses methods other than psychotherapy, is made as difficult as possible or preferably aborted on the grounds that as the truth is already known no experimentation is needed to establish it, and no alternative methods can possibly bring any enlightment or improvement. . . .
>
> This then is the position, and while it would be easy to cull quotations from the most widely used textbooks of psychiatry and psychoanalysis to illustrate my points, this is hardly necessary, as few people acquainted with the situtaion will doubt the truth of these assertions. Admittedly a small

number of analysts are much more cautious in their claims; Kubie is an outstanding example, and others might also be mentioned, but their attitude, it must be noted, is not typical, and their careful disclaimers do not find their way into the textbooks, are seldom heard by the students, and are certainly unknown to the patients, who might have second thoughts about undertaking a treatment the length and expense of which have never been shown to produce any results more favorable than no treatment at all. (See page 120.)

Take your pick of the varieties of psychotherapy—group therapy or individual analysis (Freudian, Rogerian, or Adlerian); psychotherapy alone or psychotherapy in combination with the latest fashions in chemotherapy: psychic energizers, sedatives, mood elevators, tranquilizers, or what have you. But whatever the brand of psychotherapy, virtually all of our hopes—at the individual, the local, and the national level—are pinned on this resource. We have an apparently unshakable conviction that somehow the mental doctors—the psychoanalysts, the psychiatrists, the psychologists, the psychotherapists—will be able to treat effectively the thousands upon thousands of people who so desperately need help.

But is this a valid conviction? Is it true that the solution is to be found in psychotherapy?

The fact is that while psychotherapy has a remarkably high rate of public confidence and acceptance, it has a stunningly and appallingly low rate of demonstrating any positive results at all, in connection with addiction or anything else. We are here dealing with an established fact, strictly a matter of professional record, as proved over a period of twenty-five years.

The truth of this situation is practically unknown at the public level, although it is certainly no secret within the professional ranks. It seems that the pros just can't bring themselves to tell poor little Johnny Q. Public that there is no Santa Claus. But if you are an addict you had better know the truth, or you might die chasing this particular mirage.

You may find this chapter difficult, but the difficulties are unavoidable, because we are going to give you a look at the professional mind at work, and professional thinking often is ponderous, pompous, dry, fussy, evasive, and just plain tiresome, even to the initiated.

Allowing for all of this agony, the impression nevertheless is almost universal among the common people that the professionals at any rate are careful, impartial, fair, and good judges of evidence. The burden of this chapter is to show, on their own records, that the pros are sometimes careless, partial, unfair, and incredibly bad judges of evidence—in matters of the greatest importance, for example in the matter of addiction.

In 1967, in their official publication on the subject, the U.S. Department of Health, Education, and Welfare, a very citadel of the professional viewpoint, made the following statement about alcoholism: "Available evidence seems to demonstrate that long-lasting results can be achieved primarily by a technique known generally as psychotherapy."[27]

To be clear that we are not quoting out of context we will take a fuller look at this statement and its environs a little later on. But right here, let us take note of this fact: a very large portion—a prominent and unignorable majority—of the available evidence on the effectiveness of psychotherapy points in precisely the opposite direction. It points to an inevitable conclusion that psychotherapy would be among the very last of the resources by means of which anyone dealing with alcoholism might hope to achieve "long-lasting" results—or any kind of positive results whatsoever.

The evidence is so large and so conclusive that the question forces itself upon one: Were the government spokesmen being ignorant, or were they being clever? And the least paranoid observer in the world could hardly escape some slight suspicion that they were being clever. If so, it is not a pretty picture. A lot of human suffering and a lot of human lives are involved.

We will continue with the government and their "long-lasting results" in a moment. But first, as an introduction to the general position of psychotherapy and alcohol addiction, a word from senior author John Burns:

When my addiction to alcohol and drugs finally caught up with me, I presented myself to our family doctor. And he, because I was in bad shape, rushed me off to the bughouse. It was a sophisticated and expensive mental institution, where I came under the scrutiny of other doctors and where I was given many kinds of therapy, to wit, drug therapy, hydrotherapy, vitamin therapy, occupational therapy, recreational therapy, social therapy, but chiefly psychotherapy.

The treatments improved my physical health but had no effect upon my addiction, and two weeks after my discharge I was drinking again. I drank alcoholically for the following year and was then again in such bad shape as to require another admission to the bughouse. It was a different one this time, not so sophisticated or expensive but providing many of the same therapies, and again chiefly psychotherapy.

Once more the treatments helped my physical condition but had no effect on my addiction, and I continued to drink. After that I worked with a top-flight psychiatrist, whom I liked and trusted and with whom I cooperated earnestly. He gave me several different kinds of treatment, including sodium pentathol, barbiturates, amphetamines, metrazol shock treatment, but chiefly psychotherapy. Again, there was no effect on the addiction. My psychiatrist friend finally referred me to a nonprofessional, spiritually oriented group, Alcoholics Anonymous, with whose help I recovered from my alcohol and drug addictions and have maintained recovery right up to the present day, twenty-eight years later.

In the course of all these years I have known and worked with thousands of recovered alcohol and drug addicts—in and out of Alcoholics Anonymous, men and women, old and young, black and white, rich and poor. Many of them had had treatment by psychotherapy. Some of them said that they had been helped and encouraged in their search for recovery by kindly and humane psychotherapists, but *almost none of them attributed their recoveries to psychotherapy as such.*

Nearly all addicts who had tried psychotherapy had failed and found their recoveries elsewhere.

John Burns's report can be matched by almost everyone who has experience of the addiction recovery scene. It is an impression that one cannot escape: psychotherapy is conspicuous by its *inability* to produce recoveries among alcoholics and drug addicts. Psychotherapists, the men and women doing the work, are widely appreciated as warm and helpful human beings. But the discipline itself, psychotherapy *per se,* is not among the more useful tools for dealing with addiction.

Now in the face of this situation, the United States Department of Health, Education, and Welfare[27] makes an astonishing statement. In the Department's publication, *Alcohol and Alcoholism,* the federal authorities define psychotherapy as follows: "Broadly, psychotherapy is a label covering various kinds of self-examination, counseling and guidance, in which a trained professional works with (rather than on) a patient—alone or in groups—to help him change his feelings, attitudes and behavior in order to live more effectively."[12]"Then, with fine modern fervor and contempt for everything outside their own limited view, the HEW spokesmen crank up and deliver themselves of the following pronouncement: "In the past, alcoholics have been admonished, scolded, denounced, jailed, beaten, ducked, lashed and threatened with eternal damnation. There is no evidence that any of these measures has had significant therapeutic value for more than an occasional alcoholic. Available evidence seems to demonstrate that long-lasting results can be achieved primarily by a technique known generally as psychotherapy."

Now please go back and study that statement for a moment. If they had included psychotherapy along with the scoldings, threatenings, jailings, and beatings, as having no significant therapeutic value for more than an occasional alcoholic, they would have been announcing a well-proven truth. But they are saying something quite different. Note the concluding sentence. They are saying in fact that psychotherapy is our best hope for help for the alcoholic. It is said in the usual bureaucratic jargon, but it is still saying that psychotherapy is our white hope, and that this hope is based on "available evidence."

What is this "available evidence?"

The evidence which the writers of the Government's treatise looked at is a curious compilation, not so curious for what it includes but very curious indeed for what it does not include. They give 142 bibliographical references and 17 references for supplemental reading. This assortment constitutes an interesting small library on alcoholism, but an oddly limited library so far as the effectiveness of psychotherapy is concerned. There is a great deal about the physiology, psychology, sociology, and pharmacology of alcoholism, and problems of law enforcement. But there is precious little about psychotherapy, and the really important available evidence as to the *effectiveness* of psychotherapy is simply not included. Since this evidence is prominent and extensive, it can hardly have been overlooked but must have been intentionally excluded.

We shall be taking a look at the conveniently left-out material in a moment, and you will see why it was ignored. It tends to prove precisely the opposite of the Government's shockingly irresponsible claim that "long-lasting results can be achieved primarily by a technique known generally as psychotherapy."

When you *really* take a look at the available evidence for the effectiveness of psychotherapy, what do you find?

You find the Eysenck problem.

Who is Eysenck and what is the problem? Hans J. Eysenck, Ph.D., D.Sc., is a British psychologist, an international authority in the field for many years, and obviously a heavyweight.[13n] Eysenck is a problem to the whole psychiatric and psychotherapeutic field because twenty-two years ago he had the audacity to say that psychotherapy is as good as no psychotherapy. He did not say that psychotherapy is no good. He merely said that, on his review of the evidence, you were as well off without it as with it.

In everything that follows in this chapter, note well that nobody is saying that psychotherapists do no good. Please observe the point that is being made, because it is a critical one: Psychotherapists, *as sympathetic and beneficent human beings,* certainly do good. Eysenck's conclusion—which to this day stands unrefuted— is that they do *no more* good than other sympathetic, beneficent human beings, trained or untrained. It would seem that when psychotherapists succeed in being helpful, they do so because of their humanity and regardless of, or in spite of, their professed discipline.

Eysenck's historic study was published in the *Journal of Consulting Psychology* in 1952.[7] The occasion was a culmination of his questioning of certain recommendations of the American Psychological Association. By way of introduction to his study, Eysenck questioned the association's insistence upon "the social need for the skills possessed by the psychotherapist," and he added: "In view of the importance of the issues involved, it seemed worth while to examine the evidence relating to the actual effects of psychotherapy and to seek clarification on a point of fact."

Back to Eysenck in a moment. But first a brief historical digression. Psychotherapy in the form we now know it, as a medically and scientifically oriented discipline, appeared in this country with the advent on the American scene of the ideas and influence of S. Freud and his followers in the 1920s. In spite of much opposition and criticism, Freud's theories and methods became immensely popular. By the 1930s they had acquired official medical and professional status and, with the decline of religion, had become *the* hope of almost everybody who had a mental or emotional problem.

There were early serious questionings of the *actual effectiveness* of medical-professional-psychiatric-psychoanalytic practices. In 1935 *Fortune* magazine raised the overall question and gave the then overall answer: "We have considered the causes, the symptoms, and the statistics of the nervous breakdown. What can medicine do in the way of treatment and cure? Considering the importance of the problem, the medical attack on mental diseases has been singularly ineffective. Research seems to be getting nowhere. . . . for the present, psychiatric research languishes, uncertain of its major objectives. . . . Psychotherapy, or the treatment of the mind's disorders via the mind, has one great disadvantage: it is difficult to judge any particular method by its results."

Embarrassing as the difficulties may be, it has been impossible for men calling themselves scientists to ignore the critical and urgent question of results. S. Rachman[21] summarizes the situation in the years preceding Eysenck's first paper thus: "Landis (1937), Denker (1946), and Zubin—among others—had questioned the claims made on behalf of psychotherapy and other forms of treatment prior to the appearance of Eysenck's classic paper in 1952. Prompted partly by their views, Eysenck carried out an astringent examination of the evidence on the effects of psychotherapy and came to the conclusion that the emperor had no clothes. The reactions of shock and disbelief have passed over, and now, nineteen years later, the time is suitable for a reexamination of the emperor's sartorial progress."

Rachman comes to the conclusion that the emperor, in 1971, *still* had no clothes:

> Even though psychotherapy today probably has more advocates than critics, there is a growing recognition and acknowledgement of the fact that supporting evidence is scarce. . . . with successive reports, the claims [for psychotherapeutic effectiveness] appear to become increasingly modest. . . . To sum up, it is disappointing to find that the best studies of psychotherapy yield discouraging results while the inadequate studies are over-optimistic. . . . Most writers also agree that the claims made for psychotherapy range from the abysmally low to the astonishingly high and, furthermore, they

would tend to agree that on average psychotherapy appears to produce approximately the same amount of improvement as can be observed in patients who have not received this type of treatment.[21]

What was Eysenck's 1952 statement? Having pointed out the obvious shortcomings in actuarial comparisons of the type which he had undertaken, Eysenck announced his revolutionary and now famous conclusion thus:

> Patients treated by means of psychoanalysis improve to the extent of 44 percent; patients treated eclectically improve to the extent of 64 percent; patients treated only custodially or by general practitioners improve to the extent of 72 percent. There thus appears to be an inverse correlation between recovery and psychotherapy; the more psychotherapy, the smaller the recovery rate. This conclusion requires certain qualifications, [but] these data *fail to prove that psychotherapy, Freudian or otherwise, facilitates the recovery of neurotic patients. . . . The figures fail to show any favorable effects of psychotherapy.*[7] (Italics ours.)

Now naturally, since Eysenck *was* a heavyweight and could not be ignored, there was a huge bull roar and frantic confabulation in the psychiatric and psychotherapeutic professions following his blast. If Eysenck were right, it meant that the entire psychotherapeutic enterprise, country-wide and world-wide, was doing as much good as if it didn't exist. This possibility was monstrous, unthinkable, not to be entertained. And yet—there was Eysenck's study, and it was not the work of a pip-squeak. You could not just forget about Eysenck, and so it became mightily important to prove him wrong. Eysenck himself had been critical of the data on which his study was made (as being unduly favorable to the claims of psychotherapists and having other defects). He himself called for more studies. So, with Eysenck good-naturedly cheering them on, strenuous efforts were made over the years immediately following

—1952 to 1960—to validate or invalidate the Eysenck conclusion, and you can bet your last dollar that none of the boys were trying to validate him.

Yet that is just what they did.

The net of all the studies was that Eysenck was right in the first place and was still right. There were more studies made than can be reviewed here. A good up-to-date summary of this activity is given by Rachman in the recently published Volume 15 of the International Series of Monographs in Experimental Psychology.[21] Main studies were those of Teuber and Powers (1953), Barron and Leary (1955), Rogers and Dymond (1954), Brill and Beebe (1955), Rosenzweig (1954), Meehl (1955), Ellis (1957), Phillips (1957), and Wolpe (1958). Reference data on these reports are given in Rachman's monograph.

Eight years later—in 1960—Eysenck[8] returned to the lists with a full-scale reexamination of the evidence, as refined and greatly enlarged by that time. He turned the spotlight particularly on the Teuber and Powers report of their eight-year study, employing control groups, of the effects of psychotherapy upon delinquent boys. The objective evidence of this extensive study was that "instead of confirming the expectation that the treatment group would be less delinquent than the matched control group, there is a slight difference in favor of the control group." Teuber and Powers summarized that "the data yield one definite conclusion: that the burden of proof is on anyone who claims specific results for a given form of psychotherapy."

Eysenck himself in his 1960 review[8] of the evidence and the arguments up to that date, came to certain major conclusions which, he pointed out, go "a little beyond those" of his original survey. Among his 1960 conclusions the following are noteworthy in the present context:

When untreated neurotic control groups are compared with experimental groups of neurotic patients treated by means of psychotherapy, both groups recover to approximately the same extent.

With the single exception of psychotherapeutic methods based on learning theory, results of published research with military and civilian neurotics, and with both adults and children, suggest that the therapeutic effects of psychotherapy are small or non-existent, and do not in any demonstrable way add to the non-specific effects of routine medical treatment, or to such events as occur in patients' every-day experience.

In 1960 Eysenck also made a *public* challenge on the subject in an American mass-circulation magazine. Confining himself to one aspect of psychotherapy, namely, psychoanalysis, Eysenck published an article in the January 1960, issue of *The Reader's Digest,* raising the question, "Is psychoanalytic treatment of *proven* value?" answering "Not yet," and concluding: "Psychoanalytic therapy based on these [Freudian] hypotheses has not justified itself in practice."

Since a very large part of psychiatric and psychotherapeutic practice of almost every kind is heavily based on Freudian concepts, this was a serious conclusion indeed.

Eysenck's challenge to psychotherapy—dealing with both the psychoanalytic and the so-called eclectic types of treatment—had now reached the proportions of a real scandal within the whole profession. The scandal was to persist and to grow over the years and right up to the present time. Many leading psychoanalysts and psychotherapists have agreed with Eysenck's conclusion.[10] Many have disagreed. But the striking fact—nay, the arresting and galvanizing fact—is that not one of those who have disagreed have succeeded in *disproving* the null hypothesis. In 1966, after reviewing a symposium of seventeen experts on the subject, Stuart Rosenthal, M.D., of Central Islip Hospital, New York, made the following highly pertinent comment.

It is difficult indeed to find a recent parallel in medicine wherein a "therapeutic" procedure formed the bulwark of a discipline's armamentarium and yet was without some modicum of scientific validation. Mind you, we are speaking of a procedure which is in widespread use and which is the very mainstay of private psychiatric practice. It is expensive and time-consuming, and yet it is not subject to the criteria of safety and efficacy which are applied to all medications and procedures used in medicine. I suspect it would prove very embarrassing if psychotherapy had to meet the criteria of the Federal Drug Administration. Why should psychological therapies enjoy such sanctuary? I believe that Dr. Eysenck has made a telling point—all the more so because it highlights the willingness of the profession to countenance the continued masquerade of psychotherapy as a sound therapeutic procedure. It is incumbent upon those who are the proponents of any therapy to prove its safety and efficacy, and not for others to disprove it. Therefore, I propose that specialized psychological procedures (hypnosis, psychotherapy, etc.) be subject to the same evaluation as are all the therapies used in medicine, and, if found wanting, be treated in the manner of an experimental pursuit. This would necessitate its limited application as well as disclosure of its experimental status to patients and practitioners alike. The fact that psychotherapy is practiced by physicians does not make it exempt from scientific validation.[9]

The difficulty with Eysenck was that he was not talking about opinions but about the results of scientific research. And after all the arguments about interpretation were over, the research findings undoubtedly said what Eysenck said they said. It was not *Eysenck* who was forcing the now-famous "null hypothesis" upon the attention of the psychotherapeutic profession; it was scientific research, controlled studies within the profession itself—these are what brought the "no-positive-effect" conclusion forward, with Eysenck for the most part acting merely as a gadfly and an umpire.

Of course such a problem could not be just allowed to lie there. Poor old Sanford, back in 1953, had expressed everybody's frustration and dismay when he said, "The only wise course with respect to such a challenge is to ignore it." But as it turned out it was Sanford who was ignored, and Eysenck's indications continued to be the subject of debate and of much further research. Sanford had argued that the entire question raised by Eysenck is "scientifically meaningless."[24] In point of fact, however—both to the patient seeking help and to the professional intending to supply it—it is obviously the most meaningful of all possible questions whether the resource being used is effective or not. From 1960 on, it was clear that the issue simply could not be ignored.

And it has not been ignored. A great deal of work has been done in the ensuing years—all of it, alas, adding up to the same horrible conclusion. In 1961, Lehrman[14] observed: "A great many investigations have been made to compare psychotherapeutically treated populations with similar populations that did not receive this kind of treatment. In none of them does any statistically significant over-all benefit seem to have been demonstrated as a result of the treatment." In 1963, Dr. D. H. Malan[20] of the Travistock Clinic in London said: "There is not the slightest indication from the published figures that psychotherapy has any value at all." In 1966, Eysenck[9] made another review of the evidence and summed up thus: "The position is very simply that there is not a single reviewer who has looked at the evidence and who has come to a conclusion other than the one [the 'null hypothesis'] which I elaborated in my article." And the *Psychiatry Digest,* in January 1967, summarizing a considerable study and review of other studies by researchers Truax and Wargo in the *American Journal of Psychiatry,* said it right out loud and plain for all the professional world to hear: "Controlled studies of psychotherapy have been unable to invalidate Eysenck's conclusion that no positive effect has been demonstrated for psychotherapy, when compared to spontaneous rates of improvement."

Rachman, in 1971, after an extensive review of the evidence to that date, summed it all up again, louder and clearer than ever, for all the professional world to hear:

We do not have satisfactory evidence to support the claim that psychotherapy is effective. It would seem, therefore, that those psychologists and psychiatrists who advocate and/or practice psychotherapy carry the burden of having to demonstrate the value of their views and practices. . . . The burden of producing a satisfactory case for the continued use of psychotherapy rests with those who advocate it.[21]

The *Medical Tribune,* under dates of April 4, 11, and 18, 1973, ran a series of three full-page articles under the headline: "Freudian Psychoanalysis—Dead, Alive, or Kicking?" The Eysenck conclusions were brought up to date by Eysenck himself—and left substantially unchallenged by other commentators.

The questions seem to be not, Are psychoanalytic and other forms of psychotherapy alive and kicking? but rather, Is *Eysenck* alive and kicking? Do his original and subsequent questions remain unanswered and do his conclusions stand? Does it appear that he was right in the first place, has been right all along, and is still right about the astounding fact that no positive effect has been demonstrated for psychotherapy, when compared to spontaneous rates of improvement—i.e., you are just as well off without psychotherapy as with it?

The answer on all counts is undoubtedly yes.

It is a wonder that psychotherapy stays alive in the face of all this evidence of its failure on balance to demonstrate any positive effects at all. The explanation, of course, is simple: it is a matter of faith. People *will* continue to believe in discredited practices, if it appears that there are no alternatives. And the worm's-eye view of man, with which the populace—the pros and the plebians alike—are brainwashed, keeps the real and proven-effective alternatives to psychotherapy incredible to most people.

One point remains to be clarified. The U.S. government's statement that "available evidence seems to demonstrate that long-lasting results can be achieved primarily by a technique known generally as psychotherapy," was a claim for psychotherapeutic effectiveness in regard to alcohol addiction. This statement is substantially unaltered in the 1972 revision of the HEW publication. The government evidently has learned nothing on this subject in these five years. The revised HEW bibliography, as well as the original, contains no reference to Eysenck, Rachman, Strupp, Bergin, Truax, or *any* of the numerous other investigators who have examined the evidence for the extensively researched null hypothesis concerning psychotherapy.

The data we have examined throughout this chapter relate to psychotherapeutic effectiveness (or rather, as it turns out, *lack* of demonstrated effectiveness compared to control groups) in regard to neurotic illness. Many if not all schools of psychotherapy would include alcohol addiction among the neurotic illnesses, but in order to be sure, let us see what the evidence is when psychotherapy is applied specifically to alcoholism.

In 1967, reporting on work they had been doing as far back as 1965 and earlier, Hill and Blane[12] published a study entitled "Evaluation of Psychotherapy with Alcoholics." As to the general quality of the evidence, they say: "A review of 49 studies published in the United States and Canada from 1952 through 1963 which reported evaluation of psychotherapy with alcoholics was undertaken. These studies fail to live up to their potential for contributing to knowledge in the field because of a failure to meet many methodological requirements for the conduct of evaluative research."

As a summary of the overall situation in the entire field at that date, Hill and Blane state:

> In 1942 Voegtlin and Lemere reviewed all studies published between 1909 and 1941 that evaluated any form of treatment for alcoholics. Among their conclusions they wrote: "The most striking observation is the apparent reticence with which the English-speaking psychiatrists have presented statistical data concerning the efficacy of treatment. With the

exception of [two authors], the medical profession at large is unable to form any sort of opinion, from an examination of the literature alone, as to the value of conventional psychotherapy in the treatment of alcoholism in this country or England."

More than 20 years later, we find that any "apparent reticence" in presentation of statistical data is gone; there is now little reluctance on the part of "English-speaking psychiatrists" to report statistics. We can still agree with Voegtlin and Lemere, however, that "we are unable to form any conclusive opinion as to the value of psychotherapeutic methods in the treatment of alcoholism."

We should look at two more references. Let us have our next-to-the-last word on this subject right out of the horse's mouth. Let us hear from The Joint Information Service of the American Psychiatric Association and The National Association for Mental Health. In 1967, writing under these august auspices, Chafetz, Cumming, Glasscote, Hammersley, O'Neill, and Plaut (very big guns in the field) produced a comprehensive study under the title *The Treatment of Alcoholism, a Study of Programs and Problems.*[4] Under the heading of "treatment," this study makes no reference to nonprofessional resources (there is no mention, for example, of Alcoholics Anonymous) but confines itself to professional-medical-psychotherapeutic activities. These authors do not avoid the issue of the effectiveness of psychotherapy with speciffc regard to alcoholism. They meet it head on, in clear and unambiguous terms:

Most of the facilities that provide services for alcoholics have made little, if any, attempt to determine the effectiveness of the total program or of its components. (Such lack of evaluation is not restricted to work with alcoholism facilities, of course. It is a general and serious shortcoming of virtually all American mental health services.) . . . Because of the lack of evaluation of treatment of alcoholics little is known about the relative effectiveness of different kinds of psychotherapy. One study indicates that alcoholic patients remain in psychotherapeutic types of treatment roughly as long as other psychiatric patients. But *there have been no well-designed studies comparing the response of alcoholics and other psychiatric patients to psychotherapy, either group or individual.* (Italics ours.)

For our last word, let us hear again from the horse's mouth—a different horse this time, and one that speaks out of both sides of its mouth. The U.S. Department of Health, Education, and Welfare—which said in 1967 and reaffirmed in 1972 that those famous "long-lasting results" can be achieved "primarily through psychotherapeutic techniques"—has a very remarkable thing to say out of the other side of its mouth in its First Special Report to the U.S. Congress[28] in 1971:

Many professionals treating persons with alcoholism base their techniques on the assumption that the disorder is a result of emotional or unconsciously motivated factors. This assumption is controversial. Since intrapsychic factors are studied by inference and other indirect means, hard confirming information on the validity of this theory is difficult to collect. The view that alcoholism is an intrapsychic disorder is involved in the same debates as those surrounding the typology of emotional and mental disorders, and is subject to the same degree of criticism by many persons who object to seeing it thus classified.

Treatment: At this time, well thought-out and conclusive studies on the effects of various psychological treatment techniques are lacking, equivocal, or contradictory. (Italics ours.)

Well, so that is what the available evidence is *really* saying. It is the same story right across the board—with neurotic illness as well as with alcoholism and drug addiction—"no positive results demonstrated for psychotherapy when compared to control groups."

There is one critical difference between the neurotically ill and the addicted. Neurotics tend to recover at a high rate, whether treated or not. Addicts almost never recover spontaneously, and *none* of the medical-psychotherapeutic forms of treatment does anything for the essence of their illness, the inability to stop drinking or drugging.

After reviewing over 750 research projects and studies, Stanley Rachman remarks rather wistfully, "It may turn out, in the long run, that psychotherapy does no more than provide the [neurotic] patient with a degree of comfort while [his] disorder runs its natural course." But what about the people whose disorders, in running their natural courses, lead them to skid row or to death from an overdose of heroin? Is there no answer, no effective recourse for alcoholics and drug addicts? Fortunately there is an Answer. There is a real opportunity for recovery and release. But this solution comes from a radically different source.

There is great danger in psychotherapy. The danger is that nearly everyone believes in it—so strongly and so exclusively that no other possible way of dealing with mentally ill and addicted people gets any consideration. Psychotherapy is the thing which prevents us from seeing the real, practical, effective help which is always available but which comes from a different direction. If as a nation we are ever going to do anything on a larger scale about the problems of alcoholism, drug addiction, and mental and emotional illness, we must first disabuse ourselves of the notion that psychotherapy has the Answer or is the Answer. We must open our eyes to the truth about psychotherapy—so that in turn we can see the truth about the real source for recovery.

The "psychotherapy-will-fix-it" fallacy is not a minor mistake; it is a huge, on-rolling blunder, in which our professionals persist in spite of clear warnings that they are in a blind alley, and in which alcoholics and drug addicts persist because they do not know any better.

It is high time that somebody blew the whistle on it.

CHAPTER 11

More Fallacies
Arising Out of the Disease Concept

The "I-am-not-responsible" Fallacy: *The sick man is a liar and a brat. The whole recovery question turns on responsibility. The defiance of experience and reason. Sam Abrahamson's report. The lethal old ladies. An antidotal statement.*

The "Multidisciplinary" Fallacy: *The "in" thing with the nifty name. When you put them all together, lo! it works! What has happened? The "scientific" stump blower. The dynamite in the alcoholic recovery picture. Alcoholics Anonymous is not a treatment. Why the useless stew.*

The "Education-will-fix-it" Fallacy: *The liabilities of our kind of education. Real education has gone underground. Addiction incubators. The child swindled out of his birthright. Why the majority of addicts do not want to recover.*

Along with his sickness, every addict who ever lived is a liar and a spoiled brat, whose deliberately irresponsible conduct over a long period of time finally brought him to the helpless stage of drinking or drugging. Nobody forced the drinks or the drugs on him; he took them himself of his own free will for a long time before getting hooked and losing his free will. Nobody brought the addiction on him; he brought it on himself. The addict himself, not somebody or something else, is responsible for his addiction. And the addict himself, not somebody or something else, is responsible for his recovery.*

We—your authors, who wrote that paragraph—are not looking down our noses or judging others. We ourselves are liars and spoiled brats who found our way out of the dungeon of addiction by facing and admitting the facts of our situation—as every recov-

*See O. Hobart Mowrer on the question of *sickness* vs. *moral responsibility* (page 234).

ering addict must—and taking responsibility for them.

Now the above facts *are* facts, well known to everyone who has had actual experience of addiction and release from addiction. They are hard facts, but when faced they are beautiful facts, because they lead to recovery. When the addict can say to himself, "I am responsible for my sickness and for my recovery from it," the door to freedom stands open.

There is one more hard fact, the hardest of all. If the addict says to himself, "I am *not* responsible," he has locked and barred himself in the darkness; the door remains shut. The whole tremendous question of recovery turns on whether the man will act like a man and accept responsibility, or act like a baby and reject it. His fate hangs in the balance.

In this life-and-death crisis, the addict today is overshadowed, and is in frightful danger of being overwhelmed, by a fallacy which is widely held by the professionals and public alike. It is the "I-am-not-responsible" fallacy, based on the weird assumption that if a man is sick he is *ipso facto* excused from all responsibility for his condition.

It flies in the face of all experience and all reason, but there it is. Everybody *knows* perfectly well that a sick man may be, and very often is, responsible for his illness. Out of ignorance, carelessness, or perversity he may have taken poison—or breathed bad air —or eaten wrong things or eaten too much—or entertained ugly emotions—or gotten too little exercise—or what have you; the possibilities are endless. And yet, ever since the disease concept of addiction came into vogue, the professional rehabilitators have considered it wise, right, and indeed a mark of gentility and humanity to say that because an addict is sick, he is therefore not responsible for his condition or for his recovery. The sick man is encouraged to seal his own doom by declining his God-given responsibility for his own life and its conditions. He is encouraged to say and to believe, "I am not responsible for having this disease. It is not my fault that I am sick."

This is to endorse one of the deadliest dodges of the addictive illness—the infantile refusal of the addict to play an adult's role in the world. If anything lies near the core of the problem, this does. Every addict, while he remains addicted, endlessly lies to himself about how weak and inadequate he is, how nothing much should be expected of him, and how *all of his troubles are the fault of somebody or something else.*

In recovery, this changes. The mark of an addict who is on the road to recovery is that he drops the baby role and begins to seek and assume responsibility. You can see how it works out in an individual case in the experience of freshman author Sam Abrahamson:

> I spent years resenting my parents for the poor job they did of preparing me for the world. I resented them for the money we had and the comforts I had grown used to, comforts which I wanted but was not willing to work for. I railed against the government and cursed the stupid systems and laws I was forced to obey. I nursed hatreds for schools, employers, mandatory insurance programs, speed limits, armed services, and taxes. I romanced myself as a sensitive soul cast adrift in a world of liars, cheats, bigots, perverts, and violent men. I drank and used drugs as a consolation for all the wrongs I had suffered.
>
> During this time I had some of the finest professional treatment available—private psychiatric sessions, a period in a top-flight New York City hospital, family therapy sessions, and readily accessible medical aid. I experienced brief periods of respite, but I always returned to the booze and the drugs. And over the years the consolation I found in alcohol and drugs turned to dependence, and the dependence turned to addiction.
>
> By the time I recognized what was happening to me I was caught but good. Still I had no way out. The psychiatrists were filling me full of tranquilizers to keep me cooled out, and the medical people were warning me that certain drugs I was taking were poisonous for everyone and that certain

others I was taking were specifically poisonous for me. Meanwhile I was cheating on my girl, stealing drugs and money from my father, and working only when and if I felt like it. In general, I was thumbing my nose at the world and wondering why I felt so bad.

I remained in this state until I joined Alcoholics Anonymous and came face to face with the reality of my own rotten attitudes and bad behavior. Before I came into AA, I was never brought to account for my behavior or my condition. No mention was ever made of what I might have been doing wrong, nor was it ever suggested that that might be even a part of my problem. Under the professional care I received, there simply was no question of moral responsibility. But once I began to accept responsibility, once I started trying to get honest with myself, to admit where I had been wrong, and to make amends for harm done to others, recovery was in view. At this point, I have been clean for three years—the longest time ever.

My story is not unique. Many friends of mine have been through exactly the same kind of difficulties. Those who came to grips with their own wrongdoings have recovered and are no longer addicted to or dependent upon drugs of any kind. Those who insist on being victims of life—blaming illness, the system, and other people—are still drinking and drugging and getting sick and being disillusioned.

Addicts' stories are very different in details but remarkably the same in essentials. The motif of resentment, blaming others, and stubborn irresponsibility which runs through Sam Abrahamson's report will be found prominently not only in most other addicts' life but in every addict's life without exception.

In order to protect yourself against the lethally sentimental old ladies of both sexes among the professional rehabilitators as well as among the general public who are telling you that you are not responsible, you—as an addict who hopes to recover—have got to find some means of reminding yourself of the plain old truth that you *are* responsible. The following statement is suggested as an antidote to the dangerous stuff which you are apt to hear from your morally neutral doctors, your well-meaning family, and your ignorant friends on this subject. The prescription is to read it aloud once a week:

THE ADDICT'S DECLARATION
OF FREEDOM AND RESPONSIBILITY

My name is _____. I am an addict, and I am responsible for my addiction. Nobody laid it on me. I brought it on myself.

No matter how sick or crazy I get, I am a free spirit, a child of God, and a responsible human being. My addiction was caused by my taking alcohol or drugs, by my own free will, in such a way that I got hooked and lost the use of my free will. I lost it, and with the help of God I can regain it.

My addiction is the result of my own ignorance and my own perverseness. I am responsible for acting perversely, that is, doing wrong when I knew it was wrong. I am also responsible for acting ignorantly, that is, doing wrong when I did not know it was wrong. Ignorance is no excuse, and I do not claim it as an excuse.

I blame nothing and nobody for my trouble. Granted, the society is often wrong, and other people are often wrong, but that is not what made me an addict. *I* made me an addict.

I am responsible for my recovery. Nobody is going to do it for me. I need help and will seek and accept help, but I will not turn my helpers into leaning posts or crying towels. With the help of God and my already-recovered brother and sister addicts, I can and will live one day at a time in total abstinence and freedom from alcohol or addictive drugs. It is beneath my dignity as a human being to become a leech upon the society, a guinea pig for the scientists, or a ward of the government.

Walking daily in the strength of the truth and of God, and in the love of my brothers and sisters, I will live honestly, honorably, and responsibly, and I will go forward to the discovery and fulfillment of the real meaning of life.

Now we come to one of the most "in" things in the whole addiction treatment field. It is called the "multidisciplinary approach," and it seems that in the last few years, if you did not have a "multidisciplinary" package to recommend, you couldn't get any attention from anybody in the professions—so taken is nearly everybody with this magical notion and its nifty name.

It turns out to be just another of the major fallacies deriving from the disease concept of addiction, but this one is a real cutie. In order to savor its logic, you have to go back and get yourself into the mood of the original false syllogism: "Addiction is a disease; doctors cure diseases; therefore doctors can and will cure addiction." The multidisciplinary fad originated in the alcoholism treatment field and had its main evolution there, so that is where we will examine its triumphant march to nowhere. The basic idea is, if treatments don't work separately, put 'em all together, and *then* maybe they will work. Here is how it developed:

The doctors are going to cure the alcoholics, right? So that means treatment, therapy, right? So naturally they try some chemotherapy, and—oops—that doesn't seem to work very well. All right, the next logical move is to try some psychotherapy, but —oops again—*that* doesn't seem to work very well, either. (All these recognitions of the therapies' not working are internal; what the public hears is that they are "making progress" and of course busy with "more research.") But the therapies are *not* producing recoveries, and the professionals are not such fools as not to know it, so the search continues.

Next chemotherapy and psychotherapy are tried together—but that doesn't work either. So now they start reaching out. Chemotherapy, psychotherapy, psychological testing, informative lectures, and conventional religion are tried as a package—but it is still no go. So, a few plain and fancy trimmings are added: a little psychodrama, community singing, some educational films, and Alcoholics Anonymous.

And lo! *it works!* Recoveries are produced! Here is the secret at last! No particular treatment is very good on its own, but when you put them all together, you get recoveries! So they call it "multidisciplinary," and everybody is happy. In fact, everybody is delirious.

Now what actually *has* happened? Nobody has noticed that with the introduction of Alcoholics Anonymous the one and only active ingredient has been added, and *any* combination containing this ingredient will now produce recoveries.

The situation thereafter is like this: suppose a man has to clear a field, and there are lots of stumps that need to be blown up. Now this man is of a scientific turn of mind, and upon inquiry he discovers that the best material for blowing up stumps has not been scientifically established, so he himself sets about to make a scientific study of the situation. He puts together the following mixtures of materials:

Mixture A
Dynamite
Sodium bicarbonate
Chalk

Mixture B
Dynamite
Dextrose
Fuller's earth

Mixture C
Dynamite
Magnesium sulphate
Sand

Mixture D
Dynamite
Calcium chloride
Ground coconut shells

After blowing up a large number of stumps and carefully measuring the results, our man comes to the conclusion that *all* of these combinations are equally effective and that *none* of the particular substances has any superiority as a stump-blowing agent; they all, he finds, work equally well.

We have to assume some kind of buffered idiocy or logical block in an otherwise sane man, which prevents his noticing that one particular ingredient is common to all of his mixtures and also prevents his knowing that an agent must be tested separately as well as in combination in order to determine its effectiveness. As a result the man never discovers that sodium bicarbonate, chalk, dextrose, fuller's earth, magnesium sulphate, sand, calcium chloride, and ground coconut shells are worthless as explosives—and that *dynamite* is the stuff you want to use if you intend to blow up stumps.

Now the "multidisciplinary" alcoholic rehabilitation professionals and our "scientific" stump blower are at the same level of scientific and logical integrity, and it is clearly a pretty limited level.

The dynamite in the alcoholic recovery picture is Alcoholics Anonymous. Alone and on its own, it produces large numbers of recoveries; and in combination with all kinds of assortments of "treatments" it also produces large numbers of recoveries. The fallacy is in calling AA something which it clearly is not—a "treatment"—and in failing to see that it is the only active ingredient in the "multidisciplinary" programs.

All of the medical-professional treatments are indeed—as the pros claim—about equally effective. None of them works. And the thing that does work is not a treatment but a spiritual fellowship and program. Alcoholics Anonymous is a spectacularly and consistently successful recovery resource—based on a nonmedical, nonprofessional, truth-centered, and God-centered approach to the problem. It is *in no sense whatsoever* a therapy or a treatment.

Nobody treats anybody in Alcoholics Anonymous. It is impossible—and if it were possible it would be illegal—for any member of Alcoholics Anonymous or for AA groups or for AA as a whole to treat anybody. Medical treatment is a professional, authorized practice. Alcoholics Anonymous is a nonmedical, nonprofessional, nonauthorized lay group, whose members have no wish, no competence, no authority, and *no legal right* to treat anybody for anything—by chemotherapy, psychotherapy, aversion therapy, hypnotherapy, or any other kind of "therapy" under the sun. Alcoholics Anonymous is an unorganized and officially uncredited spiritual fellowship whose power and whose widely demonstrated effectiveness to produce recoveries from alcoholism come explicitly from God, from truth, from prayer and meditation, and from the practice of honesty, humility, responsibility, selfless service, and brotherly love. And, brother—in anybody's language—that is not *treatment.*

By mixing Alcoholics Anonymous (which works) with an assortment of medical-professional treatments (which do not), the treatments are made to appear (falsely) of some value in producing recoveries. Of course nobody in his right mind would take the trouble to stir up this kind of stew—unless he happened to be a professional rehabilitator with some useless treatments to sell. Since in fact there are a lot of rehabilitators in that situation, you can see why "multidisciplinary" has become the catch phrase of the field in recent years.

Some of the fallacies arising our of the disease concept of addiction are stupid, some are clever, some are plausible, some are pretty far out. But the one now coming up for discussion is just sad. It is the "education-will-fix-it" fallacy, and it is a very weak peg indeed upon which to hang any hopes, but nevertheless some of our fondest hopes *do* hang there.

Let's face it. We twentieth-century people believe in education almost more than anything else—more than science, more than medicine, more than technology, more than power, more than money, more even than the whole "march of progress" itself— because we see that *education makes these things possible.* And therefore, if medical or psychological treatments or sociological maneuvers of one kind or another will not cure addicts of their sickness, we figure that somehow in the end our clever people will find ways to *educate* them out of it.

Alas, not so. It never has been so, and it never *can* be so. There never yet was an addict who was "educated" out of his illness, and there never will be. Our kind of education cannot prevent or cure addiction for the elementary reason that it is itself a prime *cause* of addiction.

Addicts can and do recover from addiction as a result of education—but not what *we* would call education. What releases addicts from their bondage is education of a kind which we modern men do not know and can hardly imagine, *a moral and spiritual education,* an education in honesty and responsibility—in faithful and unegotistical work—in reverence for one's family, one's elders and superiors, and one's country—in selfless love of the brethren—and in unswerving obedience to truth and to God in all the affairs of life. *That* kind of education was driven from our schools long ago, and it turns up now in locations which are not honored and indeed not recognized except by a minority who are desperate enough to look for it in unaccredited and uncertified places. Real education —training in the life of the spirit—has gone underground.

Do not imagine that a modern addict, whose need is for education in the way to God, can find it in modern religious schools any more than in secular schools. Main sections of the professing church are now apostate. Certain branches of it are actually teaching something very like atheism. (See E.F. Mascall, *The Secularization of Christianity.*) The religions have largely sold out. Fifty years ago they sold out to Freud, and ministers and priests began running around and acting like amateur psychiatrists and hustling members of their flocks off to real psychiatrists whenever a serious spiritual problem arose. Eventually people began to see what a dodo psychiatry was, so then the religions sold out to business, and for a while the ministers and priests were running around imitating, of all people, the secular executives of the world. Then the religions sold out to the hippies and the revolutionaries, and the ministers and priests ran around trying to please the teenagers and the political lunatics of the world. It is no wonder that they have no time, no effective knowledge, and no power for the cure of souls.

What we need is not more of the present kind of education but less—or better yet, none at all—if we wish to help with the addiction problem. If we closed all our schools tomorrow, the addiction rate would plummet in the next few years. Our present schools are literally addiction incubators. This is something you surely know, but do you know why? The reason why our schools hatch addicts as garbage hatches flies is that they are relentless and prime purveyors of the worm's-eye view of man. An overwhelming majority of modern educators are ardent materialists, and the whole educational system is worm's-eye oriented from its main lines down to its smallest details.

By the highly effective negative processes of ignoring the subjects and of snide and sideways scoffing, our schools teach the young human being that there is no spirit, no objective truth, no immortality, no metaphysical reality, no moral law, and no God. If the educators had the honesty to teach these denials openly and straight-on, many children, with their native intuition for sacred truth, would rebel or laugh their "teachers" to scorn. But the whole thing is done by omission, by evasion, and by indirection, in the hallowed name of science. Thus the worm's-eye philosophy—that mass of truncated guesswork and mere materialist speculation—is taught as tested, proven, and undoubted truth.

So the child hardly knows what is happening while he is being tricked and swindled out of his birthright: his instinct for sanctity and his faith in higher realities. By the time he gets to high school, and often before, he is literally a freak—in an advanced state of spiritual starvation, with his mind deformed and his inner agony so intense that he is a sitting duck for the drug experience when it becomes available to him, as it now inevitably does in most of our schools.

If you educators want to do something to help the addiction problem, at least get the worm's-eye deceit and falsehood out of your curricula. Teach, if you must, your rejection of spirit and of God, and teach your moral anarchy—but have the decency to teach these things as what they *are,* that is, as debatable philosophical viewpoints, not as established or proven truth, and for heaven's sake not as *science.*

A very large part of the real, practical education of a modern man of course is not academic but commercial in origin. The flood of newspapers, books, and magazines—the saturation with audio-visual impressions—the inescapable din of advertising and propaganda pouring in from every side—all this forms the mind of a twentieth-century human being with a power and efficiency which no school ever could match. Nevertheless, the hacks, the hucksters, and the schools speak with one voice and from common assumptions, for it is to the masters of the culture, to the men of the schools, that the popular writers and the salesmen turn for their basic ideas and for their authority. And what they all commonly assume is the worm's-eye view of man: the "scientific" validity of materialism, atheism, and "freedom" from moral concerns, that is, the "right" of man to injure himself and to harm and defraud other creatures and the world of nature without restraint. It is out of this kind of teaching that there arises the spiritual chaos and desperation which result in addiction.

So much for education and the *making* of addicts. We still have to deal with modern education—and again not as a helping factor but as a deadly obstacle—in the *recovery* of addicts.

The problem in dealing with addiction is not lack of means of recovery. Good and effective means of recovery, as we know, are now operating and are widely and readily available. By means of the recovered-addict societies—Alcoholics Anonymous, Synanon and the therapeutic communities, and Teen Challenge—a very high percentage (65 percent to 75 percent) of addicts who want to recover can and do recover. But no recovery is possible by any means without the addict's voluntary consent and cooperation. In order to get well he must *want* to get well. And the real and terrible problem arises from the fact that a very low percentage (probably under 10 percent) of all alcohol and drug addicts want to recover.

Why? Why do so many addicts—this huge and terrifying majority of addicts—not want to recover? Just as addiction itself is a product of our spirit-denying and God-denying age and its ungodly education, so also the phenomenon of addicts' not wanting to recover is a condition of our culture, its practically total immersion in the worm's-eye view of man, and its almost 100-percent-effective indoctrination of the public, beginning with the very young public, in worm's-eye principles.

The culture believes and teaches that there is no spiritual reality, no immortal soul, and no God—in short, no higher possibilities for man. Very small human beings are taught that they are merely little animals and that all other ideas on the subject are unscientific foolishness and superstition. Most of the little people (and most of the big people) don't think it out, but the implication sinks into them very deeply nevertheless: if the worm's-eye view is true—and all of the "authorities" say it is—then there is *no way out of human slavery and misery.*

Most addicts believe that no better life than their own is possible. They have been taught by their cultural mentors that a life of honor and joy in the service of the divine Majesty is a contemptible illusion—that a spiritual life, a God-centered life, is a fool's dream. And the addicts are not incapable of drawing conclusions. *They know the only other alternative to addiction:* they look at "normal" life—with its all-pervading hypocrisy and cynicism—its double-dealings, frauds, and betrayals—its brutal oppressions and crawling servilities—its envies, its hatreds, and its endless lying—its tinsel values and its meat grinder of frantic phony activities—the addicts look at the whole show, the best of it as well as the worst of it, and they decide that addiction, bad as it is, is better than that.

And they may be right.

CHAPTER 12

The Abandonment
of Recovery as a Goal

A new note. "Improvement," "control," "maintenance," and "management." Dangerous nonsense. Back to the obvious—the one formula for recovery. Temporary, forced abstinence. The hysterical mother and the naughty child. Heroin, the prototypical worm's-eye blunder. The Lexington bust. Synanon sparks a worm's-eye imitation spree. Which flops. Enter methadone, son of heroin. Early enthusiasm. The awful truth emerges. The morality of the methadone program. Where the professionals are now.

An awesome fact is emerging: with the wearing thin and gradual exposure of the "fix-it" fallacies, *the professional field is quietly in the process of abandoning recovery as a possible goal for addicts.* The bulwark of *abstinence* has been let go as unattainable, and with that the whole professional mountainside has started to slip.

It has always been considered as obvious as the sun in the sky that if an alcohol addict or a drug addict wants to recover he has to stop drinking or drugging. But recently a new note is being struck. In the last few years leading professionals have begun to suggest that it is somehow all right if the addict does *not* stop drinking or drugging.

We will look at the narcotics situation in a moment, but first let us see how this shift is working out in the field of alcoholic rehabilitation. The U.S. Department of Health, Education, and Welfare says: "Most specialists hold that no alcoholic can learn to drink moderately and regard statements to the contrary as unwise or dangerous." But "according to available information, only a small percentage—perhaps less than 20 percent of all treated patients [treated, that is, by professionals]—have been able to maintain absolute abstinence for more than three to five years." In view of this situation, "recently, some leading therapists have been using a different basis of measurement in which success is considered achieved when the patient maintains or re-establishes a good family life, a good work record and a respectable position in the community, and is able to control his drinking *most of the time.*"[27] The implication is clear. The professionals are not getting anywhere with "all treated patients" and are beginning to abandon recovery as a goal for the alcoholic.

The American Medical Association is even more forthright about the situation: "Alcoholics are treatable patients. Because their illness is a chronic disorder with tendency toward relapse, it should be approached in much the same manner as are other chronic and relapsing medical conditions. The aim of treatment is then viewed more as one of *control* than cure." That ought to be clear enough for anybody. The AMA goes on to say: "Treatment centers which have utilized this approach have achieved quite remarkable success in the management of many alcoholic patients."[1]

They are no longer talking about cure or arrest but of "management." They are now saying that "abstinence might be considered too rigid a goal" for the addict. This is like saying that getting out from under the water is too rigid a goal for a drowning man. In defense of the professionals you may assert that their long history of failure has made them desperate and that therefore they are talking this desperate nonsense. Maybe so, but for the sake of the millions of human lives involved we ought to remember that this desperate nonsense is desperately dangerous and harmful nonsense. What these professionals are saying in effect to the addict is this: "We can't show you the way to recovery, but we will be glad to 'control' you and 'maintain' you and 'manage' you, or we may even 'improve' you, while you spend the rest of your life as an addict to alcohol or drugs."

It is a matter of long, hard experience that "improvement" and "control" are deadly mirages, that they are among the cruelest and most widespread of the *delusions* from which addicts suffer. It is a tragic error that these aberrations are now encouraged, endorsed, and even made goals of "therapy." Anyone who has had firsthand experience with his own or others' addiction over any period of time knows that a shift in an addict's drinking or drugging pattern, even if it seems for the "better," does not spell improvement but on the contrary often signifies the victim's entry into deeper and more deadly levels of addiction.

If the alcoholic or drug addict reduces his intake and begins to make more or less successful efforts to mitigate disaster patterns, this is not a sign that the citizen is improving. It is a sign that he is feeling the heat and is beginning to dodge and to accommodate. For what purpose? For the sole purpose invariably of continuing in his addiction. The more he "improves" in this way the deeper he sinks into the morass of total slavery. Every addict who ever lived has gone through this terrible process. It becomes his prime objective in life to ameliorate his behavior and his environmental conditions while continuing to drink or take drugs, *in order that* he may continue to drink or take drugs.

As long as this monkey business goes on (and it will go on longer than ever if the addict hears that the experts are now calling it "improvement"), the man is not even at the threshold of recovery. Real recovery begins, and can only begin, when this desperate delusion has been shattered, when these pathetic dodges have been tried and have failed, as they always do.

There is a saying among recovered addicts that being recovered is like being pregnant—either you are or you aren't. And this is rigorously and ominously true. The notions of "improvement" which are being fostered in professional circles currently could arise only from a reading of addictive experience dangerously limited as to time span. It is like the story of the man who jumped off the Empire State Building one afternoon. As he passed the forty-first floor on his way down, somebody leaned out the window and yelled, "How are you doing?" And the man yelled back, "All right, so far!"

For the sake of mere sanity, let us hang on to this one anchor in the realm of the factual and the obvious: *abstinence is the only possible basis for recovery.* Where abstinence is not achieved and sustained, there is no recovery and there can be no recovery. This fact, proved by a huge accumulation of exhaustive and conclusive experience over many years, is surely beyond debate. The professionals, in attempting to substitute "improvement" and "control" and "management" and "maintenance" as criteria of recovery in place of abstinence, are confessing to the failure of modern treatment attempts to reach any positive goals at all.

Abstinence is the indispensable key to recovery. And spiritual conversion, in a huge majority of cases, is the indispensable condition of sustained abstinence. Hundreds of thousands of members of explicitly spiritual recovery fellowships such as Alcoholics Anonymous and Teen Challenge bear witness to this fact. Most of these addicts have tried everything else before finding recovery in spiritual conversion. Members of Synanon, Daytop, and similar groups which do not refer expressly to God have achieved the same result, recovery, by becoming converted to *truth* and *responsibility* as life-guiding principles. Spiritual conversion does not necessarily involve acceptance of a personal conception of God. Conversion to a prime spiritual principle such as *truth* is genuine and effective spiritual conversion. The success of Synanon and its offshoots and imitations is modern evidence that the great spiritual traditions of mankind are right when they say that God is truth.

One formula, and no other, produces permanent release from addiction. That formula is: conversion + abstinence = recovery. Many years of experience in trying to achieve abstinence by other means—from national Prohibition on up through the modern professional "treatment" fiasco—have proved it beyond question: sustained abstinence becomes an option *only in the wake of spiritual conversion.*

Abstinence is so clearly the only rock upon which an addict's recovery can be built that the professionals, with all their talk of "improvement" and "management," continue to try to achieve it by manipulative and coercive tricks. And of course they fail. Temporary, forced abstinence can be achieved simply enough by separating the addict from his supply, or by chemical threat and punishment with Antabuse, or by conditioning with electricity or emetics. But these devices, when they are unrelated to spiritual conversion, seldom make any contribution to recovery. The addict usually goes back to his booze or his drugs upon release from custody, and the chemical punishers and conditioners rarely hold him more than a few weeks or months after the "treatment" is stopped.

Eysenck (a proponent of behavior and conditioning therapy) admits: "There is no doubt that conditioning treatment of alcoholism has often been tried, and that it has often failed. I have no wish to take refuge in a *tu quoque* argument by pointing out that alcoholism has been particularly difficult to treat by any method whatever, and that psychoanalytic methods also have been largely unsuccessful." (He goes on to say that some conditioning workers in the field of alcoholism have used improper methods and that "this lack of rigor makes it quite impossible to adduce these so-called experiments as evidence either in favor or against conditioning therapy.")[11] These attempts to set up a mechanical or chemical substitute for the soverign and spiritual free will of the human being are bound, in the nature of things and in the nature of man, to fail.

When an addict turns his spiritual free will toward recovery, toward the truth, and toward God, then, with the right kind of help, sustained abstinence becomes possible. But *only* then. When the addict's spiritual free will remains turned toward drinking or drugging, it seems that nothing in heaven or earth can get him off the stuff and keep him off. Even inside the prisons and mental institutions, addicts' ingenuity frequently outwits the security system with everything from do-it-yourself stills to contraband drugs and booze smuggled in by "sympathetic" relatives, friends, guards, or attendants. The only effective abstinence is *voluntary* abstinence, that is, abstinence sought and sanctioned by the spiritual free will.

As we have seen, spiritual conversion is nonsense and illusion to the worm's-eye view of man and therefore can have no place in the conventional professional treatment of addicts, and this crippling handicap of the professional approach is particularly evident on the narcotics scene, where despair of recovery is now a controlling factor. You wonder why the professionals have not quit on the narcotics problem, why they have not thrown up their hands and turned the addicts back over to the preachers, the courts, and the cops. In fact, as we shall see, they *do* exactly that every so often. But in between collapses their persistence has been remarkable.

The professionals have performed very much like a hysterical mother trying to deal with an obstreperous child. The mother starts out trying to be nice to the child, patting him on the head and giving him a lollipop. The child responds by scratching her face. She flies into a rage and flails him with her purse. He falls to the floor. She tries to help him up. He kicks her in the leg. She glares at him. He bangs his head against the wall. She bursts into tears and tries to give him a hug. He bites her hand. She smacks him in the mouth. And so on.

The professional rehabilitators have been giving narcotics addicts an unending series of lollipops and smacks in the mouth since 1897, with the same result as the hysterical mother's treatment of her spoiled child. In the latter part of the nineteenth-century morphine addiction began to be a health problem of major proportions in this country. Enter lollipop number one: "In 1898 morphine was acetylated, and early trials indicated that the product cured both opium and morphine addiction. It was received with such enthusiasm and high hopes that it was named from 'hero': heroin."[5]

We all know how the "hero" fared. The early indications turned out to be tragically mistaken. Heroin solved the morphine problem all right—by replacing it as the most popular drug of abuse among narcotic addicts in America and becoming a far worse plague than morphine itself.

The heroin disaster is not an isolated mistake that some researchers made seventy-six years ago; it is the first in a whole series of blunders leading right up to the present, all following precisely the same pattern and constituting the sum total of conventional, worm's-eye view efforts to solve the addiction problem.

The faith of the medical people in the "nonaddictive" qualities of new hypnotic and narcotic drugs is remarkable. The instance of methaqualone (Quaalude, Optimil, Sopor, Parest, Somnafac) is a striking but typical case in point.

From the *New York Times,* March 25, 1973:

> The use and abuse of methaqualone . . . began about two years ago in the West and Middle West and then spread to the rest of the country. Developed in India in the early nineteen-fifties, methaqualone has had a long and disastrous history of abuse in Britain, Germany, Norway, Japan, Australia and elsewhere. It began to be used medically in this country in 1965 and was—incorrectly—hailed as a nonaddictive hypnotic.
>
> "It was one of those things we could see coming, like a train down the tracks, but we did nothing about it," observed Dr. Emil F. Pascarelli, a drug expert at Roosevelt Hospital in New York. Production of methaqualone, a prescription drug, soared from almost nothing in the late nineteen-sixties to 150 million dosage units last year, according to the Bureau of Narcotics and Dangerous Drugs. . . . Dr. Pascarelli, who has written on the "quiet epidemic" of methaqualone abuse in the United States, says most of the people he has treated for overdose have been young white and middle-class, with a scattering of Vietnam veterans mixed in.

The professionals have not come up with any worse ideas for treatment than heroin or methaqualone, but they have not come up with any better ones either. What they repeatedly do come up with is the same old deadly gimmick: one addictive substance in place of another. Heroin is the oldest addiction "treatment"; methadone is the newest. And nothing in between has done any better. So the old researchers' dream that heroin would cure morphine addiction is not some unfortunate aberration, traceable to primitive research techniques. It is par for the course.

Every time one of these professional schemes for treating addicts goes flop, not only the professionals but the nation itself reacts like our distraught mother: "You rotten kid, you want to make a mess with heroin, eh? Well, take that!" Smack! This reaction comes in the form of outraged cries for tougher laws, more arrests, and stiffer sentences from the courts. We are not saying that the smack in the mouth is any worse than the lollipop. Probably the pushers *should* get long prison terms. But let us entertain no illusions that punitive measures, of themselves, will do anything to straighten out the bad boy.

When heroin became the number one problem on the narcotics scene, the professionals for many years remained openly and admittedly at a loss as to what to do. Meanwhile laws were passed and addicts were beaten over the head and jailed, and of course that didn't help. Then a large federal treatment center was opened up in Lexington, Kentucky. The idea was to treat the addict as a sick man rather than a criminal. (Here we have the usual sentimental polarization at work. As a matter of fact the narcotics addict is usually a sick man *and* a criminal *and* a spoiled brat as well.) In spite of a large staff of well-meaning doctors and psychiatrists who struggled heroically trying to understand the addicts and to treat their sickness, the recovery rate at Lexington was abysmally low, somewhere around the rate of spontaneous remission in addicts,* that is, as effective as no treatment at all. There was a standing joke

* "In a short-term follow-up, the U.S. Public Health Service Hospital at Lexington found that between 94 and 97 percent of those they have released are back on drugs."[18] This is a spectacularly low rate, but not unusual for the professional addiction treatment scene; for example, "Riverside Hospital, a New York facility for adolescent addicts, has a reported relapse rate of 95 percent over a five-year period."[18]

among street addicts and frustrated probation officers that the cost-per-successfully-treated-addict at Lexington was about half the national debt. Actually it *was* in the hundreds of thousands of dollars. At last, in 1967, the government threw in the sponge and shut down this famous rehabilitation program.

Meanwhile, in 1958, two small nonprofessional movements succeeded in doing the undoable—getting some heroin addicts totally and permanently off the stuff. Although different in many ways, both of these movements were based on spiritual conversion coupled with complete abstinence. Teen Challenge, founded by a Protestant evangelical minister named David Wilkerson, used a straight come-to-Jesus approach. Though totally unpalatable— nay, revolting and nauseating—to the professionals, Teen Challenge continues to produce real recoveries in large numbers to this day. Synanon was a bit easier for the worm's-eye-viewers to relate to. Charles Dederich, the founder, was a flat-out agnostic, so nobody's nose got rubbed in God. But addicts going through Synanon did get a powerful dose of rigorous honesty and responsibility; those who recovered did so by becoming converted to the primary spiritual principle of truth.

Private psychiatrists, sociologists, and doctors were doing as badly as government-backed ones in helping addicts, but now several of these private professionals sprang to the Synanon banner and spearheaded various government efforts to imitate the Synanon approach. "Therapeutic communities" became the new hope for addicts.

The Synanon approach, however, did not reproduce successfully where the professionals tampered with it, throwing out elements which were distasteful to them, such as too much charisma, too tough, too long a stay required, too small an operation to be economical, etc. One of the major disasters on the tampered-with-therapeutic-community trail was Governor Rockefeller's multimillion dollar program. His experts converted a bunch of prisons into drug addict units and tried to do a watered-down therapeutic-community job on a mass scale in these centers throughout New York State. Within two years it was evident that the Rockefeller program was not working and that the public had been treated to another expensive worm's-eye failure.

By 1968 it was clear to knowledgeable people in the field that therapeutic communities could not be successfully crammed into the worm's-eye mold. Since no serious consideration was being given in high places that year to junking the worm's-eye view, and since the addiction epidemic was continuing its steady growth, the time was ripe for a fresh "solution." Enter a new "savior" drug— methadone, son of heroin!

Methadone, a synthetic narcotic, was invented as a morphine substitute during World War II. But nobody thought seriously about using it in the treatment of heroin addicts for over twenty years. Since the drug was known to be habit forming, common sense suggested that treating heroin addicts with methadone would be equivalent to attempting to extinguish a fire with gasoline.

In 1965, however, two doctors at Rockefeller University in New York triumphed over common sense and developed a program for maintaining heroin addicts on methadone. Their reasoning was plausible (as usual) and their early findings were encouraging (as usual). The big point in methadone's favor was that, while it was addictive, it did not produce the debilitating euphoria that heroin did. And here the magic word "maintenance" really got its foothold. Addicts who were being maintained on methadone could be gainfully employed; they would be getting their methadone more cheaply than they were able to get heroin on the street; stealing, mugging, and prostitution would be unnecessary; society and the addicts would both be better off. And best of all (from the worm's-eye point of view), methadone would make no demands of conversion or abstinence on the addict.

As originally conceived, methadone maintenance was to be a painless and complete answer to the heroin problem. Just switch the addict over from injected heroin to orally taken methadone, give him his new fix once a day in a glass of orange juice, and gradually reduce the amount of methadone until you ended up with a drug-free human being. No unpleasant spiritual considerations. No moral struggle on the addict's part. Just clever manipulation of drug dosage by the professionals.

Alas (here we go again) it did not work out quite as planned. The addicts, true to form, failed to follow the game plan. First it became evident that it would not be possible to get the new-made methadone addicts clean as quickly as originally intended. Then the awful truth emerged: it was not going to be possible to get them clean at all.

The program directors, however, were not deterred; they simply readjusted the game plan. "Methadone maintenance is still a good idea," they said, "even if the people in the program remain dependent on the drug indefinitely. It still benefits society. And it is good for the addict who will not accept a program like Synanon." Of course it is impossible to predetermine which addicts are going to accept one of the conversion-abstinence programs like Synanon, Teen Challenge, or Alcoholics Anonymous. So there is no way of knowing in any given case whether or not you are offering permanent methadone addiction to an addict who might otherwise have lived his way through to conversion and abstinence—that is, to real recovery. Here is "maintenance," with a vengeance. And here—in full view at last—is the abandonment of recovery as a goal.

Let us pass quickly over the question of whether it is morally acceptable to adopt as public policy the keeping of 94,000 men and women in a methadone-addicted state. If the moral outrage is not clear to you from the simple facts, no explanation will help. The principles of morality are as axiomatic as the principles of geometry. They are self-evident. One either sees them or one doesn't. The methadone experiment is an indication of the state to which our society has sunk. Only in a culture which has gone morally blind could the notion be seriously entertained that you were *helping* a man while—on the plea of mere social utility—you were condemning him to a lifetime of narcotic drug addiction.

By this time the monstrosity itself has begun to spawn its brood of related woes. As the methadone-maintenance programs have expanded (10,000 under treatment in 1970; 65,000 in 1972), so have methadone-related deaths. In New York City alone there were 45 in 1970; 330 in 1971. Many of those who are dying from overdoses of methadone are not heroin addicts and not in metha-done-maintenance programs. They are abusers of other drugs such as amphetamines and barbiturates who are looking for a new kick.

A report in the July 2nd 1974 *Wall Street Journal* by Dr. Paul Cushman Jr. sums up the methadone situation from the standpoint of its proponents: Over thirty-six thousand patients are receiving "legitimate methadone maintenance treatment" in New York City. (Note the critical term, *maintenance.*) Arrests for narcotics felo-nies and misdemeanors are down sharply from 1971 through 1973. Numbers of narcotics detainees in jails are down over the same period. There has been a reduction in narcotic overdosed patients treated in hospitals.

These ameliorations of the challenge which narcotics addiction presents to society have been purchased at what cost to the addicts themselves? At the cost, in New York City alone, of condemning thirty-six thousand of them to life-long addiction to a narcotic drug, without hope or even thought of recovery.

In Dr. Cushman's entire article of some fifteen hundred words, the word "recovery" does not appear once. The bare idea of recov-ery—the mere notion—is nowhere indicated, even by indirection or inference. It is remarkably, antiseptically absent. "Mainte-nance"—i.e., medically supervised *permanent addiction*—has won the day. For a large number of narcotics rehabilitation profession-als, recovery is now a lost cause, a totally abandoned goal. Dr. Cushman assures us solemnly that methadone maintenance, that is, permanent methadone addiction, is "highly beneficial . . . to patients." The assertion obviously is not meant as a grim jest, and yet how else can it be understood?

The methadone program is based upon a plausible but mendacious shuffle of the obvious facts. It takes its stand upon the fact that methadone addicts are easier and cheaper to manage than heroin addicts. It shamelessly and deviously ignores the fact that methadone addicts are what they are—addicts. By the methadone-addiction strategem the conscience of society may indeed be eased for a while. But the advent of widespread, officially-approved, deliberate creation of permanent methadone addiction is a simple enough thing for thousands of narcotics addicts: it is the end of all hope of recovery; it is a sentence of doom. Woe to the society that gains its ease at such a price in human degradation and human bondage.

Dr. Cushman reports that "opponents argued that . . . methadone maintenance was merely the substitution of one drug for another." In reply to this utterly factual and utterly reasonable statement, Dr. Cushman says absolutely nothing, evidently because there is absolutely nothing to say.

The professionals really ought to have been objective enough to read the history of their own past mistakes and prevent the methadone disaster before it ever got rolling. At present they are still trying to convince themselves and the public that methadone can help. But the only open questions are: How long will it take to admit defeat? How devastating will be the long-term effects of this latest piece of folly? Will methadone be a relatively self-contained failure like Lexington, or will it give birth to a new, unsolvable drug problem as heroin did?

Late bulletins make it appear that this is less and less a question and more and more an emerging fact: The following is a United Press International dispatch from Washington under date of June 21, 1973.

METHADONE MAJOR PART OF ILLEGAL U.S. DRUG TRAFFIC.
Methadone, an addictive drug used as a treatment substitute for heroin is quickly approaching marijuana and heroin as a

major part of the illegal drug traffic in the United States, the government's drug enforcement agency said.

John E. Ingersoll, director of the Bureau of Narcotics and Dangerous Drugs (BNDD), said illicit methadone use has more than doubled since last September, compared with a nearly one-third rise in heroin use. "Of approximately 325 substances on which data are collected, methadone consistently ranks in the top 10 in frequency of reported incidents," Ingersoll said, adding that marijuana and heroin led the list. "Data for an eight-month period ending in April, 1973, the more current reporting month, show that the incidents involving methadone constitute a major portion of all narcotic reports," he said. . . .

Rep. Paul G. Rogers, D-Fla., subcommittee chairman, said that the illicit market of methadone "has accounted for a staggering number of deaths from methadone overdose."

There is the usual smoke screen of conflicting publicity, but the facts are now clear enough: when it comes to treating narcotic drug addiction, the doctors and professional rehabilitators are right where they were in 1898. Nowhere. And you can see why abstinence—the only real hope for both alcohol addicts and drug addicts—is being abandoned: it is being recognized as unattainable by medical means.

We are not, however, witnessing a defeat but a sort of rescue at sea. The professional attack carrier *Recovery* is full of holes, listing to starboard, down at the bows, and sinking. But the professionals are not about to go down with the ship. The destroyers *Maintenance* and *Management* are standing by to take off the crew, bag and baggage, with evident intentions to continue the voyage as if nothing much had happened.

SECTION III

The Stunning Success and Ensuing
Difficulties of the Amateurs

The Answer to addiction—which is God himself—has always fared ill at the hands of men. He is characteristically despised and rejected of men and betrayed even by his followers. And he has a most peculiar predeliction for the company of the poor, i.e., those who really haven't got it.

While the competent, the certified, and the accredited have been trying and steadily failing to find a solution to the problem of addiction, the Answer has given himself into the hands of the incompetent, the uncertified, and the unaccredited. That is where the recoveries are taking place. The offscouring and rubbish are indeed confounding the wisdom of this world.

The bearers of the Answer to addiction, however, are amateurs only in a limited sense, and it might be more accurate to call them merely nonprofessionals. They are amateurs not out of loving choice but simply because they never had enough moxie and enough stability to become professionals—or anything else respectable or worthwhile. Infantile, selfish, grandiose, stupid, liars, irre-

sponsible, unpredictable, chaotic, perverse, partially or totally insane—the amateurs in their unregenerate state are as unlikely a lot
to do a great work as you can possibly imagine. Yet that is where
the power has lodged and where the great work is being done.

It seems reasonable to suppose that God would give himself as
readily to professionals as to amateurs, but the former in their
"wisdom" despise and reject him while the latter in their desperation finally make a little room for him.

The amateurs have the Answer. They are a sort of chosen people.
But like the chosen of old, they are a stiffnecked crowd, and their
performance has been spotty. They have made both good and bad
use of the treasure entrusted to them, and they have had a brilliant
but limited success in disbursing its blessings. The limitations do
not lie in the Answer itself but in two major areas of difficulty:

> **1.**   The amateurs have sometimes watered down or sold out the
> principles committed to their charge. They have become in-
> volved in sectarian hangups. And they have made major mis-
> takes in relating to each other, to the public, and to the profes-
> sionals.
> **2.**   And the professionals—although the facts have been star-
> ing them in the face for years and years—somehow cannot seem
> to recognize that the amateurs are doing what they really *are*
> doing, which is, regularly and consistently and increasingly pro-
> ducing large numbers of recoveries in large numbers of alcohol
> addicts and drug addicts—while the professionals, strictly on
> their own merits and with their own devices, are producing
> practically none.

The amateurs are succeeding, and their principles and methods
need only wider application to provide the long-sought solution to
the whole problem—so far as a solution at the voluntary level is
possible. (Addicts who do not want to recover will always constitute a legal-custodial problem, and a ferocious challenge to some
of the most basic assumptions of our society. But this is a far deeper
dilemma, and must be distinguished from the problem of recovery.)

The amateurs are succeeding. And how is that possible? Does it mean that they are better people than the professionals? Hardly. On any ordinary reckoning, the amateurs are certainly inferior— less educated, less trained, less honored, with less resources, indeed a lot of them only a few weeks or months out of the loony bin. What, then, is the explanation?

We think it must be this: The amateurs in their terrible need have stumbled upon the *principles* which work. They have found the principles with which recovery is possible, and without which recovery is impossible. They have found and related to the spiritual principles of truth and God and brotherly love in a way that only the lost and the damned can relate to them—in a way that ordinary people, including professionals, usually do not and cannot relate to them.

The amateurs have connected with a power that is available to all men—but available only when you approach it with your hat in your hand. This power has been said of old to have enormous tolerance for real human ills and shortcomings but at the same time not to suffer fools gladly and to have small patience with arrogant, presumptuous, overeducated, and overconfident little human beings who are enchanted with their own smarts.

The actual facts, the visible and demonstrable results, on the addiction recovery record over all the years, and particularly in the last twenty-five years, seem to prove this beyond doubt: Truth— God—cleansing and amendment of life—brotherly love—these are the principles which produce recoveries. These key spiritual principles closely involve others—honesty, fidelity, obedience, selfless service, sacred community. And now you must see where all of this leads: these principles are indices, modes, or hypostases of the single Principle of principles—the one and only Reality—the living Splendor from whom we all came and to whom we are destined to return, by light paths or dark, one way or another, in the fullness of time. It seems impossible to leave *him* out and still do any business on the recovery scene.

Evidently this is not a matter of religious inclination, personal style, or philosophical preference. It seems to be a matter of fact, and it seems to be proved rather conclusively by the comparative experience of the amateurs, who emphasize basic spiritual principles, and the professionals, who do not, in dealing with addiction. With truth and God and the love of the brethren, we have recovery. With moral laxity, atheism, and the profit motive in healing, we have practically no recovery.

CHAPTER 13

The Answer in Action:
The Recovered-Addict Societies

Addiction was always known to be incurable. Until 1934. The break-through of Alcoholics Anonymous. The breakthrough of Synanon. What does it all mean? The Answer is here. The parallel break-through of Teen Challenge. What do they all have in common? The spiritual context: some little-known history. The American business-man and the European doctor. Spiritual experience—very unlikely. The lost is found. The Oxford Groups. Thatcher and Wilson. The beginnings of AA. Regenerate School. An expression of the Way. Wilson's illumination. The marks of Real School. How long will AA last?

As we have noted earlier on, alcoholism—the inability to stop drinking and stay stopped—appeared on the human scene in the seventeenth century and soon spread throughout the world. Except during the brief Washingtonian phenomenon in mid-1800s, the condition was widely recognized to be incurable. In his historic article in the *Saturday Evening Post* in 1941, Alexander reported recoveries to be one to three out of a hundred, by all causes, mostly unknown.

If you had a real confirmed drunk on your hands, a father or a sister or an aunt or a brother (and plenty of people did), there was nothing you could do about it except hide him somewhere or put him away somewhere until, to the great relief of everyone concerned, he had the courtesy to die. In order to understand how and why this nation was finally driven to national Prohibition, you have to understand how widespread and how threatening the general level of mere bad boozing was and how *impossible* it was to deal with the burgeoning numbers of alcoholics. People everywhere were scared, and they had good reason to be.

Narcotics drug addiction, from its first widespread appearance in the late nineteenth century, was always recognized to be as incurable as alcoholism.

Beginning in 1934, there was a radical and unexpected change in this situation. In December of that year, one alcoholic, of the type everybody had given up as hopeless, began a recovery that was to endure until his death in 1971; that is to say, he never drank again.

Unlike the previous one or two or three out of a hundred who had recovered before, *this* alcoholic had two new ideas for this century (the same ideas which had flared brilliantly if briefly among the Washingtonians): (1) he thought that his own recovery would depend upon his helping other alcoholics to recover, with their recoveries in turn depending on helping others; and (2) he thought that submission to God and telling the truth and leading a spiritual life were essential to recovery.

In May of 1935 he found one other man who understood what he was talking about and who, after one slip, also began a lifelong recovery; which is to say, he never drank again. In a few weeks these two found another one, and before the year was out there were eight of them. In 1937, there were 40. By 1939, there were 100. By 1941, there were 8,000. By 1950, there were 96,000. In 1957, their numbers had reached 200,000. In 1973, it was 650,000.

This, as you may have recognized, is a brief account of the birth and growth of Alcoholics Anonymous. And there is a related development to be noted before we take a look at what this whole thing means.

In the summer of 1958 the leader of an Alcoholics Anonymous group in Long Beach, California, noticed to his amazement that several narcotics addicts who had been attending the group's meetings had gotten clean and were staying clean. This leader, Charles Dederich, took a lively new interest in the possible benefits to drug addicts of the spiritual principles by which his group were living.

The following year more than *thirty* hard narcotics addicts were clean in that group and staying clean. Here was an unheard-of thing.

Everybody by this time knew that almost any drunk who really wanted to could get dry and stay dry in Alcoholics Anonymous, but everybody also knew that no real hard narcotics addict *ever* got clean and stayed clean. Lewis Yablonsky, a criminologist and social scientist of long training and experience, has said: "In more than ten years of work with the crime problem on the East Coast, I did not know of one so-called ex-addict who had totally quit using drugs. . . . I knew that at Lexington and Chino and elsewhere the relapse of drug addicts hovered close to one hundred percent." What was happening in Dederich's little community was entirely without precedent and almost beyond belief. The only reason people believed it is because they could see it with their own eyes.

Dederich tried to keep his group within the framework of Alcoholics Anonymous, but the AA's did not like admitting narcotics addicts to their meetings, and they did not like some of the techniques which Dederich had introduced into his own meetings. So they gave him the freeze (see page 209), and he and his narcotics friends departed, to become the recovered-addict society of Synanon, in many ways as remarkable a phenomenon, and in some ways even more remarkable, than the parent society of Alcoholics Anonymous.

In 1960, there were 50 clean-and-staying-clean addicts in Synanon. In 1964, there were 400. That same year Synanon gave birth to Daytop and then to the therapeutic community phenomenon across the country, with tens and then hundreds of communities springing up everywhere, all based—more or less, but mostly more —on the Synanon model. The result of this development is that today there are about 70,000 narcotics addicts, a large percentage of whom are clean and staying clean, in Synanon and the 2,200 other therapeutic communities.

The real challenge for a spiritual community always follows upon success: will the Spirit continue to act through it in a vital ministry to suffering men, or will the community become complacent and put self-serving first?

Synanon reached the level of 1,600 residents, of whom the larger part were ex-addicts, in ten years of existence. For the last five years, this figure has been nearly constant, with people coming and going; so that Synanon, over all its fifteen years, has returned about 12,000 people to the larger society. Three-quarters of its present population are "character disorder" people: addicts, alcoholics, delinquents; the remainder are people who have come to Synanon, without major problems, in order to share the community's way of life.

About five years ago, Synanon shifted from a policy of almost exclusive emphasis on addicts to its present open policy, thereby making the kind of move to widen its application that Alcoholics Anonymous has not made. On the other hand, the size and influence of the two organizations remains disparate, with nine times as many people in AA as in Synanon and Synanon-modeled communities.

Now there is a certain kind of big news that gets fogged in the telling—good tidings of such thundering importance that while the news is to some extent communicated, the meaning is blunted, diffused, practically lost. Of such kind is the news of Alcoholics Anonymous, Synanon, and the offshoot communities.

What it means is nothing less than this: *the Answer to both alcohol addiction and narcotics addiction has been found.* The Answer is fully effective and totally satisfactory when applied; it produces complete and permanent recoveries; it enables the former addict to abstain completely from the substance to which he was addicted, to recover his sanity, to assume a responsible and productive place in life, and to live at a level of joy and creativity above that which he knew before becoming an addict and often considerably above that experienced by the generality of the population.

The Answer demands a very large investment of the addict's heart and soul and mind and strength, but it costs little or nothing in terms of money, and it is not dependent upon drugs, professional techniques, "maintenance," or any other such expensive, difficult, and prolonged substitute bondage. Not counting the spiritual commitment and work as a cost, the Answer is free.

Now all this is nobody's dream. It is a beautiful and monumental *fact*,* attested to by hundreds of thousands of alcoholics presently maintaining their recoveries in Alcoholics Anonymous and by tens of thousands presently maintaining their recoveries in Synanon and the therapeutic communities. The proof is not only large in numbers but it extends over a long span of time, leaving no doubt that the Answer really *is* the Answer and that it is successfully applicable in the vast majority of cases where its simple, nonprofessional, noncostly requirements are met.

Before asking what does the Answer consist of, what is the power that makes it work, and how can anyone connect with it, first we need to take a look at one more development—something that began to happen at almost exactly the same time that Synanon came into being, a movement entirely unconnected with either Synanon or Alcoholics Anonymous and yet throwing a bright light upon the truth and the power underlying both of these fellowships and confirming the principles upon which every recovery must be based—if it is to be permanent, a real renewal of the life, and free of the nightmare of professional "maintenance," that is, free of substitute addictions and unending governmental and medical paternalism.

---

*This massive and persistent fact is ignored as if it did not exist by the most competent and authentic of the professional spokesmen. The capacity of these people to simply overlook important and prominent facts in their field can hardly be understood as mere inadvertence. It seems to be not an accident but a technique. (See further, page 196.)

Early in 1958, a Pentecostal preacher in a small Pennsylvania town felt a call from God to help young people in the big cities. David Wilkerson's cash assets at the time were seventy-five dollars. With that in his pocket, he started for New York City, where he encountered a series of powerful rebuffs in his attempts to bring the Word of God to teenagers on the streets. He tried talking to the authorities, and he tried talking to the kids, and at first nobody would listen to him. Evidently they all thought he was just a pious nut. But then it started. . . .

It started on a street corner in Brooklyn. Wilkerson had brought a friend along to play the trumpet; he had played "Onward Christian Soldiers" four or five times, and a crowd had gathered, about half very small children and half teenagers. Wilkerson began to talk, and against all probability the teenagers began to listen. Some of them were affected. One of them said later: "You're all right, Preacher. You really bugged me." Some of them were more than affected, they were changed. They stopped fighting and they stopped taking drugs. And they stayed stopped.

Those who were changed were sent out onto the street to do for others what Wilkerson had done for them, to carry the Word and to change young lives. Thus Teen Challenge came into being. A center was opened in Brooklyn in 1961. In 1973 there were centers in fifty-four major U.S. cities and in several rural locations.

From the beginning, young narcotics addicts got clean and stayed clean under Wilkerson's challenge and the challenge of recovering brother and sister addicts. The Brooklyn experience has been that 73 percent of addicts who stay with the Teen Challenge program six months or more prove to be still clean two years later. Wilkerson wrote a book, *The Cross and the Switchblade,* about his experiences with addicts in New York. It was a publishing phenomenon. By 1973 ten million copies of it had been printed in thirty-eight languages. The Brooklyn center became a model for Teen Challenge facilities in other cities around the world.

Thus the first sustained recoveries from narcotics addiction in history occurred in very different circumstances—in the enclosed community of Synanon and in the street encounters of Teen Challenge—almost simultaneously; the Synanon beginnings were a mere matter of weeks earlier than the first Teen Challenge recoveries.

Alcoholics Anonymous, Synanon and its offshoots, and Teen Challenge have produced the only considerable numbers of recoveries from addiction. Since this is so, these movements obviously have the key to the whole addiction problem. It would seem to be of the utmost importance to find out—however unlike each other they may be in particulars—what they are all doing right. What are the factors that make them work? Can we discern common elements among Alcoholics Anonymous, Synanon, and Teen Challenge? The movements are very different in many ways, but they are at one in original basic principles and in certain essential commitments and practices:

1.   They all arise out of a *sacred context*—a community calling upon men to return to God and to live spiritually, that is, in truth, in love, in responsibility, and in righteousness. (Synanon, as we have seen, has dropped the God reference but hung on to truth and responsibility.) The spiritual factors of truth, love, and responsibility are common across the board.
2.   All of these movements are *nonprofessional*. They operate without benefit of doctors, psychologists, or government or social workers.
3.   They count on *recovered addicts themselves to do the work* of recovery, that is, with the help of God and the help of the truth to take responsibility for one's own recovery and for helping others to recover.

With regard to point number 1—the origin of these movements in a sacred context and their original grounding in an intensive and explicit God reference—it will be enlightening to review some little-known history.

Alcoholics Anonymous sprang directly out of the Oxford Group, and how that happened is quite a story. It began with a man named Roland H. Roland's last name is known, and he never was a member of Alcoholics Anonymous, but he was a prime mover in the entire chain of events, and so it has been a tacit tradition among AA's over the years to respect his anonymity just as if he had been a member.

Roland was a successful American businessman and otherwise undistinguished except that he was a hopeless alcoholic. He was an intelligent and determined fellow and had tried hard over the years to break the habit, entirely without success. Since he had some means, and since he had developed some hope that the famous European psychologist could help him, he ended up in Zurich, talking to Carl Gustav Jung.

Dr. Jung worked with him for over a year, during which time he stayed sober, and then the doctor said he thought that a return to America and the ordinary course of life was in order, with a good chance of maintaining the sobriety.

Alas, in a few weeks Roland was drunk, and as soon as he could pull himself together enough to travel he returned to Switzerland. And now Carl Jung made a confession: "I thought that I could help you. I thought that you might be the type of personality who would respond to my treatment. I see now that I was mistaken. I must tell you the truth about your situation as I see it. I believe that you have almost no chance at all to recover. Drunkards of your type almost never do recover."

"But, doctor," said Roland, "is there no chance? You said, 'almost no chance.' What does that mean?"

"There *is* a chance," said Jung, "but it is a very slim chance. Once in a great while an alcoholic of the hopeless type does recover as a result of a *spiritual experience.* You might recover if you could find your way to a spiritual experience. But it is very unlikely."

"Well," said Roland, brightening up, "that does not seem to present great difficulties. I believe in God. I have been a good churchman all my life . . ."

"Ah," Jung broke in, "I am not talking about anything like that. I am not talking about belief in spiritual things or belief in God. I am talking about *experience,* about an event which shakes a man to his foundations. It does not happen very often, and many who seek it never find it."

Roland left Jung, left Zurich, and returned to America, to look for that rare thing, a spiritual experience which would shake him out of his obsession to drink and release him from his slavery to alcohol.

Now this is a strictly true story and in no sense a fairy tale, but it has an exceedingly fey quality at this point. For it is a historical fact that in a short time Roland actually did find the highly unlikely thing he was looking for. He found it in the Oxford Group. He had his spiritual experience, and as a result he stopped drinking and stayed stopped.

The Oxford Group, although not related to any church, was a rigorously God-centered and Christ-centered movement whose members practiced a program calling for total surrender to Christ and for (1) absolute honesty, (2) absolute purity (by which they meant sexual purity), (3) absolute unselfishness, and (4) absolute love. You try, just try, practicing those principles seriously for a couple of weeks and see what happens to you. The Oxford Group was a mover and a shaker. It had real spiritual power, and it had the prime credential of a real regenerative School: it changed lives. It was the ashram, so to speak, of Frank N. D. Buchman, one of the least-known great men of our time. In 1908, Buchman was illuminated by a vision of the suffering Christ. From that day forward he believed in the primacy of personal evangelism over religious structures and doctrinal formulas, he looked for the "religion within the religions," and to the day of his death in 1961 he had extraordinary power to convey the reality of his own spiritual experience and to play a catalytic key role in inducing spiritual experience in others.

In this God-centered and Christ-centered setting, Roland H. found his experience, found the Answer, and achieved sobriety.

Alcoholism was not a central concern of the Oxford Group, but there were other people in the Group who had had drinking problems, and one of them was Ebby Thatcher. (Ebby died in 1967, so there is no question of maintaining his anonymity.) Ebby was a very far gone alcoholic indeed, but somehow he caught the spirit and secret from Roland, and somewhere along in 1933 he too got sober and began to stay sober.

Thatcher now remembered an old-time friend and fellow Vermonter named William G. Wilson. (Bill died in 1971 and his anonymity need no longer be preserved.) Wilson was an alcoholic of classical and almost heroic hopelessness. He had made the most desperate efforts over a long time to sober up and failed utterly. Ebby Thatcher visited him one late summer day in 1934 as he sat drinking gin in his kitchen on Clinton Street in Brooklyn.

Wilson, knowing Ebby from the old days, offered him a drink. Thatcher refused. Wilson said, "What is the matter with you?" Thatcher said, "I have got religion." Wilson said, "What brand?"

Ebby, unruffled by the sarcasm, proceeded to answer the further questions of Wilson, who, in spite of his cynical posture, was curious. It turned out that Ebby was sober, had been sober for some time, and was living an altogether new and rather terrific kind of life. He had had a spiritual experience. He was trying to be honest with himself, to mend past wrongs, to turn his life over to God. And without any great struggle, one day at a time, he was free from alcohol.

We should take a moment here to observe that this unnoticed meeting of two very low-profile men in a Brooklyn kitchen was one of the greatest events of the twentieth century. Because out of that meeting came Alcoholics Anonymous. And out of Alcoholics Anonymous came Synanon and the entire therapeutic community phenomenon. And the whole thing has meant life out of death for very large numbers of addicted men and women.

But it signifies something even more important than that. It reveals the emergence of *regenerate School* at the public level in the life of our times. It represents a crack in the ugly and heretofore monolithic facade of that black faith, the worm's-eye view of man, which has been the scourge and is threatening to become the doom of the present races of mankind. *Regenerate School* is the cutting edge of the universal world view of man—the God's-eye view of man—the Way, the Truth, and the Life—the sacred intelligence that is man's joy and sanity if he will have it, and the occasion of his confusion and ruin if he will reject it.

Pleas, arguments, philosophies, organizations, any appeal to reason, decency, or honor—all are powerless in the face of the influence of the worm's-eye view of man. The only light that can cut through the worm's-eye fog is the light of regenerate School—real School. And regenerate School is always a practical, effective, and apposite expression of *the Way.* And that is something so big and so important that you have to struggle to hang on to its meaning —not because it is dim or vague or remote but on the contrary because it is specific, immediate, relevant, true, and beautiful beyond our hopes.

The Way is a method, a program, a means, and a power for achieving a definite result: a radical change *(metanoia)* in human consciousness and human nature, bringing with it freedom from want and fear, regeneration of the whole person, and the true brotherhood of man. It is no small thing, but small and weak people can do it, indeed are peculiarly qualified to do it. The Way is not a religion, but all real religion springs from it—not a science, but all real science obeys its principles—not an art, but all real art is a communication of it. The Way is the power which keeps the stars in their courses, and shows men how to live. It is the way the universe works, and it is the way *you* work when you are in your right mind. It is the Norm of human life. People are sane when they obey it, and insane when they ignore it. The Way is what the rationalists call the First Principles of Practical Reason and the faithful call the Kingdom of Heaven. All things are made by it, supported by it, and received by it at death. The Way is the life

(Zoe). It is the Law (Torah) and the Presence (Shekinah), the Road (Tariqa) and the Struggle (Akbar), the Path (Tao) and its Power (Teh), the Pattern (Rita) and the Method (Dharma). It is Logos-Sophia, Atman, the ruling Power of the universe in its aspect of illuminator and guide of the human race. It is the Truth, the ultimate Reality, the Self-existent, the Suchness—Aletheia, Sat, al-Haqq, Aehyeh, Tathata. It is Christ, God himself as teacher, helper, friend, and savior of men. It is the King of kings and Lord of lords, the blessed and only Potentate. It is all this at one and the same time. And whether you like it or not, or believe it or not, you are dealing with it—positively or negatively—every hour of your life.

Remember, then, while you are reading the story of the emergence of Alcoholics Anonymous that what you are reading about is an emergence of regenerate School—real School—with everything that that implies. Alcoholics Anonymous has never called itself a school, much less a regenerate School. Nevertheless, that is what it is. From its founding in 1935, it has been able to do what only a real School can do and what ordinary schools cannot do; it has been able to change lives. That is a definition: ordinary schools instruct in various subjects; *real Schools change lives.* These life-changing Schools appear here and there and now and then. They often proceed one from another, as Alcoholics Anonymous proceeded from the Oxford Group, and as Synanon and its offshoots proceeded from AA.

Now back to the Brooklyn kitchen. Bill Wilson wasn't buying any religion of whatever brand that afternoon, and Ebby Thatcher soon went on his way. In the days following, Bill continued to drink, but he also continued to think; he couldn't get Ebby and Ebby's words and *Ebby's example* out of his mind. He went on drinking and thinking and arguing with himself, and a few weeks later in Manhattan he found his way into the Calvary Church mission to derelicts and drunkards, where he answered an altar call and gave his life to Christ. (It had been a vision of the suffering

Christ appearing to Frank Buchman that had started the Oxford Group a quarter-century earlier.)

Bill did not immediately get sober. In fact he now spun down into worse drinking than ever before. His doctor prepared his wife to face a hopeless situation. And then the impossible happened.

He was in a New York hospital drying out after a bender, when he had one of those experiences that change men radically for good. He has told the story of his theophany in a number of places,* and we will not tell it here. The point is that following this vision of God, he never drank again. He left the hospital illuminated, sober, and with a new dedication, and he began immediately to seek out points of human contact wherein to make effective use of his overwhelming experience. He turned to the Oxford Group and quickly became an active member of the teams that carried the O.G. message of spiritual renewal.

Bill's burning interest was in other alcoholics. He worked on them, in bars and out of bars, for six months—with no luck at all. But at last, in Akron, Ohio, he met Dr. Robert H. Smith, the man who was to be the cofounder of Alcoholics Anonymous. Dr. Bob was the first alcoholic to get sober directly as a result of Bill's communication of his extraordinary spiritual awakening. Bill, Bob, and their first converts stayed within the Oxford Group for a few years, then separated out and went their own way.

The AA movement grew quite slowly at first; but after a prominent article in the national press in 1941, growth was very rapid. Working from begged, borrowed, or rented space in store fronts and church basements, AAs proved to have unprecedented power to reach out and draw alcoholics into their new fellowship, to communicate the essence of its program to them, and to quickly turn them into sober workers, ready to educate the next batch of newcomers.

*See *AA Comes of Age* (New York: Alcoholics Anonymous Publishing, Inc., 1957), page 63.

All of the elements of real School are visible in the AA history.

There were antecedents in the great Tradition—in the Way. Wilson had been touched by the spiritual power that flowed through the Oxford Group and which originated in Frank Buchman's illumination. (Buchman in turn had been educated as a clergyman. The whole direction of his ministry was toward a practical Christianity that brought lost men to salvation. The Oxford Group's original name was "First Century Christian Fellowship.")

There was the experience of direct illumination. Not everyone who works in a School will achieve it, but some will; and their number is most apt to include the founders and other earliest members. School is School only because there is real knowledge in it. And real knowledge is knowledge of God. And the only way of actually knowing God is directly, through experience, so that one can say, not "I think" but "I know."

Real School has the power to attract. In this respect, AA has made a remarkable demonstration. No doubt many real Schools arise, thrive, and decline without ever reaching a tenth the number AA has. On the other hand, of course, certain great historical flowerings of regenerate School have reached incomparably greater numbers.

Real School has the power to transmit what is necessary for life change. One of Wilson's earliest concerns was whether others could get sober and stay sober with anything less than just such an illumination as he had had. It was soon clear that the power to change lives did not depend on being able to induce such an experience. The AAs found they could convey their message and convince other drunks without it. The newcomer could lean on the other fellow's strength until he got his own new life going.

AA is an unusual School, peculiarly adapted to our age. In the past most Schools required a high level of behavior and of *being* on the part of applicants. AA begins at a very much lower point; its initiates are the cast-offs of society. The only requirement for membership is a desire to stop drinking.

At the other end of the ladder, AA goes very high. Its goal is conscious contact with God. Some AAs accept the rescue from chronic drunkenness but refuse to meet the challenge to turn their lives over to the care of God. That is, they check out of School after kindergarten. The fault here obviously is with the scholar, not the School.

Real Schools release enormous quantities of energy, some of which an individual uses in putting his own life to rights but much of which works immediately for the benefit of society. There is no way of measuring the total of social good attributable to Alcoholics Anonymous. Sober AAs are indistinguishable from the general population (except for their specifically AA activity), and yet everything they do in life afterward is powerfully affected by their spiritual recovery in AA.

You can see the energy explosion more readily in certain other Schools. The whole incredible history of the Benedictine monastic tradition—possibly the single most important factor in the building of Europe—is the story of School. It was a School that frequently renewed itself over the centuries; but at its inception in the sixth century it fulfilled all of the conditions given above.

The traces, the evidences, and the monuments of regenerate School are to be found everywhere throughout history and extending into the unsearchable dawn of our times—in Lemurian and Atlantean centers*—in prehistoric Chinese patristic and oracular influences—in the ancient pre-Aryan and Aryan Indian metaphysical traditions—in the Zoroastrian, Chaldean, Egyptian, and Greek mysteries—in the patriarchs, the prophets, the suprahuman priests, the sacred kings, the Essenes, and the Therapeutae—in the Schools of Pythagoras and Plato and Ammonius Saccas—in the Khwajagan, the Bektashis, the Naq'shbandis, the Yesevis, and other brotherhoods of Central Asia—in the Kargyutpa School of

*See Guenther Wachsmuth, *The Evolution of Mankind,* (Dornach, Switzerland: Philosophic-Anthroposophic Press, 1961).

Tibet—in the hidden Western European, British, and Hibernian initiatic groups, and especially in the hidden church of the Holy Grail—in the living periods of the great monastic traditions: the Cluniacs, the Carthusians, the Cistercians, the Friars Minor, and the Order of Preachers (all of whose tremendous work we moderns hate and reject, scarcely understanding what it is we are despising). We see the work of regenerate School again in the Hesychasts and in the compilers of the *Philokalia,* whose mission was to preserve the core tradition of Eastern Christianity; we see it again in the builders of the great Gothic cathedrals of the West, whose mission was to record Christianity in as durable a form as possible before the flood of unbelief swept over Europe. Moving to the highest levels, the regenerate light flashes in the Schools that formed directly around Sri Krishna, Sri Rama, Lao Tse, the Buddha, Moses, and Muhammad—and finally and preeminently in the School of Schools, whose textbook, the supreme example, is the New Testament.

The almost unimaginable loftiness of the greatest Schools does not diminish the importance of less exalted Schools. The point is that Schools grow up, burgeon, then weaken. The outer shell of a once strong School may continue to exist for a long time after nearly all spiritual vitality and regenerate power have departed from it. What counts is the living tradition and the eternal Truth. The Spirit bloweth where it listeth. A new center is formed, new energies are released. Then, inevitably, the time of decay comes. Some Schools prevail for hundreds and even thousands of years. Some are for a generation or less.

There are many Schools which never become well known. It is axiomatic that wherever there is an illuminated man or woman—wherever, that is, there is real knowledge of God—there will shortly be a School. It may not be large, or ever become famous, or last very long, but it will be real School because *it will change lives.*

How long will Alcoholics Anonymous last? How long will it

keep its God-given power to sober up drunks and keep them sober —to break the otherwise invincible death-grip of alcohol addiction? The first signs of slow-down have long been visible. AA is growing at a declining rate. But it is still growing. Actually it is in, so to speak, its "early Christian" phase. It has had its opening success. What you would expect now is that newer Schools would emerge within the parent School, especially as the larger one necessarily loses fervor with time and extension.

When Christianity had become successful and had in fact become the state religion of Rome, anchoritic monks in the Egyptian desert—mere nobodies on the then scene—were the men carrying the live tradition. It was their experience that influenced Benedict when he set up the first lay monastic communities. Centuries after that, when large parts of the monastic enterprise had grown affluent and corrupt, the Spirit shifted to small groups of men whose mission was to get Christian Scripture and teaching over into the vernacular tongues where it would once again be available to laymen.

Real School always does the same thing. It takes ordinary sensate men and converts them into men of the Truth, men launched on the road to nothing less than union with God.

Well, you may say, that is fine for a few; what about the many? Therein lies one of the most curious facts in the history of mankind. *All of the education of the many has developed out of Schools set up to educate the few in the search for God.* American public schools are a direct result of an original commitment to teach Scripture to all men. They have been entirely subverted from that effort, of course, but that is what always happens. In time all such efforts weaken, and sometimes they turn completely around and become their own opposites. That is why new Schools appear continually: to keep the central flame alive, lest men sink beneath their own ignorance and arrogance.

In our own modern times we are clearly at the point where an elaborately developed educational system has lost inner vitality while retaining the power to proliferate bricks and mortar. But no man should mistake this for real School. The universities which were set up a millennium ago to teach theology, queen of the sciences, have come full circle: they now teach that theology doesn't matter. So the mark of death is on them. In time they will disappear. *But real School will not disappear,* because it is of God, and God has said that he will be with us even unto the end of the age.

Meanwhile, it has now been demonstrated beyond question that it is the influence of regenerate School—and no other power on earth—which is able to produce recovery from the spiritual diseases of alcoholism and drug addiction.

CHAPTER 14

Muffled Breakthrough: the Spectacular but Obfuscated Achievement of Alcoholics Anonymous

Not 5 percent but sixty-five to seventy-five percent effective. The flesh and blood reality behind the statistics. The world-wide recovery phenomenon. How effective is Alcoholics Anonymous? The facts are there, but the field believes something else. The idiotically simple calculation—and the fantastic mistake following. The error behind the error: comparing sheep and goats. Three out of four recover. The 1968 survey. A change of attitude is overdue. Industrial experience confirms the historic recovery rate.

Alcoholics Anonymous is not 5 percent effective—as widely believed by most of the alcoholism "field" in recent years. It is *sixty-five to seventy-five* percent effective—as proved by a thirty-nine-year-old world-wide demonstration and a standing army of well over half a million sober alcoholics in every quarter of the globe today. How the figures got twisted around—how the scientific and professional community has converted the smashing and ongoing AA success into a "nothing much"—into a mere one among many of their own ineffective "treatments"—is one of the great untold stories of our time.

There is nothing dry or uninteresting about statistics; they become full of sap and fascination—if your life is at stake. If you had cancer, and you had to choose between two methods of help for it, and one method produced five recoveries out of a hundred while the other method produced seventy-five recoveries out of a hundred, you surely would be glad to have these statistics before you in making your choice.

While we are talking about the statistics of recovery from alcoholism, please keep in mind that if this does not happen to be a matter of life or death for you, it is so for many millions of your fellow men and women in the United States and throughout the world at this time. First, we are going to point to the flesh and blood facts, the living beings, behind the statistics.

Up until 1935 almost nobody in this century recovered from alcoholism; the rate was one to three out of a hundred. Today, very large numbers recover from alcoholism; the rate is seven out of ten who seriously try. What has made the difference is Alcoholics Anonymous.

The flesh and blood facts of Alcoholics Anonymous are a kind of data to make your heart leap if you come into touch with their living reality. If you, the reader, could come on a journey with us, your authors, we could introduce you to thousands upon thousands of happy, rejoicing, recovered alcoholics in AA meetings and AA homes all over the earth. You could greet them, shake hands with them, talk to them far into the night, and hear from their own mouths their stories of incredible and often miraculous recovery. You could talk to their families and friends and hear their stories gratefully and joyously confirmed. You could meet these recovered alcoholics by the thousands in the large cities—by the hundreds in the smaller cities—by the scores in innumerable towns and villages —by ones and twos and threes on ships at sea and in lonely wilderness outposts from the equator to the arctics.

We could travel through all of the fifty states, all the provinces of Canada, and a great many overseas nations, and keep on introducing you to ever more and more of these responsible, hardworking, smiling, sober alcoholics. We could keep this up for years, go round the world several times, go to different AA meetings every night, and still not have introduced you to all of the hundreds of thousands of alcoholics who are sober and staying sober as a result of their participation in Alcoholics Anonymous.

The other side of the picture is this: neither we nor anyone else we know of can introduce you to any considerable number of alcoholics who are sober by any means *that does not include Alcoholics Anonymous.* Such recoveries may exist, but they are rare and isolated, as recoveries from alcoholism always were before AA came into existence. *If you leave AA out of the picture, there are no significant numbers of recoveries from alcoholism.* This is the simple truth, the clear evidence of the scientific and lay experience on the subject. There is no record that any treatment[14n] for alcoholism —leaving AA out entirely—has ever consistently produced significant numbers of recoveries.

In 1973 Alcoholics Anonymous reported that its total worldwide membership was 650,000[15n] men and women in more than 20,000 groups in more than ninety countries. The groups are unincorporated and autonomous. Any two AA members who meet together can form an AA group. The fellowship has a central office, which is a clearing house for information and a distribution center for literature, in New York City, and this may be called "official AA." Groups are asked to help support these functions, and most do. The groups also report their membership totals annually. These are tallied up in a *World Directory* which the central office publishes each year. The *World Directory* comes in two parts: one for the U.S. and Canada and one for the rest of the world. Part 1 is growing faster than part 2 nowadays. AA's expansion in various places around the world is now very rapid. AA in Mexico, for example, in just a few years has grown to 5,823 members in 383 groups. AA in Colombia has 3,057 members in 212 groups. AA in Germany has 1,500 members in 294 groups. But the U.S. and Canada total is still by far the biggest—three times larger than the rest of the world combined.

The AA *World Directory* is a fascinating publication. Looking through the pages of this book, you will marvel at the strange and wonderful places where you can go to an AA meeting. There is only one group in Chile, but there are seven in Iceland. There are 94 in Finland, 182 in New South Wales, 20 in Japan, 22 in India (11 in Bombay alone). There are 42 groups in Alaska, 16 in Newfoundland, 8 in Green Bay, Wisconsin, and 1,469 in that greatest of all AA states, California.

The AA *World Directory,* along with membership totals, gives names, addresses, and usually a telephone number for a member of the group so that a visiting AA can quickly get in touch with nearby AA members in almost any place he happens to be. The AA groups are working parts of a practical, lifesaving network that functions with a facility that is astonishing when you realize that the whole thing runs on unpaid volunteer labor. (The New York headquarters and certain other big-city AA offices do have employees, but all told there are probably not 500 paid workers in AA service organizations in the whole world.)

By mid-1973 the upsurge of AA membership around the world had created a serious record-keeping logjam in the fellowship's New York headquarters. The 1973 edition of the U.S. and Canadian parts of the *World Directory,* scheduled for April publication, was not yet out in July. There was an average of six new groups *per day* registered all through 1972 in the U.S. and Canada alone, but even greater pressure came from overseas expansion. By mid-year AA had declared a moratorium on further new editions of its *World Directory* until 1975, and during the interval it proposes to find a new way to keep abreast of the movement's growth.

In order to protect members' anonymity, the *World Directory* is not available to non-AAs, and therefore this striking record of AA's spread and effectiveness is never seen by the general public. In one way that is unfortunate, because the directory reveals AA's success and power in a way that hardly any other kind of statement can. It says in the most concrete possible terms—names, street addresses, city, state, nation, telephone number, numbers of members, and annual cash contributions to AA's New York service office—that out there in all those thousands of places are hundreds of thousands of alcoholics who have recovered from what was once considered hopeless addiction, and who stand ready to help others who also want to recover.

But now the plot thickens. Obviously there is a very large number of sober alcoholics in AA. Nobody questions that. But how many are there *proportionately to the number who join the fellowship and work the program?* In other words, how effective is AA in producing recoveries? The answer to this question is long proved and crystal clear—and at the same time strangely and mightily befogged.

There *is* a way out of alcoholism, and Alcoholics Anonymous is it. From the time of its founding thirty-nine years ago right up to the present year, AA has proved *sixty-five to seventy-five percent* effective with alcoholics who seriously undertake it. But most people in the alcoholism field today do not believe that; indeed they have convinced themselves of something very nearly the opposite of the fact. They believe that AA is relatively *ineffective.* Despite its large number of members, they believe the recovery rate of alcoholics in AA is rather low, around 5 percent. Not much better, they say, than the score for any number of other "treatments."

So goes the almost unanimous song in the field. It is sung by scientists, by government officials concerned with alcoholism, by officials of private organizations, and even by AA itself. Over and over again in learned journals, in newspapers, and in popular magazines, the point is being made that all of the different kinds of treatment are about equally effective or ineffective, including AA. It might not occur to anyone to question this commonplace generalization, except for one big—fantastically big—discrepancy. AA has hundreds of thousands of sober members, and all the other treatments together can muster no significant number of recovered alcoholics. Something has got to be very wrong.

What actually *is* wrong? Here is what the authorities are doing: they take the figure for AA's United States membership (which now rounds off at 400,000), and they set that against the U.S. total of alcoholics (presently 8 million[16n])—and they get an "effectiveness" of five percent.

This simple calculation—idiotically simple, as we shall see—has led most of the leaders in the field into a disastrous error. It is an error in which they persist year after year—an error which keeps them pouring time and money into a futile search for a "more successful therapy"—an error which blinds them to the fact that the successful resource they are looking for has been in existence for nearly four decades and that it is working beautifully for the huge majority of those who elect to use it.

It is incredible—it boggles the mind—and yet it seems to be true that *nobody* working in the alcoholism field over all these years has seen the mistake: *you do not and you cannot measure the effectiveness of a recovery resource against those who have not tried it.* You cannot measure the effectiveness of Salk vaccine against all polio cases; you can only measure it against the number who have received the vaccine. Could anything be more obvious? You cannot set AA membership against all alcoholics; you can only measure AA's effectiveness against the number of alcoholics who have actually tried AA.

This fantastic mistake needs to be examined with some care, because a life-and-death issue for millions of people hangs upon it. The erroneous method of calculating now generally accepted throughout the alcoholism field would be diagrammed as follows (all figures are for the United States):

400,000 total AA members	as a percentage of	8,000,000 total active alcoholics	equals 5 percent effectiveness

This method is wrong for reasons we have already seen (and it is also invalid on other grounds which we will see in a moment). But if this way of calculating *were* followed, it would have to be corrected for the number of active alcoholics (approximately 10 percent of 8,000,000) who at any one time are ready to seek help, and who therefore are at least *possibilities* for a recovery resource to affect. And, considering the phenomenon of "slips," the total AA membership figure would have to be corrected for sober, non-drinking membership. No statistics for this exist, but it is a reasonable guess that 90 percent of the membership are sober at a given time. So then the situation would diagram thus:

| 360,000 sober, nondrinking AA members | as a percentage of | 800,000 active alcoholics ready for help | equals 45 percent effectiveness |

But this base of calculation also must be corrected, because obviously not all active alcoholics who are ready to seek help are ready to seek it from Alcoholics Anonymous. Let us guess generously (in order to incline the figures toward a low rate of AA effectiveness) that two-thirds of them are ready to seek AA help. Then the calculation would look like this:

| 360,000 sober, nondrinking AA members | as a percentage of | 533,000 active alcoholics ready for AA help | equals 67 percent effectiveness |

But even when corrected for basic errors, this way of calculating makes no sense. The whole process is a logical and statistical monstrosity from beginning to end, because it is an attempt to make a percentage comparison of sheep and goats—a simple impossibility. A certain number of sheep (nondrinking AA members) can never be a percentage of a certain number of goats (active alcoholics). Again, nobody in the entire field over all these years has seen the glaring error: the sober, recovered, nondrinking population of Alcoholics Anonymous is taken as a percentage of a category to which it does not belong—the category of active alcoholics. Thus to the confusion of wrong numbers is added the confusion of wrong categorization, and on the basis of this monumental muddle the entire alcoholism field continues to ignore the obvious fact that in Alcoholics Anonymous it has a consistently and spectacularly successful recovery resource in its midst.

The leadership of AA has played a remarkably ambivalent role in the face of the "5-percent-effectiveness" error. Alcoholics Anonymous has repeatedly published its own calculations of its recovery rate as between 65 and 75 percent (for example, in the famous *Saturday Evening Post* article by Jack Alexander in 1941,* in the second edition of the Big Book, *Alcoholics Anonymous,* published in 1955, and in the AA *Grapevine,* the official magazine of the fellowship, in 1968.) At the same time, leading spokesmen for AA, without actually endorsing the alcoholism field's mistaken estimate of 5 percent for AA effectiveness, have nevertheless shown an odd tendency to flirt with it. This schizophrenic posture can only be understood in view of official AA's desire to exalt noncontroversy above all other virtues.

Officialdom in AA has seemed to wish at any cost, and even at the cost of the truth, to stay out of controversial issues. In an article written for a book on alcoholism in 1968, AA's cofounder Bill Wilson said: "Alcoholics Anonymous is now thirty years old, and it has brought solid recovery to 350,000 alcoholics world-wide [the 1973 figure is 650,000]. While this is no doubt a significant contribution, it cannot be considered a large one, the total problem of alcoholism considered." And Dr. John A. Norris, nonalcoholic chairman of the AA General Service Board, told a meeting of the elected delegates charged with reviewing the AA headquarters operation: "Let us use our best wits to find and develop more effective ways to attract and hold the millions of alcoholics whom AA has not yet reached effectively.... Only a fraction of alcoholics —possibly only 5 percent—become successful in AA."

This dalliance on the edges of the low-recovery-rate fallacy, this unwarranted small-singing on the part of the founder of the fellowship and the chairman of the board, is characteristic of a general

*The article is reprinted on page 300.

attitude of AA officials. The above statements amount to saying, "Don't look to us; we haven't got the Answer." They are startling communications coming from AA's leading spokesmen after more than a quarter of a century of an international demonstration that AA *does* have the Answer.

In thus bowing off the scene as a witness in its own behalf, official AA has left the field for all practical purposes to professional spokesmen who have powerful vested interests in ignoring or denigrating any and all amateur efforts, no matter how successful they in fact may be, and who are thus able to operate without challenge —with great harm to alcoholics everywhere and serious injury to our entire society.

And this whole crazy mess, this statistical stupefaction, is quite unnecessary—another one of those mighty works of professional supererogation—because the effectiveness of Alcoholics Anonymous has been well established and well known from the beginning right up to the present time. It has been ascertained by means of careful, responsible, widely published calculations which have been repeatedly made in the only valid way that such calculations *can* be made: by comparing the known number of people who stay sober in AA against the known number of people who actually try AA.

The founding members discovered that as a matter of practical fact about three-quarters of all the alcoholics who seriously undertook to live by the AA Program were able to stop drinking and stay stopped. Counting heads and judging performance was not hard in the earliest days. Three years after Bill and Dr. Bob had met and launched what was to become known as AA, the following was the score, as recorded in the minutes of the first meeting of the Alcoholic Foundation (now AA's General Service Board): there were forty-one alcoholics in touch with the fellowship who were recovered. Members were working with six alcoholics considered "questionable"; that is, they had not yet enough time sober to be counted recovered. Twelve more were still in connection with the tiny fellowship, but looked "hopeless." Ten were recovered but out of touch—presumably still okay. There were, in addition, twenty-five "prospects."

These figures boil down to fifty-one out of sixty-nine (74 percent recovered, with the prospects not counted). Very early in AA history the characteristic figure shows up: three-quarters of the alcoholics who accept the AA Program achieve recovery.

The fledgling movement was just then (in 1938) on the edge of a big breakthrough. Within a few years, membership would soar to tens of thousands, groups would proliferate, favorable publicity would flood the country. The major thrust toward the present huge size of the movement was set off by a now famous article about AA by Jack Alexander in the *Saturday Evening Post* of March 1, 1941. AA was ready for this exposure at the national level; its basic text, the Big Book, *Alcoholics Anonymous,* had been published late in 1939.

In the Alexander article, what was to become for many years the standard estimate of AA effectiveness was first clearly set forth to the national public. AA's membership by this time had climbed to 2,000. In the process of growth from the 1938 level of fifty-odd members, it had continued to be AA's closely observed experience that of every four alcoholics who sincerely tried the program, three were staying sober.

Alexander wrote: "One hundred percent effectiveness with nonpsychotic drinkers who sincerely want to quit is claimed by the members of Alcoholics Anonymous. . . . but the working percentage of recovery falls below the 100 percent mark. According to AA estimation, fifty percent of alcoholics taken in hand recover almost immediately, twenty-five percent get well after suffering a relapse or two, and the rest remain doubtful."

In other words, three out of four recover—seventy-five percent. And this same rate was observed to hold true as time went on. Fourteen years later the same estimate of effectiveness was incorporated in the second edition of *Alcoholics Anonymous,* published in 1955.

Here was a message written in letters of fire. Doctors, clergymen, and ordinary laymen all knew in those days that drunks were hopeless. And now three-quarters of them had a chance? Wonderful! There had always been a very few drunks who recovered, but no one knew how these "spontaneous remissions" occurred or how to increase them, and the best estimate of the number of such cases never exceeded two or three out of a hundred. Now here was Alcoholics Anonymous with an assurance that seventy-five percent who seriously tried it could recover!

The skyrocket of enthusiasm for AA went up. The members felt themselves endowed with the strength of ten as they went about "Twelfth-Stepping" (helping newcomers). The press, the medical profession, and religious groups in those early days sang loud praises of this extraordinary society of formerly hopeless alcoholics.

But now there enters the villain of this story: phony statistics. The AA success led to the creation of the alcoholism "field." Before AA there were just a lot of lamentable drunks, and very few self-respecting professionals were willing to make a career out of dealing with them. After AA, things began to be different. Where before practically nobody knew anything about drunks, now there arose a body of knowledge of how many, what kinds, where, what economic levels, and so on. And there arose a "field" to deal with all that these new statistics implied. This field very quickly became a full-fledged social science, with considerable numbers of professionals and paraprofessionals devoting full time to it.

One of the earliest fruits of the effort to quantify the new alcoholism field was the establishment of a figure for the total number of alcoholics. As knowledge that there were *millions* of alcoholics got around, a whole crowd of "experts" began to object that AA's recovery rate could not be 75 percent or anything like it. AA had been in existence for years by this time, but even so, its membership was only in hundreds of thousands, and therefore its recovery rate must be way down, even below 10 percent—so said the "statisticians." And thus it came about that the harebrained error of measuring AA's effectiveness against *all* alcoholics, whether or not they had ever showed up at an AA meeting, became standard operating procedure in the alcoholism field—with what results we have seen.

Meanwhile, year after year and decade after decade, Alcoholics Anonymous continued steadily to produce recoveries at the 65 to 75 percent rate, as repeatedly proved when alcoholics who had recovered in AA were measured against those who had actually tried the Program. And meanwhile also the Fellowship was doubling in numbers every few years and spreading around the globe. It took a bunch of really very brassy "statisticians" to put over on this country the idea that AA is just another "treatment," and about as ineffective as all the other "treatments."

In 1968, AA reported the results of a large-scale survey of its membership, revealing a "two-thirds success record on the one hand and plenty of new blood coming in on the other." The survey employed an extraordinarily generous sample of 11,355 members, and giving all due weight to AA's expressed caution on this point, it is clear that the results may validly be projected across the 650,000 of the whole Fellowship. (Note that the Shafer Commission, using a random sample of only 3,200, projected its findings across the nation's entire population of 200 million.) The results of the AA survey are, as usual, within the historic 65 to 75 percent figure, and later experience offers further confirmation.

The 1968 researchers discovered that 38.1 percent of the Fellowship had been sober less than a year, 34.9 percent between one and five years, 25.4 percent five years or more, with 1.6 percent unreported. Translating the survey into terms of today's membership, it means that about 247,000 people are in the crucial first year of sobriety, 227,000 have been sober between one and five years, and 165,000 have been sober for five years or longer.* There has been

*This 1968 survey has been confirmed in some of its major findings by three independent investigations of AA populations, as noted by Leach in a recent report on AA effectiveness (in Bourne and Fox, *Alcoholism,* [New York: Academic Press, 1973]).

nothing like this in history. That so many people have recovered —and have stayed recovered so long—from an addiction everywhere considered hopeless less than half a century ago, must surely be one of the most important facts in the whole field of public health in our time. If anything like AA's rate of recovery were to be achieved for cancer or for arthritis, there would be a sensation across the whole world.

In the light of AA's proved power to deal with alcohol addiction, the professionals in the field are long overdue for a change of attitude. They really ought to stop the minimization of AA's accomplishment, not because AA needs praise but because there remains a huge job to do, and they—scientists and civil servants working in government and private agencies—are the people assigned to see that the job gets done. The job is to bring the country's reluctant and recalcitrant millions of drunks within range of an effective recovery resource—and that can only mean within range of Alcoholics Anonymous.

Whenever anyone proposes a vigorous promotion of AA to drunks, present members of the fellowship have a tendency to bristle. "The man has got to want it," they say. "You can't shove it down his throat." They are apt to remind you that AA works by attraction and not by promotion. And of course this position is wise. It just would not do to have the sober members out proselytizing and begging and pressuring active alcoholics to please get sober and join up. But if AA itself should not apply pressure to the drunk, *just about everybody else should.* Studies made of the effects of getting people into AA with a threat behind them prove that real recovery often can begin that way. For example, a city judge suspends sentence on a drunk-and-disorderly charge, and orders the man or woman to go to AA meetings for a period. Not all who start this way stay the course, but enough *do* to make it a very valuable approach. It needs to be widely copied.

On another front the fine art of urging people into AA is also working very well: a number of large industrial firms are producing phenomenally good results by *requiring* alcoholic workers at all levels to deal with their problem. In this connection, confirmation of the 65 to 75 percent calculation of AA's recovery rate came to light in one of the most important articles on alcoholism in recent years, "The Beginning of Wisdom about Alcohol," by Herrymon Maurer, in the May, 1968, issue of *Fortune*. Maurer's article was the first full-dress report on the fact that enlightened industrial alcohol programs were achieving a recovery rate of 65 to 70 percent by "crisis precipitation" and *referral of the alcoholic employee to Alcoholics Anonymous*. The company puts heavy pressure on the employee, up to and including threat of loss of his job. The company insists that he cooperate in his own recovery by full-scale participation in AA. It wisely attempts to do for a man what disaster will inevitably do for him if he keeps on drinking: it shows him that the only alternative to cooperating in his own recovery is loss of status, chronic sickness, and total failure in life.

So the wheel comes full circle. AA is proved as effective as always—wherever and whenever it is applied. In these industrial alcoholism programs the number of alcoholics who actually try the AA program is known. The number who succeed and the number who fail are likewise known. And right here, where the figures can be the most carefully checked, the results conform precisely to the original and frequently reiterated AA statement that three out of four who really try can find lasting recovery in the program. It is the best news that an alcoholic and his family ever heard, and it is a shame that the news gets lost or muffled.

Well—whatever happens to the statistics, the *fact* of the AA demonstration is there, and it cannot by any means be refuted. But it can be ignored. And this is indeed the way in which the addiction "field" has chosen to cope with the situation. Studied ignorance is the professionals' method of dealing with the amateurs' results.

The evidence that the only way to recover from addiction is by spiritual means has been in front of the scientific community in this country for nearly forty years. Starting in 1936 with the AA demonstration and continuing with the founding of Synanon and Teen Challenge in 1958 through to the present, the only significant numbers of recoveries from alcoholism and drug addiction have occurred in one or another of these spiritually centered recovered-addict societies or their offshoots. But the professional fraternity taken altogether—psychiatrists, ordinary MDs, psychologists, and social scientists of all sorts—simply cannot see it.

An individual scientist here and there may happen to recognize that addicts recover only by spiritual means, but he knows better than to say so in public or to write about it—and thereby expose himself to the raised eyebrows of his colleagues. As a result, in the scientific literature on alcohol addiction and drug addiction there is a nervous and superstitious avoidance of serious discussion and evaluation of the only approach to recovery that in fact works. There is an almost complete self-imposed ignorance on the part of the professionals in the field of the real meaning of AA and the other recovered-addict societies, and this blindness carries over powerfully into information for the general public which is based on professional views.

Two recently published major studies in the field of drug abuse illustrate this phenomenon in a remarkable way. The first of these studies is probably the most important government-financed overview of the nation's drug problem ever issued. It is *Drug Abuse in America: Problem in Perspective—The Second Report of the National Commission on Marihuana and Drug Abuse* (popularly known as the Shafer Report).[25]

The other is *Licit and Illicit Drugs: The Consumers Union Report on Narcotics, Stimulants, Depressants, Inhalants, Hallucinogens, and Marijuana—including Caffeine, Nicotine, and Alcohol,* by Edward M. Brecher and the editors of *Consumer Reports*[2] (hereinafter called *Licit*).

The Shafer Report represents the best that federal funds, high-level direction, and a large research and writing staff can do. *Licit* presents the findings of one of the most distinguished and impartial independent research groups in the country. Both books are massive: 481 pages for the Shafer Report, 623 for *Licit*. Both are comprehensive, dealing with all principal drugs that produce abuse, dependency, and addiction. Both give major space to alcohol, marijuana, and heroin. The Shafer Report leans favorably toward use of methadone maintenance as a treatment for heroin addiction; *Licit* is a virtual brief for it.

Despite differences of coverage and emphasis, an extraordinary unanimity emerges from these two books, written by quite different people, working from different bases, at about the same time. Both books are sharply critical of the nation's narcotics laws; both view our present drug-education programs as probably "counterproductive"; both look toward at least partial legalization of marijuana; and both, as noted, support methadone maintenance for heroin addicts.

But perhaps the most curious area of unanimity in the two books concerns the place and utility of the spiritually based recovery programs. *Neither report considers them significant.* Several pages are devoted in *Licit* to a systematic minimization of Synanon and Synanon offshoots, using as a main target of criticism not Synanon itself but an obviously minor league Synanon-like program in New Jersey. The authors set it up as a straw man and then knock it down. The Shafer Report concludes that the "therapeutic community method is suitable for very few [heroin addicts]." Thus the recovered-addict societies modeled on Synanon are left out of consideration because they are not big enough. (With 70,000 addicts involved and with demonstrated high recovery rates, they are not big enough!) At the same time, Teen Challenge, with its network of more than half a hundred recovery centers, is simply not mentioned.

And neither report deals with the subject of recovery from alcoholism—*at all.* In a total of 1,104 pages, the subject is simply left out. This, in the teeth of the fact that both reports stress that alcohol is without any question the worst drug problem facing the nation today.

The Shafer document makes two passing mentions of Alcoholics Anonymous, but the report fails entirely to draw on the AA example and from it to develop any recommendations for dealing with alcoholics or alcoholism.

But *Licit* furnishes the truly astonishing example of the "avoidance syndrome." Here, in an otherwise encyclopedic work on drug and alcohol abuse, the index of which alone occupies 28 pages, *there is not a single mention of Alcoholics Anonymous.* The hundreds of thousands of sober AA members—irrefutable evidence that there can be lasting recovery from addiction—carry absolutely no weight *at all* with Consumers Union. Since it is impossible to minimize AA on grounds that it has too few members, the device of total ignorance is employed. It is as if one were to report on new-model cars and leave out General Motors.

In the end these two authoritative, detailed, expensive, top-drawer studies of the drug and alcohol problem in America have *nothing at all* to recommend as a means of recovery to those caught in alcoholism. They have nothing more to recommend as social policy with respect to alcohol than the obviously futile hope that the liquor and advertising industries either will reform themselves or somehow be reformed by government action. And their recommendation for drug addicts is the substitution of one narcotics drug addiction for another.

CHAPTER 15

Synanon and the Therapeutic Communities —Born While AA Slept

The enthusiastic AA member. The AA group with the special emphasis on truth. The first addicts recover. Why it was unbelievable. Synanon games. Why the "encounter" movement went nowhere. Dederich's spiritual conversion. The influence of Emerson. The break with Alcoholics Anonymous. The parallel with the untouchables. Sectarianism all around. Synanon and AA could learn a lot from each other.

The entire therapeutic community movement in this country—now involving 2,200 communities and 70,000 narcotics addicts—started with one man, Charles Dederich. He was a member of Alcoholics Anonymous, and, to put it mildly, an enthusiastic member.

> When I eventually threw myself head over heels into the whole AA thing, I was excited as the devil. And didn't know why, because it didn't seem to be the answer I was looking for. [For years he had been thinking about how the world needed a "cheap and effective psychoanalysis" to clean up the "neuroses that develop as a result of growing up in a complicated culture."] But at least it [AA] seemed capable of doing something that had looked impossible. It had stopped me from drinking, that was for sure. So maybe there was a mechanism in AA that could not only stop people from doing certain things, but maybe start them doing something else. . . .
>
> And I loved it! "This is for me," I said to my sponsor. And he said, "Fatso, believe me: it had better be for you. Because

I am telling you, if you don't go to an AA meeting every day of your life from now on—you're going to die. And fast." So that's exactly what I did. I went every day. And twice on Saturdays and Sundays. I became a frantic, fanatical AA fellow. I lived it, I breathed it, I slept it, I ate it. For weeks I did nothing else but AA work. . . .[6]

In January 1958 there were thousands of meetings of Alcoholics Anonymous going on weekly all across the country. One of them was a meeting regularly scheduled in Charles Dederich's small apartment near the beach in Ocean Park, California:

With some friends from AA I had set up a Wednesday night "free association" discussion group. The group was set up to explore a "line of no line." The meetings were loud and boisterous. Attack of one another was a keynote of the sessions, with everyone joining in. I could detect considerable lying and self-deception in the group. I began to attack viciously—partly out of my own irritations and at times to defend myself. The group would join in, and we would let air out of pompously inflated egos, including my own. The sessions soon became the high point in everybody's week.[29]

This was the group that was to become Synanon—the first, the most famous, and the most successful of the therapeutic communities for drug addicts—and the example out of which all the other communities arose. Now a nonprofit California corporation with facilities in six cities*(San Diego, Santa Monica, San Francisco, Tomales Bay, Oakland, and Detroit), Synanon has a total resident population of 1,600, of whom about 1,000 are recovered heroin or other drug addicts. Synanon operates a number of businesses that bring in a large measure of self-support for the community, with gross sales of about six million dollars a year.

Many AAs are not aware even now that Synanon was founded by an AA member (who was never a drug addict), and that it actually existed within AA for a time before its separate incorpora-

*A very different situation as of 1990: Synanon is practically out of business. See Note, page 214.

tion. Synanon is AA's most vigorous offspring, but its parturition went largely unnoticed by the fellowship at large. Most AAs do not realize that Synanon is really an extension of their own movement, that its history is part of their history, and that it came into being to fill the vacuum created when AA, challenged to extend its ministry to heroin addicts, declined to do so.

In the beginning, Dederich and the dozen or so AA friends who helped him form Synanon had no intention of leaving AA. They were just another AA group, trying some unusual experiments with the format of their meetings. But in eight short months Dederich was out of AA, and Synanon was incorporated as a completely separate organization for the recovery of heroin addicts. The issue between the Synanon group and AA was bluntly simple: Could heroin addicts be members of AA? AA's answer was no. Dederich chose to go with the addicts.

There were far fewer drug addicts then than now, and they were nearly all in the biggest cities. In those days few AAs had probably ever met one. So the question of admitting drug addicts to AA membership seemed a remote issue. Surely—official AA told itself —there was no real problem. The addicts would no doubt work out something for themselves. It could hardly be the responsibility of an organization calling itself *Alcoholics* Anonymous to devote its members' time and energy to the needs of drug addicts.

And so the matter has rested for fifteen years. It now requires another look. The answers are no longer quite so obvious. There is a growing, uneasy sense that a mistake may have been made. Perhaps AA made a wrong turning, out of that most fertile of all grounds for wrong turnings, complacency.

By 1958, AA was already large, successful, and even in a sense wealthy. In twenty-three years its membership had gone into the hundreds of thousands; for twenty-three years the press had lavished favorable attention upon it; the movement was cited across the world as one of the truly great humanitarian enterprises of this century. With all this, almost any movement would find it hard to avoid a certain amount of complacency, and AA was no exception. It was into this AA complacency of the late 1950s that Synanon dropped like a small but powerful bomb.

The Synanon story begins with those unusual AA discussion groups in Dederich's apartment. AA had always insisted on a commitment by members to rigorous honesty as *the* precondition for sobriety. But over the years the convention had grown up that discussion of the seamier parts of one's story was reserved for the intimate relationship between an AA member and a single, trusted, fellow-AA sponsor, or perhaps a doctor, priest, rabbi, or minister. By universal agreement many subjects were taboo in the open or closed general meetings—sex, notably, but there were others. In fact the only shabby behavior that by custom got a full airing in regular AA meetings was *drinking* behavior.

The Dederich AA meetings reversed this policy. Everything was to be out in the open. It was a harking back to absolute honesty, a radical commitment to truth. You could bring up any subject, use any language. The one inviolable ground rule was that there be no actual violence. Physical fighting, no. Brutal verbal disagreement, yes. The "attack" or "encounter" feature of the group sessions was important. People were free to express their best or worst feelings about others, and they could expect the same in return. Dederich noted early in his experience with these new groups that "positive change in people in the group . . . resulted more from the intense verbal attacks than from the analytic approach. As a result of these vicious [verbal] haircuts, people seemed to grow before my eyes."

Dederich's group of AAs would also gather in his apartment at other times for sessions on religion and philosophy that they began to call seminars. One visitor mixed up "seminar" and "discussion" and came out with "synanon." This term stuck as the name of their intensified AA meetings, and finally, when the group was incorporated early in August of 1958, it became the name of the new organization. Later on the group encounter sessions were renamed Synanon "games." From the start Dederich was the leader in these extraordinary experiments. He had a peculiar genius for it, for getting to the truth of his own and others' feelings and attitudes.

Synanon games evolved through a whole lexicon of variations: the "extended game," the forty-eight-hour-long "dissipation" (later called trips), the "perpetual stew" (an endless game that runs night and day with people coming and going at will). All the variations are details of limited importance. The earth-shaking thing at the core of the whole phenomenon is the insistence on absolute honesty. The revolutionary strength of Synanon, its power to change behavior and to keep addicts clean, came from this.

With Synanon leading the way, an ill-fated passion for "encounter groups" swept the country in the 1960s. A major fact emerging from the wreckage of that hope for a universal kind of help is this: *dedication to truth is easy to lose in a welter of gimmicks and techniques.* The Synanon game has proved to be relatively unexportable. Dederich said that one step in its evolution was to eliminate the AA-style meeting moderator. But as he also said, he himself had to play thousands of games over a five-to-ten-year period before he had trained a sufficient number of experienced, strong players in Synanon so that games could go on there without him.

The secret of the Synanon game, or any such work groups, is that there must always be, in every one, enough people with deep experience and unwavering commitment to rigorous truth-telling to hold out against—and finally overturn—the automatic lying and massive weakness of the inexperienced majority in the session. Strength of this kind is developed and maintained only when people work together in a spiritual community. Without such strength, the encounter groups everywhere tend to degenerate into trivial thrill-seekers' playgrounds.

Only the truth sets men free. Certainly, only the truth sets an addict free. And for the truth you give your whole life: you cannot win freedom for a couple of hours' effort a week. The hobbyist encounter-grouper and weekend therapy-hound are pretty largely out of luck. What they lack is what AA (and later Synanon) always had: a hard core of participants whose lives depended on staying sober or off drugs, and whose commitment to the truth was therefore of life-and-death seriousness. In this kind of setting, the Spirit unmistakably moves; enormous forces for good and for healing are released; ordinary people become extraordinary people. Where the dedication to truth and to service to others is deep enough, men arise from the dead. Dederich's group of AAs was to find out how true that is.

Early on they were joined in their truth-telling sessions by some heroin addicts. By March of 1958 it was clear that they had in their midst a rare bird indeed: an addict who was clean and *staying clean*. By mid-year there were several more. Dederich and the others recognized the extreme importance of this at once. They were well aware of what the current score on recovery from heroin addiction was: zero. There was no known way for a heroin addict to recover—that is, to get off the drug and *stay off*. Years later one of the original AAs in the group recalled their excitement when they realized what they had got hold of:

> And now picture us in the grip of this all-consuming faith [in the truth] that caused us to shed every vestige of selfishness, with everyone's purse open to everyone else, freely stripping ourselves down to our most hidden moments, the most intimate and secret details of our lives, and pitching into each other with verbal weapons that loving friends had never before used against each other, in order to compel ourselves to this state. Who needed alcohol? . . . We were drunk with ideas. Drunk with the possibilities that this method was opening upon every side. And then this test case, just walking into our hands, straight out of jail. And with that first one, I mean Rex [the first addict who recovered], this thing revealed to us unimagined vistas.[6]

Dederich was not slow to see that in a few short months his intensified AA meeting had evolved into something the world had not witnessed before: a working approach to recovery from heroin addiction. He was to be the midwife in bringing a means of salvation for hopeless heroin addicts out of Alcoholics Anonymous, which, in its turn, a quarter-century earlier, had brought hope to the then completely hopeless alcoholics.

Dederich himself had been salvaged by AA only a year or two previously. He credited AA with saving his life, and he had had a profound spiritual connection with it. He had been utterly down and out, at the end of a long drinking career. His second wife had just left him; both of his children were lost to him:

> I went on a month-long bender of such proportions that everything went to pot and I wound up all over the floor, a real jibbering idiot, with every blood vessel in my eyeballs hemorrhaging, and myself so sick with the dry heaves that I could have wished for death to release me from this agony. . . . I knew that some AA literature had been left around. Somehow I managed to find this stuff, and somehow I managed to read the telephone number, but the number had been changed meanwhile and it took me forty minutes to reach the club. But by chance it was the very same sponsor who was sent to help me. [He had rejected AA help when his wife called for it three years earlier.]
>
> Only this time I was ready to welcome him. He nursed me through four days of horror, summoned a doctor to shoot me full of vitamins and tranquilizers, and finally on the fifth day, dragged me to an AA meeting in Beverly Hills, where he propped me against a wall close to the john, so I could get there quickly. . . .
>
> Thus I stayed while the meeting went on, feeling totally out of the picture. Utterly friendless and alienated. Totally alone. . . . I guess that can explain what I did next. I had been through a long period of silence, and apparently a great stock of unused vocabulary had accumulated just inside my vocal chords, and it had to come out. And so, suddenly, I shoved myself out into the meeting and started to harangue the audience, delivering a violent religious diatribe of which all I can remember is that it brought me bursts of laughter and

finally a terrific hand, and that afterwards people swarmed up to me, congratulating me, slapping me on the back, and saying that I was great.

Life became nothing but certain hours of financially necessary work—or what I then still considered necessary work—and then a rapid change of clothes and a quick run to the nearest AA house, which happened to be on Twenty-sixth Street in Santa Monica. Lunchtime, evenings, every spare moment, found me either there or at some other AA meeting sounding off on the Bible, on the Talmud, on cybernetics, even on the telephone book if no other topic was at hand. Didn't make any difference to me so long as I was doing the talking.[6]

Dederich is one of the great talkers of the age. He makes fun of himself for his volubility, and evidently his takeover ways in AA meetings were a severe trial for the AA brethren in the years when he was an active member. But there is little doubt he talked Synanon into existence, and that means that as a direct result of all his talking thousands of the world's most hopeless and totally unreformable human beings have been led back to clean, moral, responsible lives. From its start until the present, Synanon has made one consistent and unimpeachable demonstration: under its roofs live more clean narcotics addicts than can be found in one constellation anywhere else in the world.

It is impossible to tell the whole extraordinary Synanon story here; there are three books available for anyone who wants to get it in detail.[7n] Here the focus is on the crucially important transformations in Synanon's founder that accompanied his spiritual conversion in AA and the resulting impact on the recovery of narcotics addicts across the land.

In his progress from falling-down drunk to leader of men, Dederich had about made it to the caterpillar stage by the time he was haranguing the Santa Monica AA members with his great talk. There was to be a next stage. Out of the chrysalis was to come a completely different kind of creature. His experience was very much like those recorded in William James's *Varieties of Religious Experience* or in Richard Bucke's *Cosmic Consciousness.* The scene of this change was Santa Barbara, where Dederich's firm had transferred him:

> But something happened in Santa Barbara. Something very strange. A feeling of impending doom took hold of me. I couldn't understand it—I was just plain scared. Scared to death. So I never unpacked my suitcase. Every spare hour I had I spent in my room, frightened out of my wits. And I couldn't discover why.
>
> I happened to have with me an old copy of Emerson's essay on self-reliance[18n]. . . . I took to carrying that little book around with me. And whenever I had nothing else to do I would take it out and do a bit of reading in it. As often as ten times a day. With some kind of inexplicable drive to read passage after passage over and over again. Until suddenly it dawned on me that this was no mere literary flight, this was a book of directions. It was as technical for the human psyche as a mechanic's manual was for the repair and running of a car.
>
> And what the book said was you—you, the reader—you have a piece of God in you. Why then don't you rely on your own thinking and your own impulses? Trust yourself, man! Be a convert to your own inborn religion. . . .
>
> The moment, up in Santa Barbara, when I realized that I wanted to spend the rest of my life rescuing drunks, my terror left me. I had no more fear. I went back to Los Angeles and got right to work. I sat in an AA club and took every incoming call, doing for other people what my sponsor had done for me, wiping away their tears, talking philosophy to them, cleaning up their vomit. I suppose lots of guys are living in misery to this day who might be happily drunk or happily dead, if I hadn't jerked them off some barstool.[6]

Living on thirty-three-dollar unemployment checks, Dederich set himself to reading all the books he "should have read and hadn't": Emerson, Thoreau, Lao Tse, Freud, St. Thomas. By now it was the middle of the winter of 1957–58, and AA friends began dropping into his small apartment near the beach. Here he started the special Wednesday night meetings; and here Synanon was born. By early summer the group had its first clean addicts. By mid-summer Dederich and his Synanon flock, now numbering about twenty, had pulled out of AA for good. Dederich tells how it happened:

The break with Alcoholics Anonymous occurred about the middle of August (1958). It happened right in the middle of an AA meeting. Our whole gang had taken over the Saturday night meeting of the Santa Monica AA group at 26th and Broadway and built it up from its attendance of ten people to an attendance of about forty-five or fifty. There was some objection on some issue by the members of the Board of Directors of the AA club. I recall the leader stopping the meeting. They didn't like us. The alkies didn't like the addicts and they didn't like me in particular because, among other things, I had been through an LSD experience. I had committed the unpardonable sin—I had taken a drug. . . .

They made things difficult for us. I remember getting up in the meeting and saying, "All right, let's go home—the hell with this." So the whole meeting got up, and we all got into our automobiles and came down to the club and never went back to AA again.[6]

"The alkies didn't like the addicts." These words of Dederich's are a kind of shorthand. It was not so much a matter of personal likes and dislikes as a question of policy: did drug addicts belong in AA meetings at all? In the late 1950s addicts had begun to show up at some big-city AA meetings, not only heroin addicts but people addicted to barbiturates and other drugs. It was a logical move on the part of the drug addicts; why not see if what worked for so many alcohol addicts would work for them.

At the level of the ordinary AA group, there was a good deal of confusion. Addicts would get cordial acceptance, nervous acceptance, or no acceptance—strictly on the basis of local option. Finally the dilemma they presented worked its way up to AA's New York headquarters. A policy opposing entry of addicts into the Fellowship was laid down in an article by the late Bill Wilson, AA's senior cofounder, in the February 1958 issue of the AA *Grapevine,* the Fellowship's monthly magazine. This was six months before the Synanon split. It seems reasonable to suppose that Bill's stance had some effect on the Santa Monica AAs and on the trouble between them and the Synanon AAs and addicts.

At first reading Bill's article might seem a very simple statement of something AAs had assumed all along: AA is for alcoholics. The matter-of-factness, however, tended to conceal the fact that the article also announced a critically important change of emphasis. It was the first time that official AA formally stated that *the welfare of the organization should come ahead of the recovery of individuals.* "Our first duty, as a society," Bill wrote, "is to insure our own survival." It is a straight commitment to corporate egotism—and an ill-starred turningpoint in the history of a great altruistic movement.

In subsequent sentences Bill retreats from other important positions that he himself first laid down in the Twelve Steps, AA's great formulation of its recovery program. Perhaps the most serious of these strategic withdrawals is in his statement that sobriety—freedom from alcohol through the teaching and practice of the Twelve Steps—is the sole purpose of an AA group. But the steps themselves make clear that sobriety is a mere prerequisite of the AA program, which has spiritual awakening as its goal (Twelfth Step), with prayer, meditation, and *service to others* (Eleventh and Twelfth Steps) as the primary means to that end.

The net effect of Bill's article is that AA decided to turn away from drug addicts, not because AA cannot help them—there is the implicit recognition that the AA Program is precisely what they need—but because *the addicts represented a threat to AA's organization.* History is full of examples of great spiritual movements that have at some point taken a similar turning; they have chosen safety, and in the end the instinct for mere self-preservation has suffocated them.

It is no doubt true that heroin addicts indeed *were* a real threat to AA's composure. Remember that they were considered completely incurable by people who knew the facts about them best. Lewis Yablonsky had been advised by other professionals not to associate with Synanon, because working with hopeless addicts could never help his career. It took Synanon itself a year after its incorporation to put an end to "chipping," the light use of various drugs by many of its residents. These addicts were unregenerate conmen, thieves, and liars of a kind to make ordinary drunks look almost nice. Could AA really be expected to get a spiritual message across to them? Would it not be upset or even destroyed by letting these addicts into the Fellowship?

Gandhi once faced a situation that offers a remarkable parallel, on a considerably larger scale, to the AA-versus-drug-addict dilemma. The case is instructive because, despite the size of the stakes, Gandhi was able to avoid the mistake of putting organization ahead of the truth and the people it was set up to serve.

Hinduism from very ancient times right down to the present had always consisted of four castes—and then a fifth, which did not really have caste rating at all but was "outcaste." These were the sixty million "untouchables." Gandhi called them *harijans,* children of God. The untouchables' situation in mid-twentieth century Indian society was, on the whole, probably worse than the condition of black slaves in the U.S. before the Civil War. Gandhi's sense of truth and justice finally rebelled at any further countenancing of this enormity, sanctioned though it was by religion and ancient custom.

There were powerful practical arguments for leaving the situation alone. By forcing the issue, Gandhi would certainly jeopardize everything he had built up over so many years—organization, friends, financial support. The way it worked out, he put not only these things but his own life into the balance. He went on a fast to the death in protest against harijan exclusion from Hindu life.

The people understood his message: that untouchability was a violation of God's truth, a vicious sectarianism, a division of society into mutually exclusive groups on ostensibly religious grounds but actually for the convenience and safety of the powerful. And the people understood Gandhi's demand: that they end the age-old discrimination *at once.* The entire nation swung round in a single week. Temples which for centuries had been closed to untouchables were opened to them. Social and economic barriers of all kinds were dismantled. Gandhi had won. But he had been prepared to sacrifice *everything*—all personal and organizational welfare—to the demands of the right and the truth.

The parallel is striking. In his *Grapevine* article Bill was speaking as chief of the *sect* of Alcoholics Anonymous, the "main nation" among the addicted. By 1958 the recovered alcoholics in AA were indeed the safe, the successful, and the strong. The heroin addicts, on the other hand, were precisely the untouchables. The decision came down that they would stay on the outside. The claims of organizational "purity" and safety came ahead of raw human needs. Sectarianism carried the day.

Christianity has splintered itself into sects over the last thousand years. In our time the pace of entropic dissolution quickens; the recovered-addict fellowships have accomplished the same process in a mere thirty years. (The process of splintering into sects became hectic with the proliferation of Synanon's offshoots—all the Daytops, Gateways, Topic Houses, Phoenix Houses, Harmonie Houses, and all the other Houses of the land.) Each adopts a posture of total independence of the others, denies its debt to the others, and is in turn denied.

Wilson and Dederich, two of the most remarkable men of the century, sat behind desks on opposite ends of the continent, effectively walled off from what might have been mutually helpful interaction by the fact of their sectarianism. This is no mere matter of how nice it would have been if great fellows had got together. Big issues, big stakes—a huge number of lives—were involved. And although it may be that everybody did as well as he humanly could, sectarianism nevertheless looms in this picture as the divisive force it always is. There is an extremely difficult and dangerous situation in this country with respect to addiction, and in all these years two of the most successful and powerful movements for dealing with the problem—Alcoholics Anonymous and Synanon —have had nothing to do with each other. And yet they desperately need each other's strengths.

There is much that AA could learn from Synanon. Wherever AA has grown weak and ineffective—and many AA groups suffer from complacency and conventionality—it has done so because the truth has been dishonored. Many AAs will argue that life can be compartmentalized. It is not necessary, they say, to try to correct *all* one's character defects, just the drinking. Synanon's demonstration of the enormous power released by dealing with the truth as it concerns *one's whole life* ought to have been, and could have been, a stimulus to reform within AA, a return to the original sense of AA's Twelve Steps, which clearly point to moral reform in *all* areas of one's life. Bill Wilson said that he "built the four absolutes of the Oxford Group—absolute truth, absolute love, absolute unselfishness, and absolute purity—into the Sixth and Seventh Steps of the Program."

A major asset of Alcoholics Anonymous is its huge number of groups. It is an international network, an effective subculture, reaching almost everywhere, where alcoholics can go for recharging of their spiritual batteries and for fellowship in the work of staying sober and helping others stay sober. A major Synanon weakness is its isolation. It has limited facilities; for all practical purposes Synanon is confined to California; most addicts who leave Synanon have to go back to trying to live unaided in the same society that was the theatre of their original addiction and failure. Dederich himself has estimated that 90 percent of those who leave

Synanon, even after considerable periods of time in the program, return to drugs.*

Suppose for a moment that the AAs had not decided so flatly to have nothing to do with victims of other drugs, and suppose that the huge AA power base—all of those 18,000 groups spread all over the world—was available for addicts to plug into and to draw strength from. Think what that would mean in saved lives!

There is a story out of AA's early days. A new member confessed to the group that along with his alcoholism he had been involved in some very ugly behavior of a kind so scandalous that some of the members were for drumming him out of the Fellowship. But one of them said, "No, wait. What would the Master do?" And that turned the verdict in favor of the new man.

It is by no means too late for AA to ask itself now, with respect to opening its membership to drug addicts—What would the Master do?

*Note: In the years following the first publication of *The Answer to Addiction*, Synanon has undergone a well-publicized decline through the phases of the merely bizarre—shaved heads required for all its members, male and female, as of 1975—to the shockingly out of balance—mandated spouse-swapping, vasectomies, and abortions, as of 1977—to the criminally violent, culminating in the famous attack against Los Angeles attorney Paul Morantz on October 10, 1978. In connection with this attack, in which a live rattlesnake was placed in the attorney's mailbox, Dederich and two other Synanon members pleaded no contest to the charge of conspiracy to commit murder. At the time of his arrest in the Morantz case, Dederich was drunk. His own recovery from alcoholism had gone by the boards, along with everything else.

APPENDIX A

A Sampler of Some of Our Schoolmasters' Teachings in the Lifesavers Way of Life

Robert Mendelsohn *on*

the escalation of the AIDS controversy and
the gamma globulin fiasco

(From "The People's Doctor Newsletter")

A wire service story dated August 30, 1986, begins with the words, "Turmoil among AIDS experts at the Federal Centers for Disease Control."

In case your newspaper did not carry this important article, CDC's AIDS squad has been plagued by personality conflicts, firings of eminent scientists, an exodus of researchers, and delayed studies of ways to halt the deadly epidemic. The intensity of infighting in the CDC research laboratories has been demonstrated by experts sabotaging each other's experiments and suppressing research to combat the deadly disease. Virus cultures have turned up missing or contaminated. There have been petty squabbles over authorship of papers. Top scientific officials have ordered that their names be added to studies they never worked on.

While this sorry state of affairs at the top level of U.S. government health agencies may come as a shock to many people, it should come as no surprise to regular readers of this Newsletter. A decade ago, I brought you early warnings about what was to become the CDC's swine flue fiasco. Later, I revealed how that same bunch fumbled the ball on Legionnaire's disease. More recently, the CDC vaccine enthusiasts have forced mandatory immunizations on this country's children, without telling parents the risks of the vaccines and without requiring doctors to report vaccine reactions. So why

216

should we expect any different behavior when it comes to AIDS?

I often have referred to the personnel at the CDC as second-rate doctors. Now, reporter Steve Sternberg, who wrote this article for Knight-Ridder Newspapers, supports my evaluation by pointing out that those scientists who have been forced to leave the CDC rank among the nation's most prestigious researchers. Indeed, few of the laboratory's original scientists remain. Perhaps these remaining lesser lights in medicine account for the strange behavior of the CDC in giving gay rights priority over public health.

Lest you think that the CDC is unique in the world of medicine because it places personality conflicts over scientific progress, ask your own doctor how often he angrily has watched scientists in his own medical schools and hospitals graft their own names onto published research with which they had practically nothing to do.

What's the point of government-funded research if the researchers have no integrity?

(From the same Newsletter)

Question, from M.R.: My doctor suggests I have a gamma globulin shot before I travel overseas. I know this shot is made from blood, and I wonder whether, in view of the AIDS epidemic, it's safe for me to take it.

Answer, from Dr. Mendelsohn: Many doctors still are using gamma globulin to ameliorate chicken pox in children and to protect Americans traveling abroad.

If your doctor assures you this human blood product is safe, ask him if he has read the February 7, 1986, issue of the *Journal of the American Medical Association*. That issue contains the information that the entire supply of gamma globulin available in the United States is positive for the AIDS (HTLV-III) antibody.

Donald Steele, M.D., of Newport Beach, California, comments: "I am appalled that the Food and Drug Administration, the Centers for Disease Control, local health services or the drug companies have not informed physicians throughout the United States that administration of gamma globulin to their patients or employees may entail the risk of converting them to a false-positive reaction for the HTLV-III antibody.... Without advance knowledge, however, the liability imposed on each of us is potentially enormous. Each of us can envision innumerable scenarios that might put us at grave risk if we fail to inform the patient in advance...."

While I am all in favor of giving patients information, perhaps a simpler solution would be to dump all gamma globulin down the drain.

From Robert Mendelsohn,
The People's Doctor Newsletter

Robert Mendelsohn, M.D., was a life-long faithful and responsible servant of modern medicine. He was at the same time a life-long faithful and fair critic of modern medicine.

Dr. Mendelsohn practiced medicine for over thirty-five years. He was Chairman of the Medical Licensing Committee for the State of Illinois. He was National Director of the Medical Consultation Service of Project Head Start. And he was the recipient of numerous awards for excellence in medicine and medical teaching. At the time of his death in 1988 he was Associate Professor of Preventive Medicine and Community Health in the School of Medicine of the University of Illinois.

He was also a stoutly self-proclaimed medical heretic. Dr. Mendel-sohn believed that the greatest danger to your health was usually your own doctor. Modern medicine's methods, he argued, are rarely effective, and in many instances are more dangerous than the diseases they are designed to diagnose and treat.

Mendelsohn's basic book is *Confessions of a Medical Heretic*. Equally important are the monthly newsletters which he wrote beginning in 1977. You can get any or all of the newsletters from *The People's Doctor Newsletter*, 1578 Sherman Avenue, Suite 318, Evanston, Illinois 60201.

Harry M. Tiebout *on how*
psychotherapists and psychiatrists can learn
something from Alcoholics Anonymous

*(From "Psychological Factors Operating
in Alcoholics Anonymous")*

In recent years AA has been shining brightly if at times un-
evenly in the firmament of psychotherapy. No one can as
yet be sure whether it is a meteor, a comet, or a star of
some considerable magnitude, but it should be observed with
respect and interest, and assayed for the light it may shed
upon the therapeutic process. As with other new and striking
phenomena, investigators initially tend to examine it from
the perspective of known or relatively proved principles of
psychotherapy. Hence there is a flood of explanations as to
what makes AA tick—explanations which run from homosexual outlet, dependency upon a father person, opportunity to exploit exhibitionistic, narcissistic trends, through to
vague and rather pontifical assertions about the therapeutic
influence of the group. No one professes to be quite clear
about his opinion, and everyone generally concedes that there
must be an X factor, the presence of which is assumed by
conjecture.

Now the strange fact in all this picture of uncertainty and
conjecture is that very few of the investigators have studied
AA carefully, nor have they availed themselves of opportu-
nities to talk to members who have made the grade over a
sufficient period to have achieved a long-time slant on what
goes on and what is essential. If they had, they would have
learned what that X factor is. They would have discovered

that a religious component, a spiritual development, a belief in a God, was considered by AAs the one cardinal element without which there could be no permanent sobriety.

Failure to accept repeated testimony of the more experienced AAs is in itself an interesting phenomenon and attests to the stranglehold which Freud and his dicta have upon current psychotherapeutic thinking. Fairly early in his career, for reasons best known to himself and his own unconscious, Freud took the position that religious beliefs and feelings were signs of dependency and immaturity, sedulously to be avoided and decried. This "opiate-for-the masses" attitude he maintained unflinchingly to the day of his death, and it is this attitude which has influenced present-day psychiatry to the point of excluding the possibility of religion and religious forces having any valid therapeutic effect or function. It is my belief that here, as in his insight into feminine psychology, Freud suffered from certain blind spots and biases which prevented him from seeing the role of religion in human affairs. It is my further belief that the phenomenon of AA can never be understood until more insight is gained into the phenomenon of religion and spiritual growth.

In this paper, therefore, I plan to present some material plucked from AA which supports pretty conclusively the AA conviction that this religious factor is the essential X quantity. I shall then set forth my own tentative explanation as to why such is the case.

In offering you the following account of AA experience, I wish first to express my indebtedness to some of the older members who have provided the information on which these stories are based.

Some six or seven years ago there was a new member who, according to reports, was one of the toughest-minded men ever to enter AA. However, he became quickly enthusiastic about the program, at the same time violently opposing the "spiritual angle." "Damn this God business" was his constant cry, to the consternation of the others in the group who felt he was a disturbing influence in that he seemed to prove that sobriety could be maintained without God. He remained dry for many months, got his family together, worked hard and successfully with other alcoholics. He finally felt secure enough to leave AA work and go back into his old business of selling on the road. Within three weeks he began drinking, and after a terrific bat, while writhing with an awful hangover in a cheap hotel, "something cracked," as he put it, and "I gave in and admitted that the boys must have something with their God stuff," as he later reported. This man has since stayed sober and five years ago founded one of the most successful and active current AA groups.

Many other individual members have been through similar experiences, but it is also true of groups, as the history of one in a Western city clearly indicates. This group was started by an AA member who was one of the very few able to stay dry without the "spiritual angle." In other respects this man is a most enthusiastic member with a sobriety record running at least six years. Some five years ago, while taking a business trip through this community, he assembled a group of alcoholics and sold them the idea of AA minus the need for a belief in "a power greater than themselves." This he insisted was not necessary. After he left the group hung together and got in quite a few new members, but a year later, when they numbered perhaps twenty, they were, with one exception, all drunk at the AA Christmas party.

Later, and largely on the basis of AA literature and letters from the central office in New York, the group went straight AA, accepting the necessity of the religious or spiritual slant. Now, four years later, there are a dozen groups in this area numbering several hundred members with a record of seventy-five percent sober.

The third illustration is perhaps even more telling, as it concerns the efforts of a psychiatrist to use most of the AA program but without any emphasis on the "God angle." Club houses, group activities, discussions were all offered, but the record over a considerable period of time was far from satisfactory until some of the men surreptitiously visited the local AA group and started to spread straight AA among the others. Before the "higher power" idea was introduced, the secretary reports, the results were small. Although everyone who wanted to stop drinking felt he had been much helped by the instruction received from the doctor, and although the doctor personally was both popular and respected professionally, the alcoholics with one or two exceptions could not seem to stay dry on his regimen. After the contact with AA, progress was much greater. Now about twenty men who could do nothing with the club program are AAs and are progressing far more satisfactorily.

These examples, which are typical of AA experience, lend solid support to the opinion that the religious element is essential.

What the religious element may be, therefore, becomes the real nub of the question as to why AA succeeds where others fail. In attempting to determine the answer to this question I have developed certain speculations which seem to some extent to supply the answer sought for.

Before detailing the facts on which my speculations are based, one source of confusion must be eliminated, namely, the distinction between religious practice and religious feeling. Religious practice frequently produces religious feeling, but it does not inevitably do so. In order to avoid two such conflicting usages of the word "religious," the word "spiritual" will be employed to refer to the feeling which may arise during the course of religious observance. In other words, a spiritual feeling should result from religious practice.

The question now reads, "What is a spiritual feeling?" The answer to this question, an essential preliminary to any discussion of AA, is most difficult. It cannot be stated directly, but it must be attempted, because it is only by appreciating the nature of a spiritual feeling that one can arrive at an understanding of what goes on in AA.

The first series of facts which focused my attention upon the spiritual factor sprang from observations made upon what I have come to call conversion experiences. Differing slightly from more customary usage, I define a conversion experience as a psychological event in which there is a major shift in inner response or affectivity. Whereas, before, the patient was swayed by a set of predominantly hostile, negative attitudes, after the conversion process the patient is swayed by a set of predominantly positive, affirmative ones. This change is generally although not necessarily religious both in inspiration and in expression. It may take place with sweeping, almost cataclysmic suddenness, or it may occur slowly over a period of time. The important fact for the purpose of this paper is that as a result of this change there develops a new type of inner response. This new type is spiritual in quality.

To date, I have been in a position to study at least thirteen patients who have exhibited this response. Incidentally, not all of these patients were alcoholic. From these observations, I have gathered a picture of the new feelings which arise and how they affect the individual.

It is these new, positive, affirmative feelings, spiritual in nature, which I now must attempt to describe even though to describe a feeling kills it and in no way creates it. Unfortunately, also, the feeling I must discuss has to be seen or felt before it can be realized and, therefore, thought about in all its aspects.

The outstanding quality to appear is a frame of mind for which patients use words such as "peaceful," "quiet," "contented," "calm," "serene," "tranquil," and the like. Pressed further, they fall back on words and phrases which show that the tense, roused, anxious state so characteristic of the alcoholic has gone without a trace. Characteristically they report, "I feel different; I'm not tense and nervous like I used to be. I don't have to get everything settled at once, I'm not so impatient. Things don't bother me like they used to. I now don't think that when things don't go my way, it's aimed at me." Some will say further, "It's astonishing what it [the new emotional viewpoint] does to your outlook on life. Before I used to think about the future and how I could enjoy that. Now I enjoy the present and let the future take care of itself. It's much simpler that way because your thinking does not have to be all clogged with what may happen in the future. You don't ignore the future but it isn't a burden any more." One patient carried this point further by adding, "If you're not so full of demands as to what you should get out of life, you can live in the present because you're satisfied with it. You're not always hoping that the future will bring you what you want; even though you know that, when you get it, you won't be satisfied long." The tense, driving, goal-pushed person has disappeared and in his place there is an individual who can be patient, relaxed, and much more tolerant.

Along with this new type of inner feeling response go changes in many of the personality or character attributes formerly in the ascendancy. For instance, there may be a loss, temporary or lasting, of most of the overt signs of what may be designated as "automatic hostility." As an example, patients are frequently victims of what may be called the "sucker" complex. They will complain of a sense of isolation and loneliness which they frequently offer as an explanation for their drinking. They then proceed to explain their loneliness as follows: They are basically friendly, trusting souls who have tried to get close to other people, but they have always been disappointed sooner or later so that now they are cautious about really going "all out" for anyone. They have been "suckers" too often and now they are going to wait until they see what is real underneath. The interesting fact is that, with the changed emotional status, the problem of hostility and its associated mechanisms drops out; the "sucker" fear vanishes and patients remark, "I feel easier with people; I'm not so suspicious, and I realize they do things because they are themselves and it is not directed against me. I can like them and I think they can like me and I don't get all upset when I find that there are things about them that I don't like. I don't fear that my feelings will change because I don't go all out for people in the same way. I know they have faults, but that's because they are human. I don't fear being a sucker any more."

Fully as striking is the disappearance of the perfectionistic drive. The mechanism for this disappearance is easy to decipher and interestingly clear. During the automatically negative phase the patient projects the feeling of hostility into the world about him and, therefore, finds it filled with hostility, for which the world always affords plenty of factual support. When the new phase comes up, instead of automatic hostility there is an automatic positive note which in turn projects a friendly feeling into the environment. It is then possible to view the bad with kindlier eyes and call it a human tendency to err. Furthermore, the good is seen as real and genuine and not as a hypocritical mask which covers a basic hostility and selfishness.

With the submergence of the hostility components and the consequent disappearance of the perfectionistic drive, there is also a corresponding dimming of the idealistic overtones. In retrospect, it becomes apparent that the search for the true, the good and the perfect is a naïve, unconscious effort to neutralize the projected hostility. The unconscious thinking seems to run as follows: "If the world is perfect or I can find enough perfection in it, then the badness (or hostility) of the world cannot continue to prevail."

Along with the cessation of the idealistic pressures, there is a corresponding shift in the feelings of guilt. Whereas prior to the conversion change the patient is burdened by a sense of guilt which can be called truly sadistic and punishing, after the change the individual acknowledges guilt and wrongdoing but accepts his own human tendency to err as he does that of other people. One patient pointed up this particular aspect when she said, "Before I always knew what was right and wrong. I would always be trying to live up to ideals. I was sort of blank about what I *wanted* to be. I would have doubts. I would put on a front to be what I wanted to be. Then something came along and I had to stay up there; that's when I became tense. Now I know I have been doing right and wrong all my life but I don't have to be so virtuous about being good or guilty about being bad." Commenting on her former sense of righteousness, she said, "Before if there were any Ten Commandments, I had to be at the bottom of them. I was a queen without a kingdom." Her final thought on her perfectionism was, "It made me sit on many things which would have helped me to grow."

Along with the amelioration of the hostility component, there is an equally striking loss of the egocentric power drive. Prior to the shift, happiness is the goal and happiness is pictured as independence, freedom, and doing what you please. Happiness, it is unconsciously assumed, can only be achieved through being strong enough to get what one wants. It can never be attained by a weakling who is doomed to unhappiness because he must always be frustrated. Since the feeling of inner strength automatically implies the opposite weakness, the individual involved in the dilemma of securing happiness through power inevitably suffers from a superiority-inferiority conflict. When he feels strong, he feels superior; when he feels weak, he feels inferior.

Logically, if the power drive is diminished or changed in quality, the goal of happiness disappears and so does the striving for superiority with its accompanying inferiority reaction. Instead of happiness as a goal, patients find contentment in the present. Furthermore, with the departure of the pressure for power, the superiority-inferiority issue sinks into a proper recognition of the fact that some people are better in one thing, others in another. The patient can then add, "I have my weaknesses and my own good points or strengths."

Another and quite unexpected feature of the new state is the change which comes in the capacity to work. Before, work had been resented as duty, put up with as a boring, cramping routine, entered into with a competitive drive for power and superiority. Characteristically, alcoholics work either under the relentless pressure of superior attainment or in spurts as an outlet for their inner tension states. Once a goal has been reached and an outside incentive is lacking, the drive for work promptly vanishes and in its place their so-called "lazy streak" makes its appearance. At this point they demand fun, amusement, and freedom from responsibility.

After the conversion shift, the work picture is quite different. With the absence, or at least marked decline, of the drive for superiority and the concern for what the job can do for and with the ego, there comes an interest in the job itself. The job is viewed more objectively, it becomes "my responsibility, which I assume without question because it is one place where I fit into life and am a part of things." With the development of this attitude, work habits become steadier and more predictable.

Patients themselves are surprised at this change and comment as follows: "Before I used to be busy, now I am just occupied." Another, a student and in no way alcoholic, said,

"Now I can plug at my lessons [her work] and not mind it."
Asked to define plugging, she replied, "Plugging is working
without lift." Still another patient said, "I guess I've got to re-
vamp my ideas about myself. I thought I was a hard worker.
I was, but only to get what I wanted. Now I can see there
is fun in doing the job, not so I can outshine anybody else
but so I know inside I've been doing my honest best." The
shift to a more consistent, even output of energy is always an
unexpected increment.

The last attribute of the change is a markedly greater degree
of objectivity. This has already been hinted at, first by the
patient who remarked concerning her perfectionism, "It made
me sit on many things which would have helped me to grow."
It was also noted in the new attitude toward work.

The change which makes the objectivity possible is a basic
switch from nonreceptivity to receptivity. The nonreceptive
egocentric individualist is too busy maintaining his own status, too wrapped in his own affairs, to be able to perceive
what is going on about him. Instead he must impose his own
thoughts and feelings upon circumstances. When the shift
takes place and the individual is no longer dominated either
by idealistic demands or hostile presumptions, a receptivity
to experience, to one's self appears. The individual can accept
facts without inner argument or resistance; he can remain
open-minded about ideas, neither totally excluding them nor
wholly accepting them and then not being able to alter them
as the facts require.

The difference in response is most notable in the learning
situation, and it is here that the patients' remarks are the
most pointed. As one patient put it, "Learning is after all a
matter of cooperation, and I don't believe I've ever cooperated in any thing all my life. I've thought I had, but I always
did it with reservations." Another said, "I now pray to let my
mind see and hear all and to let my mind stay open. I want

to find out what's wrong. I want to know the facts, but I now know there are many different outlets from a fact." Her final comment, made as her ability to think became more firmly ingrained, was, "The deterioration of me was the inability to think. There were times when I couldn't will myself to think. Before I used to plan, now I can think without planning. Before it was to let me think of what I could do."

To sum up, the change in emotional state which follows the conversion experience is characterized primarily by altered response in which quiet and serenity predominate. It was also pointed out that associated with that altered response are other changes, the following of which were mentioned and discussed: (1) the loss of automatic hostility; (2) the disappearance of the perfectionistic drive; (3) the disappearance of the egocentric power drive; (4) the appearance of a better response to work demands; and finally, (5) the appearance of a much greater capacity for objectivity.

Other changes in attitude accompany the new state. I have, however, perhaps described enough to give you some slant as to what follows after the conversion shift has taken place. The new feelings which appear are distinctly spiritual in quality and alter the psychic picture in the direction of what it must be conceded are healthier reactions. Experience has furthermore demonstrated that these reactions furnish a substantial base for continued sobriety.

Having pointed out and described the true nature and extent of spiritual feelings, I am now in a position to answer the original question, "What is the X factor which the program of AA contains above and beyond that of other therapeutic efforts?" The answer is that the program supplies through its religious emphasis a source of spiritual strengthening, a conversion, if you will, either quick or gradual, which, coupled with the rest of the activities, provides a new basis of emotional orientation in which the former egocentric hostile pattern is supplanted by a more object-centered approach in which positive and affirmative attitudes prevail.

Obviously, this answer leaves much unsaid. There is no discussion of what causes a conversion which, in turn, brings out the spiritual manifestations; neither is there any explanation of the altered psychology which appears with the conversion switch. Moreover, I have said nothing about the permanence or impermanence of these reactions. These are questions with which, naturally, I have been much occupied, but in this paper I have limited myself to stressing the significance of the spiritual development in members of Alcoholics Anonymous. I have also tried through a description of the changed personality attributes to indicate that along with the development of the spiritual feelings there are new features in personality make-up which are decidedly healthier attitudes.

In conclusion, therefore, I can only reiterate what I initially set forth: namely, that the success of the AA program may be understood only in the light of a recognition of the religious practices it encourages and the consequent spiritual awakening. All the other parts of the AA program are valid and important, but I am convinced that a true understanding of its effectiveness depends upon insight into the source and nature of what has been called the X factor, or "spiritual feeling."

> From Harry M. Tiebout, *Psychological Factors*
> *Operating in Alcoholics Anonymous*

(For Harry M. Tiebout biog, see next page)—

Harry M. Tiebout, M.D., was the first psychiatrist to endorse Alcoholics Anonymous as a means of recovery from alcoholism, even though AA's methods were directly opposed to much of psychoanalytic theory. Recognizing the soundness and effectiveness of AA's methods, Dr. Tiebout altered his entire professional approach to the treatment of alcoholism and other behavior disorders, in conformity to the AA model. He laid special stress on the need for ego deflation and reliance upon God.

Dr. Tiebout was born in Brooklyn in January 1896. He received a B.S. degree from Wesleyan University in 1917, was married in 1920, and completed his medical and psychiatric training at Johns Hopkins University in 1922. He was associate professor of psychiatry at Cornell Medical College from 1932 to 1935, medical director of Blythewood Sanitarium in Greenwich, Connecticut, from 1935 to 1950, and a member of the advisory panel on mental health and alcoholism for the World Health Organization in Geneva from 1954 to 1959. Dr. Tiebout was president and chairman of the board of the National Committee on Alcoholism from 1950 to 1952, and chairman of the American Psychiatric Association's committee of alcoholism. He was a trustee of Alcoholics Anonymous from 1957 until his death in 1966.

Dr. Tiebout's best-known article is "Surrender Versus Compliance in Therapy." A listing of the numerous articles he published in medical, scientific, and psychiatric journals is available from *The Quarterly Journal of Studies on Alcohol* (Rutgers University, P.O. Box 969, Piscataway, New Jersey).

O. Hobart Mowrer *on*
the place of sin in modern religion and modern psychiatry

(From "The Crisis in Psychiatry and Religion")

As long as one adheres to the theory that psychoneurosis implies no moral responsibility, no error, no misdeed on the part of the afflicted person, one's vocabulary can, of course, remain beautifully objective and "scientific." But as soon as there is so much as a hint of personal accountability in the situation, such language is, at the very least, wide of the mark and, conceivably, quite misleading. Therefore, if "moral judgment" does enter the picture, one might as well beard the lion and use the strongest term of all, sin....

But there is also a deeper objective here. "Sickness," is a concept which generates pervasive pessimism and confusion in the domain of psychopathology; whereas sin, for all its harshness, carries an implication of promise and hope, a vision of new potentialities. Just so long as we deny the reality of sin, we cut ourselves off, it seems, from the possibility of radical redemption ("recovery").

In some ways it is perhaps not surprising that we are ... [exploring] the question of whether real guilt, or sin, is relevant to the problem of psychopathology and psychotherapy. For half a century now we psychologists, as a profession, have very largely followed the Freudian doctrine that human beings become emotionally disturbed, not because of their having *done* anything palpably wrong, but because they instead *lack insight*. Therefore, as would-be therapists we have set

234

out to oppose the forces of repression and to work for *understanding*. And what *is* this understanding, or insight, which we so highly prize? It is the discovery that the patient or client has been, in effect, *too* good; that he has within him impulses, especially those of lust and hostility, which he has been quite unnecessarily inhibiting. And health, we tell him, lies in the direction of recognizing and expressing these impulses.

But there are now widespread and, indeed, ominous signs that this logic and the practical strategies it seems to demand are ill-founded. The situation is, in fact, so grave that we are even willing to consider the possibility that misconduct may, after all, have something to do with the matter and that the doctrine of repression and insight are more misleading than helpful.

However, as soon as we psychologists get into a discussion of this problem, we find that our confusion is even more fundamental than might at first appear. We find that not only have we disavowed the connection between manifest misconduct and psychopathology; we have, also, very largely abandoned belief in right and wrong, virtue and sin, in general.

On other occasions when I have seen this issue under debate and anyone has proposed that social deviousness is causal in psychopathology, there is always a chorus of voices who clamor that sin cannot be defined, that it is culturally relative, that it is an unscientific concept, that it is a superstition—and therefore not to be taken seriously, either in psychopathology or in ordinary, everyday experience. And whenever an attempt is made to answer these objections, there are always further objections—often in the form of reductions to absurdity—which involve naivety or sophistry that would ill-become a schoolboy. Historically, in both literate and non-literate societies, human beings are supposed to have reached the age of discretion by early adolescence; yet here we have the spectacle of grown men and women soberly insisting that, in effect, *they* cannot tell right from wrong—and that no one else can.

Now I realize how futile it is to try to deal with this kind of attitude in a purely rational or logical way. The subversive doctrine that we can have the benefits of orderly social life without paying for it, through certain restraints and sacrifices, is too alluring to be counteracted by mere reason. The real answer, I believe, lies along different lines. The unassailable, brute fact is that personality disorder is the most pervasive and baffling problem of our time; and if it *should* turn out that persons so afflicted regularly display (or rather *hide*) a life of too *little*, rather than too much, moral restraint and self-discipline, the problem would take on an empirical urgency that would require no fine-spun argument.

Sin used to be—and, in some quarters, still is—defined as whatever one does that puts him in danger of going to Hell. Here was an assumed cause-and-effect relationship that was completely metaphysical and empirically unverifiable; and it is small wonder that it has fallen into disrepute as the scientific outlook and method have steadily gained in acceptance and manifest power. But there is a very tangible and very present Hell-on-this-earth which science has not yet helped us understand very well; and so I invite your attention to the neglected but very real possibility that it is *this* Hell—the Hell of neurosis and psychosis—to which sin and unexpiated guilt lead us and that it is *this* Hell that gives us *one* of the most, perhaps *the* most realistic and basic criteria for defining sin and guilt. If it proves empirically true that certain forms of conduct characteristically lead human beings into emotional instability, what better or firmer basis would one wish for labeling such conduct as destructive, self-defeating, evil, sinful?*

If the Freudian theory of personality disorder were valid, one would expect neurotic and psychotic individuals to have led exemplary, yea saintly lives—to have been just too good for this world. The fact is, of course, that such individuals typically exhibit lives that have been disorderly and dishonest in extreme degree. In fact, this is so regularly the case that one cannot but wonder how so contrary a doctrine as that of Freud ever gained credence. Freud spurned The Wish and exalted Reality. What he regarded as Reality may yet prove to have been the biggest piece of wishfulness of all.

Or, it may be asked, how is it if sin and psychic suffering are correlated that not *all* who sin fall into neurosis or psychosis? Here the findings of the Kinsey studies are likely to be cited, showing that, for example, many persons have a history of sexual perversity who are later quite normal. In other words, the argument is that since sin and persistent suffering do not always go hand-in-hand, there is perhaps no relationship at all. The answer to this question is surely obvious. *Some* individuals, alas, simply do not have enough character, or conscience, to be bothered by their sins. These are, of course, the world's psychopaths. Or an individual may have been *caught* in his sin and punished for it. Or it may have weighed so heavily on his conscience that he himself has *confessed* it and made appropriate expiation. Or, quite conceivably, in some instances the individual, without either detection or confession, may have set upon a program of service and good works which has also brought him peace and

*There is, admittedly, an element of circularity in the above argument. If it is maintained that mental illness is caused by unacknowledged and unexpiated sin, or real guilt, then it adds nothing to our knowledge to *define* sin as that which causes mental illness. In fact, there is a sense in which such a definition is not only circular but misleading. Obviously, what is needed is an *independent criterion* for identifying sin or guilt.

redemption. In other words, there is, surely, no disposition on the part of anyone to hold that sin, as such, necessarily dooms a person to interminable suffering in the form of neurosis or psychosis. The presumption is rather that sin has this effect only where it is acutely felt but not acknowledged and corrected.

Also, it is sometimes contended that individuals who eventually come to the attention of psychotherapists have, to be sure, been guilty of major errors of conduct; but, it is held, the illness was present first and the misconduct was really just an expression or symptom thereof. If this were true, where then would we draw the line? Is there no such thing as moral responsibility and social accountability at all? Is every mean or vicious thing that you or I, as ordinary individuals, do not sin but rather an expression of "illness"? Who would seriously hold that a society could long endure which consistently subscribed to this flaccid doctrine?

Then there is, of course, the view that, in the final analysis, all psychopathology—or at least its profounder forms—have a constitutional or metabolic basis. One must, I believe, remain open-minded with respect to this possibility—indeed, perhaps even somewhat hopeful with respect to it; for how marvelous it would be if all the world's madness, stupidity, and meanness could be eliminated through biochemistry. But over the years we have seen one approach after another of this kind come into prominence, with much heralding as the long-awaited break-through on the problem of mental disease, only to fade out as manifestly not quite the panacea we had imagined it to be. Some of us may, at this point, even suspect that today the main incentive for keeping the biochemical hypothesis alive is not so much the supporting empirical evidence, which is meager enough, but instead the fact that it at least obliquely justifies the premise that the whole field of mental disorder is the proper and exclusive domain of medicine.

Also, and again somewhat obliquely, it excuses the clergy from facing squarely the responsibilities that would devolve among them if neurosis and psychosis should indeed turn out to be essentially *moral* disorders.

The conception of personality disturbance which attaches major etiological significance to moral and interpersonal considerations thus faces formidable resistance, from many sources; but programs of treatment and prevention which have been predicated on these other views have gotten us nowhere, and there is no clear reason to think they ever will. Therefore, in light of the total situation, I see no alternative but to turn again to the old, painful, but also promising possibility that man is preeminently a *social* creature and that he lives or dies, psychologically and personally, as a function of the openness, community, relatedness, and integrity which by good action he attains and by evil action destroys.

As long as we could believe that the psychoneurotic's basic problem was not evil but a kind of ignorance, it did not seem too formidable a task to give him the requisite enlightenment or insight. But mental hospitals are now full of people who have had this kind of therapy, in one guise or another, and found it wanting; and if we are thus forced to reconsider the other alternative, the therapeutic or redemptive enterprise, however clear it may be in principle, is by no means simple in practice. If the problem is genuinely one of morality, rather than pseudo-morality, most of us in the secular healing professions, of psychology, psychiatry, or social work, find ourselves reduced to the status of laymen, with no special training or competence for dealing with or even approaching the problem in these terms. We know something, of course, about procedures for getting disturbed persons to talk about themselves, free-associate, "confess"; but the whole aim of this strategy has been insight, not redemption and personal reformation. And clergymen themselves have so often been told, both by their own leaders and by members of the secular healing professions, that they must recognize their own "limitations" and know when to "refer" that they, too, lack the necessary confidence and resources for dealing with these problems adequately.

Many present-day psychoanalysts will offer no serious objection to the way in which classical Freudian theory and practice have been evaluated in this paper; but they will insist that many "advances" have been made since Freud's time and that these put the whole problem in a very different light. If we ask, "Precisely what *are* these advances?" we are told that they have to do with the new emphasis upon "ego psychology" rather than upon "the unconscious." But what did Emalian Gutheil (1958) tell us at our convention last year in Washington about ego psychology? He said that although analysts now recognize the ego as much more important than formerly, they know next to nothing about the conditions for modifying or strengthening it; and the same position has been voiced earlier by Lawrence Kubie (1956) and in one of his very last papers (1937) even by Freud himself.

Therefore, I do not see how we can avoid the conclusion that at this juncture we are in a real crisis with respect to the whole psychotherapeutic enterprise. But I do not think we are going to remain in this crisis, confused and impotent, indefinitely. There is, I believe, growing realism with regard to the situation on the part of both psychologists and psychiatrists, on the one hand, and ministers, rabbis, and priests, on the other; and I am hopeful and even confident that new and better ways of dealing with the situation are in the making.

What precisely, these ways will be I do not know; but I venture the impression that Alcoholics Anonymous provides our best present intimation of things to come and that the therapeutic programs of the future, whether under religious or secular auspices, will, like AA, take guilt, confession, and expiation seriously and will involve programs of *action* rather than mere groping for "insight."

From O. Hobart Mowrer,
The Crisis in Psychiatry and Religion

 O. Hobart Mowrer's life work was to correct, both in theory and in practice, the failure of professional religion and professional psychiatry to deal effectively with the problems of mental and emotional disturbances in modern times. He was quoted by *Time* Magazine in 1976 as summing up his vision of a new direction in psychic healing, in the following terms: "Future treatment of the emotionally disturbed will, like Alcoholics Anonymous, take guilt, confession, and expiation seriously and will involve programs for action rather than mere groping for insights."

Hobart Mowrer was born in 1907 in Unionville, Missouri. He received an A.B. degree from the University of Missouri in 1929, was married in 1931, and received a Ph.D. from Johns Hopkins University in 1932. Between 1932 and 1948 he served on the faculties of Northwestern, Yale, and Harvard Universities. He was research professor of psychology at the University of Illinois from 1948 to 1975. A dean in the field of psychology, Dr. Mowrer was a member of the board of directors of the American Psychological Association from 1952 through 1955 and was president of that organization in 1953 and 1954. From 1951 through 1954 he was a consultant to the National Institute of Mental Health. He died in June, 1982.

Dr. Mowrer published hundreds of articles over the years in professional journals. His basic books are *The Crisis in Psychiatry and Religion*, *The New Group Therapy*, and *Morality and Mental Health*.

Martin Gross *on the*
alteration of the nature of our civilization
brought about by modern psychology

(From "The Psychological Society")

Much has been said about the awesome *external* transformation in our modern world. These changes are obvious. But the *internal* shift in man's psyche has altered both our actions and expectations more than any technological force. This change in inner man has taken place quietly, yet it has altered the nature of our civilization beyond recognition.

The major agent of change has been modern psychology. At the time of Sigmund Freud's visit to Clark University in Massachusetts in 1909, psychology was an infant discipline. Today, psychology is an art, science, therapy, religion, moral code, life style, philosophy and cult. It sits at the very center of contemporary society as an international colossus whose professional minions number in the hundreds of thousands.

Its ranks include psychiatrists, psychoanalysts, clinical psychologists, psychotherapists, social workers, psychiatric nurses, school psychologists, guidance counselors, marriage and family therapists, educational psychologists, Sensitivity T-Group and Encounter leaders, and assorted lay therapists. Recently, it has added a number of newly hyphenated professionals including psycholinguists, biopsychologists and psychobiographers.

Its experimental animals are an obliging, even grateful human race. We live in a civilization in which, as never before, man is preoccupied with *Self.* We have become fascinated with our madness, motivations and our endless, sometimes wearying search for normality. Modern psychology and psychiatry seek to satisfy that fascination by offering us a full range of systems, from the serious to the whimsical, with which we can understand our confused psyche, then seek to heal it.

The contemporary Psychological Society is the most vulnerable culture in history. Its citizen is a new model of Western man, one who is dependent on others for guidance as to what is real or false. In the unsure state of his mind, he is even doubtful of the authenticity of his own emotions. As the Protestant ethic has weakened in Western society, the confused citizen has turned to the only alternative he knows: the psychological expert who claims there is *a new scientific standard of behavior* to replace fading traditions.

In the 1950s, David Riesman spoke of the "other directed" man as receiving his life cues from outside sources. Today, we can see a new *psychologically directed* man in operation. His antennae are thrust continually outward for hints from experts who are handsomely paid to tell him what to make of himself and others, how best to live, even feel.

The citizen-patient has been told, and usually believes, that his tormenting doubts about love, sex, work, interpersonal relations, marriage and divorce, child raising, happiness, loneliness, even death, will yield to the new technology of the mind. Mouthing the holy name of *science*, the psychological expert claims to know all.

This new truth is fed to us continuously from birth to the grave. Childhood, once a hardy time of adventure, is now seen as a period of extreme psychological fragility. A U.S. Senate subcommittee warns us that premature emotional disturbance will strike one in ten of our children. The nation's child guidance clinics have trebled in number over the last twenty years. One physician, Dr. Arnold Hutschnecker, even suggests a grand scheme to screen all the nation's children to find those who need preventive psychotherapy.

The schoolhouse has become a vibrant psychological center, staffed not only by schoolteachers trained in "educational psychology" but by sixty thousand guidance workers and seven thousand school psychologists whose "counseling" borders on therapy. In one case, virtually an entire first-grade class at P.S. 198 in New York City has been given free psychotherapy at nearby Mount Sinai Hospital.

The need for psychological expertise follows us doggedly through life. Erik Erikson's *identity crisis* has become a symbol for millions of adolescents, an age group which is increasingly concerned about its psyche. A CBS-TV special on youth reported that uppermost in the minds of those interviewed were nagging doubts about mental health. The college-age population is also heavily into its psyches as "drop-in" counseling centers handle record numbers of anguished youth. Columbia University reports a threefold increase in student use of psychological services in a decade.

The adult is, of course, the mainstay of the new Society, for his anxieties are endless. The enormity of that need is only hinted at in a George Washington University study which showed that Americans ingest tons of psychochemicals, mainly minor tranquilizers, in a continuous search for tranquillity.

This frenetic quest is part of modern man's search for the elusive goal of normality. It is a state which Freud once called an *ideal fiction* and which society hopelessly confuses with happiness and peace of mind. "The quest for peace of mind—or good mental health, which is another name for it—is universal," the National Association of Mental Health informs an eager public.

Modern psychological-mindedness springs from many origins, one of which is the breakdown in the separation between health and sickness when applied to the mind. Historically, insanity was an affliction that struck the few. The remainder felt spared. They may have been mean, or unhappy, or even eccentric, but they were considered sane.

Today, that boundary between the well and the sick has been blurred by psychology and psychiatry. Emotional illness is now seen as an ugly but natural manifestation that strikes us all in varying degrees. "Now every normal person is only approximately normal," Freud reminded us shortly before his death. "His ego resembles that of the psychotic in one point or another, in a greater or lesser degree." In modern parlance, we are all, to some extent, *sick*.

Impressionable citizens of the Society have even falsely equated mental health with the usually unreachable *ideal* state which combines success, love and lack of anxiety. The Psychological Society thus creates its own self-fulfilling prophecy. *We are all sick, for normality is almost unattainable.*

This might be called *the theory of universal madness*. We have increasingly directed suspicion of mental instability against our friends, family and, eventually, ourselves. In New York City, a ten-year study, *Mental Health in the Metropolis*, claimed that approximately 80 percent of adults showed some symptoms of mental illness, with one in four actually impaired.

In 1977 the President's Commission on Mental Health confirmed these dire diagnoses. It concluded that the state of our psyches is worse than believed, and that one-quarter of all Americans suffer from severe emotional stress. They warn that up to 32 million Americans are in need of professional psychiatric help.

A National Institute of Mental Health psychologist even portrays universal madness as a statistical certainty. "Almost no family in the nation is entirely free of mental disorders," he stated in a recent federal study. The NIMH psychologist estimates that in addition to the 500,000 schizophrenics in hospitals, there are 1.75 million psychotics not hospitalized, and up to *60 million Americans who exhibit deviant mental behavior related to schizophrenia.* He speaks of the "psychological turbulence that is rampant in an American society that is confused, divided and concerned about its future."

Despite these warnings, mental illness has not increased significantly since 1955, when complete records first began. The annual mental hospitalization rate of 8.5 per 1000 population is remarkably steady and consistent throughout much of the developed world. What the Psychological Society has done is to redefine *normality.* It has taken the painful reactions to the normal vicissitudes of life—despair, anger, frustration—and labeled them as maladjustments.

The semantic trick is in equating happiness with normality. By permitting this, we have given up our simple right to be both *normal and suffering* at the same time. Instead, we have massively redefined ourselves as *neurotic,* even as incipient mental cases, particularly when life plays its negative tricks. It is a tendency which gives modern America, and increasingly much of the Western world, the tone of a giant psychiatric clinic.

This is only one legacy of modern psychology. Its pervasiveness in the fabric of our culture has become near total as it absorbs new disciplines each year. Armed with what it claims are the hidden truths about man's behavior, it has impressed its philosophical stamp on virtually all of contemporary life: mental health and illness, the arts, education, religion, medicine, the family, child care, business, the social sciences, history, government, language, advertising, law, crime and punishment, even architecture and economics.

Its most obvious impact is on what are now collectively called *the helping professions,* a mental health team that includes perhaps a dozen professionals headed by the psychi-

atrist. Much as the ministry did for years, the superprofes-
sionals of psychology and psychiatry have now assumed the
supreme watchdog role. Not only have we entrusted them
with the care of so-called neurotics and our mentally ill, but
delinquents, drug addicts, the low-achieving student, the stut-
terer, the confused collegian, the suicidal, the homosexual,
the criminal, the alcoholic, even the aged and the poor are all
considered their natural patients.

In the Psychological Society, human problems are no longer
seen as normal variations or unseemly twists of fate. We
now view them as the products of internal psychological maladjustments. We are even encouraged to believe that there
would be no failure, no crime, no malevolence, no unhappiness if man could only understand his psyche, then set it for a
metaphysical condition called *adjustment*. As more of us find
that ideal state defeated by life's pressures, psychology offers
its ultimate remedy—*psychotherapy*.

"The demand for psychotherapy is non-ending. It's unbelievable," states Dr. Donald M. Kaplan, a New York
teaching and practicing psychologist-analyst. "Individual
psychotherapy was once an elitist privilege, but it has now
been democratized. The general population now feels entitled to it, and is seeking it out. In prior times, people would
take care of ordinary life crises by themselves, or with the
help of their families. Now they all want psychotherapy."

Millions receive psychotherapy each year in a multitude of
forms, from psychoanalysis to simple supportive therapy, in
groups or alone. Others seek the Nirvana in the new wave
of *humanistic* therapies including scores of imaginative ideas
from Gestalt Therapy to nude marathons. We are offered almost a hundred different psychotherapies for every healing
taste. Each proclaims a somewhat different method, sworn to
be the superior key.

The outpatient psychiatric clinics are busy sites of this new therapy rush. In 1955 they treated a total of 233,000 people. Since then, the number has risen dramatically to 2.4 million patients annually. This figure does not include another 1.5 million patients treated each year in the 570 federally supported Community Mental Health Centers.

The establishment bases of psychotherapy are the psychiatrists, the majority of whom see patients in their private offices, clinical psychologists and the psychiatric social workers (M.S.W. degree), the burgeoning third rung of the helping professions. Judging from a 1973 American Psychiatric Association study of private practice, and a more recent report on health services from the American Psychological Association, we can estimate that one and a half million Americans take their psychic repair in the private offices of these practitioners.

In all, some six million Americans each year receive psychotherapy in clinics and hospitals and from private therapists. To find the total number in therapy, however, we must also look at the growing legions of *lay therapists* who offer a psychological inventory from *est* to primal workshops and encounter. At least a million more Americans take their therapy from these sources, or a total of seven million who receive psychological intervention annually.

This balm is not evenly distributed, for the therapy professions have a geographic bias. Almost half the psychiatrists, for example, practice in New York, California, Illinois, Pennsylvania or Massachusetts. Nearly one-third are in New York and California alone. But the profession is expanding rapidly into the rest of the country. Once psychologically isolated Nebraska now boasts over a hundred psychiatrists.

Psychology is now an international movement which cuts across national and class boundaries. With the demise of the belief in immortality and the end of absolute morality, it is becoming the most generally accepted substitute.

Its power level in each nation varies with how well its theme of magical human improvement matches the indigenous ethic.

It has not yet gained a strong hold in southern Europe, but its strength increases as one progresses northward into France, Germany, Holland, Scandinavia and Britain. Even the Soviet Union, a consistent critic of Western insight psychology, has begun to recant. In *Kommunist*, the official ideological journal, Soviet psychologists have recently called for more research into applications of the unseen *unconscious*.

America, however, has been the warm, natural host for modern psychology. It has nurtured the young colossus from its infancy to its current adulthood. In fact, the American sponsorship of psychology may be setting a pattern for world society as definitive as America's earlier leadership in industrial technology.

Psychology has taken hold in the Protestant world mainly because both the psychological and Protestant ethics insist that a method be found for the perfectibility of men. That perfectibility was once sought through the intervention of God, but is now accomplished by supposed scientific adjustment of the psyche. Long before the Psychological Society, the nineteenth-century social historian Alexis de Tocqueville saw this urgent need for perfectibility in the American character. "Aristocratic nations are liable to narrow the scope of human perfectibility; democratic nations to expand it beyond reason," he observed.

This democratic hope has encouraged our desperate search for psychic understanding and repair. Instead of increasing our stability as a culture, that search has paradoxically accelerated man's tendency toward anxiety and insecurity, shaking the very underpinnings of Western civilization. It is now apparent that the Judeo-Christian society in which psychology began its ascendancy is atrophying under the massive impact of several forces, particularly that of modern psychology. In its place stands a new culture of a troubled and confused citizenry, the Psychological Society.

For many, this Society has all the earmarks of a potent new religion. When educated man lost faith in formal religion, he required a substitute belief that would be as reputable in the last half of the twentieth century as Christianity was in the first. Psychology and psychiatry have now assumed that special role. They offer mass belief, a promise of a better future, opportunity for confession, unseen mystical workings and a trained priesthood of helping professionals devoted to servicing the paying-by-the-hour communicants.

Not only is the new Society attempting to fill the void left by Christianity, but it has created images that parallel older spiritual ones. The traditional religious idea of *sin* is becoming obsolete. But the medico-psychological concept of *sick* has replaced it almost intact. We now speak glibly of murderers, addicts, even the personality-distorted as being "sick" or "neurotic" as effortlessly as neighbors once gossiped about the sinfulness of the local alcoholic.

Even though psychology and psychiatry are at the core of this new Society, surprisingly they have been the least analyzed of all disciplines. While attention has been focused on their customers, psychology and psychiatry themselves have escaped outside scrutiny, leaving their extraordinary control over our lives less than understood.

This book [*The Psychological Society*] hopes to correct that oversight and explain the psychologization of our culture. It will probe the Psychological Society, its operations, origins, claims, manifestations, customs, mores, shortcomings, validity, aspirations and ultimate significance. *This evaluation has become essential, for not an idea, not a style, not a personal or cultural relationship exists which has not been drastically affected by the new supremacy of the Psychological Society.*

From Martin Gross, *The Psychological Society*

Martin Gross is a foremost defender of our rights to protection against professional arrogance, incompetence, and error in the fields of medicine and psychiatry. His first book, *The Brain Watchers*, was such an effective critique of the abuses of psychological testing that it triggered a Congressional investigation which resulted in the Civil Service Commission's discontinuing the use of psychological tests.

Martin Gross was born and brought up in New York City. He received his undergraduate degree from City College of New York, and completed two years of graduate study at Columbia University. He served in the Air Corps as a navigator and radar operator during World War II. Gross has published more than 250 articles in national magazines, most of them critical commentaries on psychology, medicine, education, and national affairs.

Martin Gross's three basic books are:

The Doctors, which is an incisive, fair, understanding, appreciative, and practically very helpful critique of modern medicine;

The Psychological Society, which is an incisive, fair, understanding, appreciative, and practically very helpful critique of modern psychology and modern psychiatry;

The Brain Watchers, which is an incisive, fair, understanding, appreciative, and practically very helpful critique of modern psychological testing techniques.

The Lifesavers Groups
Are Self-Help Groups
Based on the Motto:
In God We Trust

Lifesavers Associates, Box 75, White Lake, NY 12786

APPENDIX B

The Lifesavers
Way of Life

With the coming of Alcoholics Anonymous, millions of alcoholics, otherwise hopeless, have found their way back to sanity. But there is far greater lifesaving power in the AA principles than has yet been widely recognized, because what is involved is *the practice of the ethical and spiritual principles common to all mankind*, and applicable to all mankind.

The original program of Alcoholics Anonymous consisted of the Four Absolutes and the Twelve Steps (see next page). The Absolutes were in use several years before the Steps were formulated. In a real sense, the Absolutes were the foundation on which the Steps were built. The Absolutes and the Steps together constituted the primitive program, and it was a world-shaker. This is the program by which co-founders Bill W. and Dr. Bob S. got sober, by which the first hundred AAs recovered, by which the whole movement was launched.

As a matter of experience, it has been found that these original principles produce recovery not only from addictive drinking but also from a broad spectrum of the spiritual ills of life. This original program—applied not only to alcohol problems but to a wide range of other problems—is called the Lifesavers way of life. It is so called because in many cases it is the only means by which people who are floundering in deep trouble can get their heads above water and keep them above water.

The following are statements of Lifesavers principles as practiced in effective Lifesavers groups in our critical times:

The Four Absolutes: Used in the Oxford Group and in the pioneering years of Alcoholics Anonymous, these life-transforming principles in one form or another have been the foundation of the spiritual life in all ages and all cultures. They were the basis, for example, upon which Gandhi's ashram operated; they are among the essentials of the first of the traditional eight limbs of yoga (the *yamas*); and they are clearly the principles to which a life in Christ requires adherence:

1. Absolute honesty—non-lying to oneself or others; fidelity to the truth in thought, word, and actions.
2. Absolute purity—purity of mind, purity of body, purity of the emotions, purity of heart, sexual purity.
3. Absolute unselfishness—seeking what is right and true in every situation above what I want.
4. Absolute love—loving God with all your heart, all your soul, all your mind, and all your strength, and your neighbor as yourself.

The Absolutes, of course, are not claims of attainment. They are *aims, levels of commitment* for daily conduct. When they are maintained faithfully as *goals*, they become powerful transformers of conduct, character, and consciousness.

The Twelve Steps: One of the most effective and most widely applied statements of the Lifesavers principles in modern times, and one of the great working statements of the spiritual life of all times, this fundamental version of the program of Alcoholics Anonymous was in general use throughout the AA Fellowship even before the publication of the "Big Book" (*Alcoholics Anonymous*, AA's basic text) in April 1939. The shorter statements which had preceded it are now forgotten, and the Twelve Steps have become the universally accepted and only generally known version of the AA program.

These Steps are a lifeline for alcohol addicts, many of whom, lacking opportunity to contact an AA group, have recovered by the mere knowledge and application of these twelve principles. From the standpoint of the whole world of recovery from addiction, it is impossible to exaggerate the importance of the Twelve Steps of Alcoholics Anonymous. If an addict who is sincerely seeking a way out had no other tool than a working knowledge of these Steps, he would have a very good chance of recovery. Do not let the simple language in which they are stated fool you. They are a spiritual powerhouse to which hundreds of thousands of addicts, now walking the streets as free men and women, owe their lives and their liberty.

Adapted versions of the Steps have been used by non-alcoholics for many years—by the Al-Anon Family Groups, Neurotics Anonymous, Narcotics Anonymous, Gamblers Anonymous, Overeaters Anonymous, and many others. The original version of the Steps, for use by alcoholics only, may be found in the Big Book, *Alcoholics Anonymous* (1976: Alcoholics Anonymous World Services, Inc.). The Steps as adapted here can be used by anyone:

1. We admitted we were powerless, that our lives had become unmanageable.
2. Came to believe that a Power greater than ourselves could restore us to sanity.
3. Made a decision to turn our will and our lives over to the care of God *as we understood him.*

4. Made a searching and fearless moral inventory of ourselves.

5. Admitted to God, to ourselves, and to another human being the exact nature of our wrongs.

6. Were entirely ready to have God remove all these defects of character.

7. Humbly asked him to remove our shortcomings.

8. Made a list of all persons we had harmed and became willing to make amends to them all.

9. Made direct amends to such people wherever possible, except when to do so would injure them or others.

10. Continued to take personal inventory and when we were wrong promptly admitted it.

11. Sought through prayer and meditation to improve our conscious contact with God *as we understood him,* praying only for knowledge of his will for us and the power to carry that out.

12. Having had a spiritual awakening as the result of these Steps, we tried to carry this message to others, and to practice these principles in all our affairs.

Altogether (leaving aside the commentaries) there is not a lot of material here. In the entire Lifesavers program—the Four Absolutes and the Twelve Steps—there are only sixteen things to remember. The Lifesavers way of life is based on an astonishingly simple program. *But it embodies the very power of life over death.*

The Lifesavers experience proves that *anyone* who is suffering from hopelessness, resentment, depression, fear, burnout, or loss of direction in life—can attain spiritual awakening, self-control, freedom, peace, and joy if he or she will go to sufficient lengths in adopting these principles as a way of life.

(The Upstate Lifesavers Group—located in Hankins, New York, 120 miles northwest of New York City—offers sponsoring help to anyone, anywhere, who wants to get started on the Lifesavers way of life. To get in touch, write: Upstate Group, Box 225, Hankins, NY 12741. Or call 914-887-5499, ask for Trudy, and just say you want some information about the Lifesavers way of life.)

The Lifesavers way of life, essentially, consists of the Four Absolutes of the Oxford Group and the Twelve Steps of Alcoholics Anonymous, as adapted for anyone (see pages 254–256). Seven pioneers, with a couple of hundred close associates (see pages 291–299), did the major work in formulating these principles for effective rescue work in the modern world. Here they are—

Pioneers in the Lifesavers Way of Life

Frank Buchman, former Dutch Reformed minister, founder and director of the Oxford Group—which was the basic intellectual and practical ground in which Bill and Dr. Bob developed the principles and practices of Alcoholics Anonymous.

*William G. Wilson—
"Bill" to his innumerable
friends—former New
York stockbroker, and
co-founder of Alcoholics
Anonymous.*

*Robert H. Smith, M.D.—
"Dr. Bob" to his innumer-
able friends—physician
and surgeon, and co-
founder of Alcoholics
Anonymous.*

Father Edward Dowling, S.J., the Roman Catholic priest who worked closely with Bill and Bob in formulating the Steps and the Traditions of Alcoholics Anonymous.

Dr. Harry M. Tiebout, the psychiatrist who understood the spiritual and medical aspects of Alcoholics Anonymous and presented them to modern medicine (see page 220).

Dr. William D. Silkworth, the physician who understood Bill's spiritual experience and its practical relationship to modern medicine.

Father Samuel Shoemaker, the Episcopal priest and Oxford Group leader who worked closely with Bill and Bob in formulating the principles and practices of Alcoholics Anonymous.

A further word about
the pioneers—

The Lifesavers way of life was pioneered by deeply religious men and women, and the Lifesavers way—although in itself is no sense a religion—is necessarily a deeply religious way of life. The pioneers, although working in different schools, were agreed upon one source for faith and basic help—the Bible.

The pioneers and early members looked to certain key Bible texts (see below) for inspiration and comfort—

Frank Buchman found the following particularly useful: Psalm 23 (p. 265), Psalm 32 (p. 266), Psalm 103 (p. 267), Psalm 121 (p. 267), John 17 (p. 279), and II Timothy 2 (p. 283).

Bill found the following particularly useful: the Sermon on the Mount (p. 272), I Corinthians 13 (p. 281), and the Epistle of James (p. 285).

Dr. Bob found the following particularly useful: the Sermon on the Mount (p. 272), I Corinthians 13 (p. 281), and the Epistle of James (p. 285).

Father Dowling found the following particularly useful: John 19:25–27 (p. 280).

Dr. Tiebout found the following particularly useful: Psalm 1 (p. 263), Psalm 23 (p. 265), and Proverbs 1:2–7 (p. 268).

Dr. Silkworth found the following particularly useful: II Kings 6:8–17 (p. 263).

Father Shoemaker found the following particularly useful: John 17:1–26 (p. 279) and 19:25–27 (p. 280).

These key texts are given in full on the following pages.

Excerpt from
THE SECOND BOOK
OF THE KINGS

CHAPTER 6:8–17

Elisha reveals Ben-hadad's plans.

⁸Then the king of Syria warred against Israel, and took counsel with his servants, saying, In such and such a place shall be my camp.

⁹And the man of God sent unto the king of Israel, saying, Beware that thou pass not such a place; for thither the Syrians are come down.

¹⁰And the king of Israel sent to the place which the man of God told him and warned him of, and saved himself there, not once nor twice.

¹¹Therefore the heart of the king of Syria was sore troubled for this thing; and he called his servants, and said unto them, Will ye not shew me which of us is for the king of Israel?

¹²And one of his servants said, None, my lord, O king: but Elisha, the prophet that is in Israel, telleth the king of Israel the words that thou speakest in thy bedchamber.

Elisha at Dothan.

¹³And he said, go and spy where he is, that I may send and fetch him. And it was told him, saying, Behold, he is in Dothan.

¹⁴Therefore sent he thither horses, and chariots, and a great host: and they came by night, and compassed the city about.

¹⁵And when the servant of the man of God was risen early, and gone forth, behold, an host compassed the city both with horses and chariots. And his servant said unto him, Alas, my master! how shall we do?

¹⁶And he answered, Fear not: for they that be with us are more than they that be with them.

¹⁷And Elisha prayed, and said, Lord, I pray thee, open his eyes, that he may see. And the Lord opened the eyes of the young man; and he saw: and, behold, the mountain was full of horses and chariots of fire round about Elisha.

Excerpts from
THE BOOK OF PSALMS

PSALM 1

Psalm of the two ways: introductory to entire Psalter

Blessed is the man that walketh not in the counsel of the ungodly, nor standeth in the way of sinners, nor sitteth in the seat of the scornful.

²But his delight is in the law of the Lord; and in his law doth he meditate day and night.

³And he shall be like a tree planted by the rivers of water, that bringeth forth his fruit in his season; his leaf also shall not wither; and whatsoever he doeth shall prosper.

⁴The ungodly are not so: but are like the chaff which the wind driveth away.

⁵Therefore the ungodly shall not stand in the judgment, nor sinners in the congregation of the righteous.

⁶For the Lord knoweth the way of the righteous: but the way of the ungodly shall perish.

PSALM 22

To the chief Musician
upon Aijeleth Shahar,
A Psalm of David.

My God, my God, why hast thou forsaken me? why art thou so far from helping me, and from the words of my roaring?

²O my God, I cry in the daytime, but thou hearest not; and in the night season, and am not silent.

³But thou art holy, O thou that inhabitest the praises of Israel.

⁴Our fathers trusted in thee: they trusted, and thou didst deliver them.

⁵They cried unto thee, and were delivered: they trusted in thee, and were not confounded.

⁶But I am a worm, and no man; a reproach of men, and despised of the people.

⁷All they that see me laugh me to scorn: they shoot out the lip, they shake the head, saying,

⁸He trusted on the Lord that he would deliver him: let him deliver him, seeing he delighted in him.

⁹But thou art he that took me out of the womb: thou didst make me hope when I was upon my mother's breast.

¹⁰I was cast upon thee from the womb: thou art my God from my mother's belly.

¹¹Be not far from me; for trouble is near; for there is none to help.

¹²Many bulls have compassed me: strong bulls of Bashan have beset me round.

¹³They gaped upon me with their mouths, as a ravening and a roaring lion.

¹⁴I am poured out like water, and all my bones are out of joint: my heart is like wax; it is melted in the midst of my bowels.

¹⁵My strength is dried up like a potsherd; and my tongue cleaveth to my jaws; and thou hast brought me into the dust of death.

¹⁶For dogs have compassed me: the assembly of the wicked have inclosed me: they pierced my hands and my feet.

¹⁷I may tell all my bones: they look and stare upon me.

¹⁸They part my garments among them, and cast lots upon my vesture.

¹⁹But be not thou far from me, O Lord: O my strength, haste thee to help me.

²⁰Deliver my soul from the sword; my darling from the power of the dog.

²¹Save me from the lion's mouth: for thou hast heard me from the horns of the unicorns.

²²I will declare thy name unto my brethren: in the midst of the congregation will I praise thee.

²³Ye that fear the Lord, praise him; all ye the seed of Jacob, glorify him; and fear him, all ye the seed of Israel.

²⁴For he hath not despised nor abhorred the affliction of the afflicted; neither hath he hid his face from him; but when he cried unto him, he heard.

²⁵My praise shall be of thee in the great congregation: I will pay my vows before them that fear him.

²⁶The meek shall eat and be satisfied: they shall praise the Lord that seek him: your heart shall live for ever.

²⁷All the ends of the world shall remember and turn unto the Lord: and all the kindreds of the nations shall worship before thee.

²⁸For the kingdom is the Lord's: and he is the governor among the nations.

²⁹All they that be fat upon earth shall eat and worship: all they that go down to the dust shall bow before him: and none can keep alive his own soul.

³⁰A seed shall serve him; it shall be accounted to the Lord for a generation.

³¹They shall come, and shall declare his righteousness unto a people that shall be born, that he hath done this.

PSALM 23

A Psalm of David.

The Lord is my shepherd; I shall not want.

²He maketh me to lie down in green pastures: he leadeth me beside the still waters.

³He restoreth my soul: he leadeth me in the paths of righteousness for his name's sake.

⁴Yea, though I walk through the valley of the shadow of death, I will fear no evil: for thou art with me; thy rod and thy staff they comfort me.

⁵Thou preparest a table before me in the presence of mine enemies: thou anointest my head with oil; my cup runneth over.

⁶Surely goodness and mercy shall follow me all the days of my life: and I will dwell in the house of the Lord for ever.

PSALM 32

A Psalm of David, Maschil.

Blessed is he whose transgression is forgiven, whose sin is covered.

²Blessed is the man unto whom the Lord imputeth not iniquity, and in whose spirit there is no guile.

³When I kept silence, my bones waxed old through my roaring all the day long.

⁴For day and night thy hand was heavy upon me: my moisture is turned into the drought of summer. Selah.

⁵I acknowledged my sin unto thee, and mine iniquity have I not hid. I said, I will confess my transgressions unto the Lord; and thou forgavest the iniquity of my sin. Selah.

⁶For this shall every one that is godly pray unto thee in a time when thou mayest be found: surely in the floods of great waters they shall not come nigh unto him.

⁷Thou art my hiding place; thou shalt preserve me from trouble; thou shalt compass me about with songs of deliverance. Selah.

⁸I will instruct thee and teach thee in the way which thou shalt go: I will guide thee with mine eye.

⁹Be ye not as the horse, or as the mule, which have no understanding: whose mouth must be held in with bit and bridle, lest they come near unto thee.

¹⁰Many sorrows shall be to the wicked: but he that trusteth in the Lord, mercy shall compass him about.

¹¹Be glad in the Lord, and rejoice, ye righteous: and shout for joy, all ye that are upright in heart.

PSALM 46:1–7

To the chief Musician
for the sons of Korah,
A Song upon Alamoth.

God is our refuge and strength, a very present help in trouble.

²Therefore will not we fear, though the earth be removed, and though the mountains be carried into the midst of the sea;

³Though the waters thereof roar and be troubled, though the mountains shake with the swelling thereof. Selah.

⁴There is a river, the streams whereof shall make glad the city of God, the holy place of the tabernacles of the most High.

⁵God is in the midst of her; she shall not be moved: God shall help her, and that right early.

⁶The heathen raged, the kingdoms were moved: he uttered his voice, the earth melted.

⁷The Lord of hosts is with us: the God of Jacob is our refuge. Selah.

PSALM 103

A Psalm of David.

Bless the Lord, O my soul: and all that is within me, bless his holy name.

²Bless the Lord, O my soul, and forget not all his benefits:

³Who forgiveth all thine iniquities; who healeth all thy diseases;

⁴Who redeemeth thy life from destruction; who crowneth thee with lovingkindness and tender mercies;

⁵Who satisfieth thy mouth with good things; so that thy youth is renewed like the eagle's.

⁶The Lord executeth righteousness and judgment for all that are oppressed.

⁷He made known his ways unto Moses, his acts unto the children of Israel.

⁸The Lord is merciful and gracious, slow to anger, and plenteous in mercy.

⁹He will not always chide: neither will he keep his anger for ever.

¹⁰He hath not dealt with us after our sins; nor rewarded us according to our iniquities.

¹¹For as the heaven is high above the earth, so great is his mercy toward them that fear him.

¹²As far as the east is from the west, so far hath he removed our transgressions from us.

¹³Like as a father pitieth his children, so the Lord pitieth them that fear him.

¹⁴For he knoweth our frame; he remembereth that we are dust.

¹⁵As for man, his days are as grass: as a flower of the field, so he flourisheth.

¹⁶For the wind passeth over it, and it is gone: and the place thereof shall know it no more.

¹⁷But the mercy of the Lord is from everlasting to everlasting upon them that fear him, and his righteousness unto children's children;

¹⁸To such as keep his covenant, and to those that remember his commandments to do them.

¹⁹The Lord hath prepared his throne in the heavens; and his kingdom ruleth over all.

²⁰Bless the Lord, ye his angels, that excel in strength, that do his commandments, hearkening unto the voice of his word.

²¹Bless ye the Lord, all ye his hosts; ye ministers of his, that do his pleasure.

²²Bless the Lord, all his works in all places of his dominion: bless the Lord, O my soul.

PSALM 121

A Song of degrees.

I will lift up mine eyes unto the hills, from whence cometh my help.

²My help cometh from the Lord, which made heaven and earth.

³He will not suffer thy foot to be moved: he that keepeth thee will not slumber.

⁴Behold, he that keepeth Israel shall neither slumber nor sleep.

⁵The Lord is thy keeper: the Lord is thy shade upon thy right hand.

⁶The sun shall not smite thee by day, nor the moon by night.

⁷The Lord shall preserve thee from all evil: he shall preserve thy soul.

⁸The Lord shall preserve thy going out and thy coming in from this time forth, and even for evermore.

Excerpts from

THE PROVERBS

CHAPTER 1

Part I. Instruction and exhortation to sons.

The proverbs of Solomon the son of David, king of Israel;

²To know wisdom and instruction; to perceive the words of understanding;

³To receive the instruction of wisdom, justice, and judgment, and equity;

⁴To give subtilty to the simple, to the young man knowledge and discretion.

⁵A wise man will hear, and will increase learning; and a man of understanding shall attain unto wise counsels:

⁶To understand a proverb, and the interpretation; the words of the wise, and their dark sayings.

⁷The fear of the Lord is the beginning of knowledge: but fools despise wisdom and instruction.

⁸My son, hear the instruction of thy father, and forsake not the law of thy mother:

⁹For they shall be an ornament of grace unto thy head, and chains about thy neck.

¹⁰My son, if sinners entice thee, consent thou not.

¹¹If they say, Come with us, let us lay wait for blood, let us lurk privily for the innocent without cause:

¹²Let us swallow them up alive as the grave; and whole, as those that go down into the pit:

¹³We shall find all precious substance, we shall fill our houses with spoil:

¹⁴Cast in thy lot among us; let us all have one purse:

¹⁵My son, walk not thou in the way with them; refrain thy foot from their path:

¹⁶For their feet run to evil, and make haste to shed blood.

¹⁷Surely in vain the net is spread in the sight of any bird.

¹⁸And they lay wait for their own blood; they lurk privily for their own lives.

¹⁹So are the ways of every one that is greedy of gain; which taketh away the life of the owners thereof.

²⁰Wisdom crieth without; she uttereth her voice in the streets:

²¹She crieth in the chief place of concourse, in the openings of the gates: in the city she uttereth her words, saying,

²²How long, ye simple ones, will ye love simplicity? and the scorners delight in their scorning, and fools hate knowledge?

²³Turn you at my reproof: behold, I will pour out my spirit unto you, I will make known my words unto you.

²⁴Because I have called, and ye refused; I have stretched out my hand, and no man regarded;

²⁵But ye have set at nought all my counsel, and would none of my reproof:

²⁶I also will laugh at your calamity; I will mock when your fear cometh;

²⁷When your fear cometh as desolation, and your destruction cometh as a whirlwind; when distress and anguish cometh upon you.

²⁸Then shall they call upon me, but I will not answer; they shall seek me early, but they shall not find me:

²⁹For that they hated knowledge, and did not choose the fear of the Lord:

³⁰They would none of my counsel: they despised all my reproof.

³¹Therefore shall they eat of the fruit of their own way, and be filled with their own devices.

³²For the turning away of the simple shall slay them, and the prosperity of fools shall destroy them.

³³But whoso hearkeneth unto me shall dwell safely, and shall be quiet from fear of evil.

CHAPTER 3:5–6

⁵Trust in the Lord with all thine heart; and lean not unto thine own understanding.

⁶In all thy ways acknowledge him, and he shall direct thy paths.

CHAPTER 8

Part II. In praise of wisdom.

Doth not wisdom cry? and understanding put forth her voice?

²She standeth in the top of high places, by the way in the places of the paths.

³She crieth at the gates, at the entry of the city, at the coming in at the doors.

⁴Unto you, O men, I call; and my voice is to the sons of man.

⁵O ye simple, understand wisdom: and, ye fools, be ye of an understanding heart.

⁶Hear; for I will speak of excellent things; and the opening of my lips shall be right things.

7For my mouth shall speak truth; and wickedness is an abomination to my lips.

8All the words of my mouth are in righteousness; there is nothing froward or perverse in them.

9They are all plain to him that understandeth, and right to them that find knowledge.

10Receive my instruction, and not silver; and knowledge rather than choice gold.

11For wisdom is better than rubies; and all the things that may be desired are not to be compared to it.

12I wisdom dwell with prudence, and find out knowledge of witty inventions.

13The fear of the Lord is to hate evil: pride, and arrogancy, and the evil way, and the froward mouth, do I hate.

14Counsel is mine, and sound wisdom: I am understanding; I have strength.

15By me kings reign, and princes decree justice.

16By me prices rule, and nobles, even all the judges of the earth.

17I love them that love me; and those that seek me early shall find me.

18Riches and honour are with me; yea, durable riches and righteousness.

19My fruit is better than gold, yea, than fine gold; and my revenue than choice silver.

20I lead in the way of righteousness, in the midst of the paths of judgment:

21That I may cause those that love me to inherit substance; and I will fill their treasures.

22The Lord possessed me in the beginning of his way, before his works of old.

23I was set up from everlasting, from the beginning, or ever the earth was.

24When there were no depths, I was brought forth; when there were no fountains abounding with water.

25Before the mountains were settled, before the hills was I brought forth:

26While as yet he had not made the earth, nor the fields, nor the highest part of the dust of the world.

27When he prepared the heavens, I was there: when he set a compass upon the face of the depth:

28When he established the clouds above: when he strengthened the fountains of the deep:

29When he gave to the sea his decree, that the waters should not pass his commandment: when he appointed the foundations of the earth:

30Then I was by him, as one brought up with him: and I was daily his delight, rejoicing always before him;

³¹Rejoicing in the habitable part of his earth; and my delights were with the sons of men.

³²Now therefore hearken unto me, O ye children: for blessed are they that keep my ways.

³³Hear instruction, and be wise, and refuse it not.

³⁴Blessed is the man that heareth me, watching daily at my gates, waiting at the posts of my doors.

³⁵For whoso findeth me findeth life, and shall obtain favour of the Lord.

³⁶But he that sinneth against me wrongeth his own soul: all they that hate me love death.

CHAPTER 9

(The praise of wisdom,
continued.)

Wisdom hath builded her house, she hath hewn out her seven pillars:

²She hath killed her beasts; she hath mingled her wine; she hath also furnished her table.

³She hath sent forth her maidens: she crieth upon the highest places of the city.

⁴Whoso is simple, let him turn in hither: as for him that wanteth understanding, she saith to him,

⁵Come, eat of my bread, and drink of the wine which I have mingled.

⁶Forsake the foolish, and live; and go in the way of understanding.

⁷He that reproveth a scorner getteth to himself shame: and he that rebuketh a wicked man getteth himself a blot.

⁸Reprove not a scorner, lest he hate thee: rebuke a wise man, and he will love thee.

⁹Give instruction to a wise man, and he will be yet wiser: teach a just man, and he will increase in learning.

¹⁰The fear of the Lord is the beginning of wisdom: and the knowledge of the holy is understanding.

¹¹For by me thy days shall be multiplied, and the years of thy life shall be increased.

¹²If thou be wise, thou shalt be wise for thyself: but if thou scornest, thou alone shalt bear it.

¹³A foolish woman is clamorous: she is simple, and knoweth nothing.

¹⁴For she sitteth at the door of her house, on a seat in the high places of the city,

¹⁵To call passengers who go right on their ways:

¹⁶Whoso is simple, let him turn in hither: and as for him that wanteth understanding, she saith to him,

¹⁷Stolen waters are sweet, and bread eaten in secret is pleasant.

¹⁸But he knoweth not that the dead are there; and that her guests are in the depths of hell.

Excerpts from

ECCLESIASTES or THE PREACHER

CHAPTER 5:18

18Behold that which I have seen: it is good and comely for one to eat and to drink, and to enjoy the good of all his labour that he taketh under the sun all the days of his life, which God giveth him: for it is his portion.

CHAPTER 12:12–13

12And further, by these, my son, be admonished: of making many books there is no end; and much study is a weariness of the flesh.

13Let us hear the conclusion of the whole matter: Fear God, and keep his commandments: for this is the whole duty of man.

Excerpt from

THE SONG OF SOLOMON

CHAPTER 3:1–5

By night on my bed I sought him whom my soul loveth: I sought him, but I found him not.

2I will rise now, and go about the city in the streets, and in the broad ways I will seek him whom my soul loveth: I sought him, but I found him not.

3The watchmen that go about the city found me: to whom I said, Saw ye him whom my soul loveth?

4It was but a little that I passed from them, but I found him whom my soul loveth: I held him, and would not let him go, until I had brought him into my mother's house, and into the chamber of her that conceived me.

5I charge you, O ye daughters of Jerusalem, by the roes, and by the hinds of the field, that ye stir not up, nor awake my love, till he please.

Excerpts from

THE GOSPEL ACCORDING TO ST. MATTHEW

CHAPTER 5

*The sermon on the mount.
The beatitudes.*

And seeing the multitudes, he went up into a mountain: and when he was set, his disciples came unto him:

2And he opened his mouth, and taught them, saying,

3Blessed are the poor in spirit: for theirs is the kingdom of heaven.

4Blessed are they that mourn: for they shall be comforted.

5Blessed are the meek: for they shall inherit the earth.

6Blessed are they which do hunger and thirst after righteousness: for they shall be filled.

7Blessed are the merciful: for they shall obtain mercy.

8Blessed are the pure in heart: for they shall see God.

9Blessed are the peacemakers: for they shall be called the children of God.

10Blessed are they which are persecuted for righteousness' sake: for theirs is the kingdom of heaven.

11Blessed are ye, when men shall revile you, and persecute you, and shall say all manner of evil against you falsely, for my sake.

12Rejoice, and be exceeding glad: for great is your reward in heaven: for so persecuted they the prophets which were before you.

Similitudes of the believer.

13Ye are the salt of the earth: but if the salt have lost his savour, wherewith shall it be salted? it is thenceforth good for nothing, but to be cast out, and to be trodden under foot of men.

14Ye are the light of the world. A city that is set on an hill cannot be hid.

15Neither do men light a candle, and put it under a bushel, but on a candlestick; and it giveth light unto all that are in the house.

16Let your light so shine before men, that they may see your good works, and glorify your Father which is in heaven.

Relation of Christ to the law.

17Think not that I am come to destroy the law, or the prophets: I am not come to destroy, but to fulfill.

18For verily I say unto you, Till heaven and earth pass, one jot or one tittle shall in no wise pass from the law, till all be fulfilled.

19Whosoever therefore shall break one of these least commandments, and shall teach men so, he shall be called the least in the kingdom of heaven: but whosoever shall do and teach them, the same shall be called great in the kingdom of heaven.

20For I say unto you, That except your righteousness shall exceed the righteousness of the scribes and Pharisees, ye shall in no case enter into the kingdom of heaven.

21Ye have heard that it was said by them of old time, Thou shalt not kill; and whosoever shall kill shall be in danger of the judgment:

22But I say unto you, That whosoever is angry with his brother without a cause shall be in danger of the judgment: and whosoever shall say to his brother, Raca, shall be in danger of the council: but whosoever shall say, Thou fool, shall be in danger of hell fire.

23Therefore if thou bring thy gift to the altar, and there rememberest that thy brother hath ought against thee:

24Leave there thy gift before the altar, and go thy way; first be reconciled to thy brother, and then come and offer thy gift.

25Agree with thine adversary quickly, whiles thou art in the way with him; lest at any time the adversary deliver thee to the judge, and the judge deliver thee to the officer, and thou be cast into prison.

26Verily I say unto thee, Thou shalt by no means come out thence, till thou hast paid the uttermost farthing.

27Ye have heard that it was said by them of old time, Thou shalt not commit adultery:

28But I say unto you, That whosoever looketh on a woman to lust after her hath committed adultery with her already in his heart.

29And if thy right eye offend thee, pluck it out, and cast it from thee: for it is profitable for thee that one of thy members should perish, and not that thy whole body should be cast into hell.

30And if thy right hand offend thee, cut it off, and cast it from thee: for it is profitable for thee that one of thy members should perish, and not that thy whole body should be cast into hell.

Jesus and divorce.

31It hath been said, Whosoever shall put away his wife, let him give her a writing of divorcement:

32But I say unto you, That whosoever shall put away his wife, saving for the cause of fornication, causeth her to commit adultery: and whosoever shall marry her that is divorced committeth adultery.

33Again, ye have heard that it hath been said by them of old time, Thou shalt not forswear thyself, but shalt perform unto the Lord thine oaths:

34But I say unto you, Swear not at all; neither by heaven; for it is God's throne:

35Nor by the earth; for it is his footstool: neither by Jerusalem; for it is the city of the great King.

36Neither shalt thou swear by thy head, because thou canst not make one hair white or black.

37But let your communication be, Yea, yea; Nay, nay: for whatsoever is more than these cometh of evil.

38Ye have heard that it hath been said, An eye for an eye, and a tooth for a tooth:

³⁹But I say unto you, That ye resist not evil: but whosoever shall smite thee on thy right cheek, turn to him the other also.

⁴⁰And if any man will sue thee at the law, and take away thy coat, let him have thy cloke also.

⁴¹And whosoever shall compel thee to go a mile, go with him twain.

⁴²Give to him that asketh thee, and from him that would borrow of thee turn not thou away.

⁴³Ye have heard that it hath been said, Thou shalt love thy neighbour, and hate thine enemy.

⁴⁴But I say unto you, Love your enemies, bless them that curse you, do good to them that hate you, and pray for them which despitefully use you, and persecute you;

⁴⁵That ye may be the children of your Father which is in heaven: for he maketh his sun to rise on the evil and on the good, and sendeth rain on the just and on the unjust.

⁴⁶For if ye love them which love you, what reward have ye? do not even the publicans the same?

⁴⁷And if ye salute your brethren only, what do ye more than others? do not even the publicans so?

⁴⁸Be ye therefore perfect, even as your Father which is in heaven is perfect.

CHAPTER 6

Sermon on the mount,
continued: *mere externalism
in religion condemned.*

Take heed that ye do not your alms before men, to be seen of them: otherwise ye have no reward of your Father which is in heaven.

²Therefore when thou doest thine alms, do not sound a trumpet before thee, as the hypocrites do in the synagogues and in the streets, that they may have glory of men. Verily I say unto you, They have their reward.

³But when thou doest alms, let not thy left hand know that thy right hand doeth:

⁴That thine alms may be in secret: and thy Father which seeth in secret himself shall reward thee openly.

⁵And when thou prayest, thou shalt not be as the hypocrites are: for they love to pray standing in the synagogues and in the corners of the streets, that they may be seen of men. Verily I say unto you, They have their reward.

⁶But thou, when thou prayest, enter into thy closet, and when thou hast shut thy door, pray to thy Father which is in secret; and thy Father which seeth in secret shall reward thee openly.

[7]But when ye pray, use not vain repetitions, as the heathen do: for they think that they shall be heard for their much speaking.

The new revelation concerning prayer.

[8]Be not ye therefore like unto them: for your Father knoweth what things ye have need of, before ye ask him.

[9]After this manner therefore pray ye: Our Father which art in heaven, Hallowed be thy name.

[10]Thy kingdom come. Thy will be done in earth, as it is in heaven.

[11]Give us this day our daily bread.

[12]And forgive us our debts, as we forgive our debtors.

[13]And lead us not into temptation, but deliver us from evil: For thine is the kingdom, and the power, and the glory, for ever. Amen.

[14]For if ye forgive men their trespasses, your heavenly Father will also forgive you:

[15]But if ye forgive not men their trespasses, neither will your Father forgive your trespasses.

Externalism again rebuked.

[16]Moreover when ye fast, be not, as the hypocrites, of a sad countenance: for they disfigure their faces, that they may appear unto men to fast. Verily I say unto you, They have their reward.

[17]But thou, when thou fastest, anoint thine head, and wash thy face;

[18]That thou appear not unto men to fast, but unto thy Father which is in secret: and thy Father, which seeth in secret, shall reward thee openly.

The kingdom law of riches.

[19]Lay not up for yourselves treasures upon earth, where moth and rust doth corrupt, and where thieves break through and steal:

[20]But lay up for yourselves treasures in heaven, where neither moth nor rust doth corrupt, and where thieves do not break through nor steal:

[21]For where your treasure is, there will your heart be also.

[22]The light of the body is the eye: if therefore thine eye be single, thy whole body shall be full of light.

[23]But if thine eye be evil, thy whole body shall be full of darkness. If therefore the light that is in thee be darkness, how great is that darkness!

[24]No man can serve two masters: for either he will hate the one, and love the other; or else he will hold to the one, and despise the other. Ye cannot serve God and mammon.

The cure of anxiety:
trust in the Father's care.

²⁵Therefore I say unto you, Take no thought for your life, what ye shall eat, or what ye shall drink; nor yet for your body, what ye shall put on. Is not the life more than meat, and the body than raiment?

²⁶Behold the fowls of the air: for they sow not, neither do they reap, nor gather into barns; yet your heavenly Father feedeth them. Are ye not much better than they?

²⁷Which of you by taking thought can add one cubit unto his stature?

²⁸And why take ye thought for raiment? Consider the lilies of the field, how they grow; they toil not, neither do they spin:

²⁹And yet I say unto you, That even Solomon in all his glory was not arrayed like one of these.

³⁰Wherefore, if God so clothe the grass of the field, which to day is, and to morrow is cast into the oven, shall he not much more clothe you, O ye of little faith?

³¹Therefore take no thought, saying, What shall we eat? or, What shall we drink? or, Wherewithal shall we be clothed?

³²(For after all these things do the Gentiles seek:) for your heavenly Father knoweth that ye have need of all these things.

³³But seek ye first the kingdom of God, and his righteousness; and all these things shall be added unto you.

³⁴Take therefore no thought for the morrow: for the morrow shall take thought for the things of itself. Sufficient unto the day is the evil thereof.

CHAPTER 7

Sermon on the mount,
continued: *judgment of others*
forbidden.

Judge not, that ye be not judged.

²For with what judgment ye judge, ye shall be judged: and with what measure ye mete, it shall be measured to you again.

³And why beholdest thou the mote that is in thy brother's eye, but considerest not the beam that is in thine own eye?

⁴Or how wilt thou say to thy brother, Let me pull out the mote out of thine eye; and, behold, a beam is in thine own eye?

⁵Thou hypocrite, first cast out the beam out of thine own eye; and then shalt thou see clearly to cast out the mote out of thy brother's eye.

⁶Give not that which is holy unto the dogs, neither cast ye your pearls before swine, lest they trample them under their feet, and turn again and rend you.

Encouragements to pray.

[7]Ask, and it shall be given you; seek, and ye shall find; knock, and it shall be opened unto you:

[8]For every one that asketh receiveth; and he that seeketh findeth; and to him that knocketh it shall be opened.

[9]Or what man is there of you, whom if his son ask bread, will he give him a stone?

[10]Or if he ask a fish, will he give him a serpent?

[11]If ye then, being evil, know how to give good gifts unto your children, how much more shall your Father which is in heaven give good things to them that ask him?

Summary of O.T. righteousness.

[12]Therefore all things whatsoever ye would that men should do to you, do ye even so to them: for this is the law and the prophets.

The two ways.

[13]Enter ye in at the strait gate: for wide is the gate, and broad is the way, that leadeth to destruction, and many there be which go in thereat:

[14]Because strait is the gate, and narrow is the way, which leadeth unto life, and few there be that find it.

Warning against false teachers: the test.

[15]Beware of false prophets, which come to you in sheep's clothing, but inwardly they are ravening wolves.

[16]Ye shall know them by their fruits. Do men gather grapes of thorns, or figs of thistles?

[17]Even so every good tree bringeth forth good fruit; but a corrupt tree bringeth forth evil fruit.

[18]A good tree cannot bring forth evil fruit, neither can a corrupt tree bring forth good fruit.

[19]Every tree that bringeth not forth good fruit is hewn down, and cast into the fire.

[20]Wherefore by their fruits ye shall know them.

The danger of profession without faith.

[21]Not every one that saith unto me, Lord, Lord, shall enter into the kingdom of heaven; but he that doeth the will of my Father which is in heaven.

[22]Many will say to me in that day, Lord, Lord, have we not prophesied in thy name? and in thy name have cast out devils? and in thy name done many wonderful works?

[23]And then will I profess unto them, I never knew you: depart from me, ye that work iniquity.

The two foundations.

24Therefore whosoever heareth these sayings of mine, and doeth them, I will liken him unto a wise man, which built his house upon a rock:

25And the rain descended, and the floods came, and the winds blew, and beat upon that house; and it fell not: for it was founded upon a rock.

26And every one that heareth these sayings of mine, and doeth them not, shall be likened unto a foolish man, which built his house upon the sand:

27And the rain descended, and the floods came, and the winds blew, and beat upon that house; and it fell: and great was the fall of it.

28And it came to pass, when Jesus had ended these sayings, the people were astonished at his doctrine:

29For he taught them as one having authority, and not as the scribes.

Excerpts from
THE GOSPEL ACCORDING TO ST. JOHN
CHAPTER 17

The prayer of intercession.

These words spake Jesus, and lifted up his eyes to heaven, and said, Father, the hour is come; glorify thy Son, that thy Son also may glorify thee:

2As thou hast given him power over all flesh, that he should give eternal life to as many as thou hast given him.

3And this is life eternal, that they might know thee the only true God, and Jesus Christ, whom thou hast sent.

4I have glorified thee on the earth: I have finished the work which thou gavest me to do.

5And now, O Father, glorify thou me with thine own self with the glory which I had with thee before the world was.

6I have manifested thy name unto the men which thou gavest me out of the world: thine they were, and thou gavest them me; and they have kept thy word.

7Now they have known that all things whatsoever thou hast given me are of thee.

8For I have given unto them the words which thou gavest me; and they have received them, and have known surely that I came out from thee, and they have believed that thou didst send me.

9I pray for them: I pray not for the world, but for them which thou hast given me; for they are thine.

10And all mine are thine, and thine are mine; and I am glorified in them.

11And now I am no more in the world, but these are in the world, and I come to thee. Holy Father, keep through thine own name those whom thou hast given me, that they may be one, as we are.

¹²While I was with them in the world, I kept them in thy name: those that thou gavest me I have kept, and none of them is lost, but the son of perdition; that the scripture might be fulfilled.

¹³And now come I to thee; and these things I speak in the world, that they might have my joy fulfilled in themselves.

¹⁴I have given them thy word; and the world hath hated them, because they are not of the world, even as I am not of the world.

¹⁵I pray not that thou shouldest take them out of the world, but that thou shouldest keep them from the evil.

¹⁶They are not of the world, even as I am not of the world.

¹⁷Sanctify them through thy truth: thy word is truth.

¹⁸As thou hast sent me into the world, even so have I also sent them into the world.

¹⁹And for their sakes I sanctify myself, that they also might be sanctified through the truth.

²⁰Neither pray I for these alone, but for them also which shall believe on me through their word;

²¹That they all may be one; as thou, Father, art in me, and I in thee, that they also may be one

in us: that the world may believe that thou hast sent me.

²²And the glory which thou gavest me I have given them; that they may be one, even as we are one:

²³I in them, and thou in me, that they may be made perfect in one; and that the world may know that thou hast sent me, and hast loved them, as thou hast loved me.

²⁴Father, I will that they also, whom thou hast given me, be with me where I am; that they may behold my glory, which thou hast given me: for thou lovedst me before the foundation of the world.

²⁵O righteous Father, the world hath not known thee: but I have known thee, and these have known that thou hast sent me.

²⁶And I have declared unto them thy name, and will declare it: that the love wherewith thou hast loved me may be in them, and I in them.

CHAPTER 19:25–27

The scene at the foot of the cross.

²⁵Now there stood by the cross of Jesus his mother, and his mother's sister, Mary the wife of Cleophas, and Mary Magdalene.

²⁶When Jesus therefore saw his mother, and the disciple standing by, whom he loved, he saith unto

his mother, Woman, behold thy son!

27Then saith he to the disciple, Behold thy mother! And from that hour that disciple took her unto his own home.

Excerpts from

THE FIRST EPISTLE OF PAUL THE APOSTLE TO THE CORINTHIANS

CHAPTER 11:23–29

The order and meaning of the Lord's table.

23For I have received of the Lord that which also I delivered unto you, That the Lord Jesus the same night in which he was betrayed took bread:

24And when he had given thanks, he brake it, and said, Take, eat: this is my body, which is broken for you: this do in remembrance of me.

25After the same manner also he took the cup, when he had supped, saying, This cup is the new testament in my blood: this do ye, as oft as ye drink it, in remembrance of me.

26For as often as ye eat this bread, and drink this cup, ye do shew the Lord's death till he come.

27Wherefore whosoever shall eat this bread, and drink this cup of the Lord, unworthily, shall be guilty of the body and blood of the Lord.

28But let a man examine himself, and so let him eat of that bread, and drink of that cup.

29For he that eateth and drinketh unworthily, eateth and drinketh damnation to himself, not discerning the Lord's body.

CHAPTER 13

The ministry gifts must be governed by love.

Though I speak with the tongues of men and of angels, and have not charity, I am become as sounding brass, or a tinkling cymbal.

2And though I have the gift of prophecy, and understand all mysteries, and all knowledge; and though I have all faith, so that I could remove mountains, and have not charity, I am nothing.

3And though I bestow all my goods to feed the poor, and though I give my body to be burned, and have not charity, it profiteth me nothing.

4Charity suffereth long, and is kind; charity envieth not; charity vaunteth not itself, is not puffed up,

5Doth not behave itself unseemly, seeketh not her own, is not easily provoked, thinketh no evil;

⁶Rejoiceth not in iniquity, but rejoiceth in the truth;

⁷Beareth all things, believeth all things, hopeth all things, endureth all things.

⁸Charity never faileth: but whether there be prophecies, they shall fail; whether there be tongues, they shall cease; whether there be knowledge, it shall vanish away.

⁹For we know in part, and we prophesy in part.

¹⁰But when that which is perfect is come, then that which is in part shall be done away.

¹¹When I was a child, I spake as a child, I understood as a child, I thought as a child: but when I became a man, I put away childish things.

¹²For now we see through a glass, darkly; but then face to face: now I know in part; but then shall I know even as also I am known.

¹³And now abideth faith, hope, charity, these three; but the greatest of these is charity.

Excerpt from

THE SECOND EPISTLE
OF PAUL THE APOSTLE
TO THE CORINTHIANS
CHAPTER 4

The ministry: honesty.

Therefore seeing we have this ministry, as we have received mercy, we faint not;

Because the truth taught is commended by the life.

²But have renounced the hidden things of dishonesty, not walking in craftiness, nor handling the word of God deceitfully; but by manifestation of the truth commending ourselves to every man's conscience in the sight of God.

Because not self but Christ Jesus as Lord is preached.

³But if our gospel be hid, it is hid to them that are lost:

⁴In whom the god of this world hath blinded the minds of them which believe not, lest the light of the glorious gospel of Christ, who is the image of God, should shine unto them.

⁵For we preach not ourselves, but Christ Jesus the Lord; and ourselves your servants for Jesus' sake.

⁶For God, who commanded the light to shine out of darkness, hath shined in our hearts, to give the light of the knowledge of the glory of God in the face of Jesus Christ.

Because the power is of God alone.

⁷But we have this treasure in earthen vessels, that the excellency of the power may be of God, and not of us.

The ministry: suffering.

8We are troubled on every side, yet not distressed; we are perplexed, but not in despair;

9Persecuted, but not forsaken; cast down, but not destroyed;

10Always bearing about in the body the dying of the Lord Jesus, that the life also of Jesus might be made manifest in our body.

11For we which live are always delivered unto death for Jesus' sake, that the life also of Jesus might be made manifest in our mortal flesh.

12So then death worketh in us, but life in you.

13We having the same spirit of faith, according as it is written, I believed, and therefore have I spoken; we also believe, and therefore speak;

14Knowing that he which raised up the Lord Jesus shall raise up us also by Jesus, and shall present us with you.

15For all things are for your sakes, that the abundant grave might through the thanksgiving of many redound to the glory of God.

16For which cause we faint not; but though our outward man perish, yet the inward man is renewed day by day.

17For our light affliction, which is but for a moment, worketh for us a far more exceeding and eternal weight of glory;

18While we look not at the things which are seen, but at the things which are not seen: for the things which are seen are temporal; but the things which are not seen are eternal.

Excerpt from

THE SECOND EPISTLE OF PAUL THE APOSTLE TO TIMOTHY

CHAPTER 2

Part II. The path of a good soldier in the time of apostasy.

Thou therefore, my son, be strong in the grace that is in Christ Jesus.

2And the things that thou hast heard of me among many witnesses, the same commit thou to faithful men, who shall be able to teach others also.

3Thou therefore endure hardness, as a good soldier of Jesus Christ.

4No man that warreth entangleth himself with the affairs of this life; that he may please him who hath chosen him to be a soldier.

5And if a man also strive for masteries, yet is he not crowned, except he strive lawfully.

6The husbandman that laboureth must be first partaker of the fruits.

[7]Consider what I say; and the Lord give thee understanding in all things.

[8]Remember that Jesus Christ of the seed of David was raised from the dead according to my gospel:

[9]Wherein I suffer trouble, as an evil doer, even unto bonds; but the word of God is not bound.

[10]Therefore I endure all things for the elect's sakes, that they may also obtain the salvation which is in Christ Jesus with eternal glory.

[11]It is a faithful saying: For if we be dead with him, we shall also live with him:

[12]If we suffer, we shall also reign with him: if we deny him, he also will deny us:

[13]If we believe not, yet he abideth faithful: he cannot deny himself.

[14]Of these things put them in remembrance, charging them before the Lord that they strive not about words to no profit, but to the subverting of the hearers.

[15]Study to shew thyself approved unto God, a workman that needeth not to be ashamed, rightly dividing the word of truth.

[16]But shun profane and vain babblings: for they will increase unto more ungodliness.

[17]And their word will eat as doth a canker: of whom is Hymenaeus and Philetus;

[18]Who concerning the truth have erred, saying that the resurrection is past already; and overthrow the faith of some.

[19]Nevertheless the foundation of God standeth sure, having this seal, the Lord knoweth them that are his. And, Let every one that nameth the name of Christ depart from iniquity.

[20]But in a great house there are not only vessels of gold, and of silver, but also of wood and of earth; and some to honour, and some to dishonour.

[21]If a man therefore purge himself from these, he shall be a vessel unto honour, sanctified, and meet for the master's use, and prepared unto every good work.

[22]Flee also youthful lusts: but follow righteousness, faith, charity, peace, with them that call on the Lord out of a pure heart.

[23]But foolish and unlearned questions avoid, knowing that they do gender strifes.

[24]And the servant of the Lord must not strive; but be gentle unto all men, apt to teach, patient,

[25]In meekness instructing those that oppose themselves; if God peradventure will give them repentance to the acknowledging of the truth;

[26]And that they may recover themselves out of the snare of the devil, who are taken captive by him at his will.

THE GENERAL EPISTLE
OF JAMES

CHAPTER 1

Part I. The testings of faith:
The purpose of testings.

James, a servant of God and of the Lord Jesus Christ, to the twelve tribes which are scattered abroad, greeting.

²My brethren, count it all joy when ye fall into divers temptations;

³Knowing this, that the trying of your faith worketh patience.

⁴But let patience have her perfect work, that ye may be perfect and entire, wanting nothing.

⁵If any of you lack wisdom, let him ask of God, that giveth to all men liberally, and upbraideth not; and it shall be given him.

⁶But let him ask in faith, nothing wavering. For he that wavereth is like a wave of the sea driven with the wind and tossed.

⁷For let not that man think that he shall receive any thing of the Lord.

⁸A double minded man is unstable in all his ways.

⁹Let the brother of low degree rejoice in that he is exalted:

¹⁰But the rich, in that he is made low: because as the flower of the grass he shall pass away.

¹¹For the sun is no sooner risen with a burning heat, but it withereth the grass, and the flower thereof falleth, and the grace of the fashion of it perisheth: so also shall the rich man fade away in his ways.

¹²Blessed is the man that endureth temptation: for when he is tried, he shall receive the crown of life, which the Lord hath promised to them that love him.

Solicitation to do evil
is not of God.

¹³Let no man say when he is tempted, I am tempted of God: for God cannot be tempted with evil, neither tempteth he any man:

¹⁴But every man is tempted, when he is drawn away of his own lust, and enticed.

¹⁵Then when lust hath conceived, it bringeth forth sin: and sin, when it is finished, bringeth forth death.

¹⁶Do not err, my beloved brethren.

¹⁷Every good gift and every perfect gift is from above, and cometh down from the Father of lights, with whom is no variableness, neither shadow of turning.

¹⁸Of his own will begat he us with the word of truth, that we should be a kind of firstfruits of his creatures.

¹⁹Wherefore, my beloved brethren, let every man be swift to hear, slow to speak, slow to wrath:

20For the wrath of man worketh not the righteousness of God.

21Wherefore lay apart all filthiness and superfluity of naughtiness, and receive with meekness the engrafted word, which is able to save your souls.

The test of obedience.

22But be ye doers of the word, and not hearers only, deceiving your own selves.

23For if any be a hearer of the word, and not a doer, he is like unto a man beholding his natural face in a glass:

24For he beholdeth himself, and goeth his way, and straightway forgetteth what manner of man he was.

25But whoso looketh into the perfect law of liberty, and continueth therein, he being not a forgetful hearer, but a doer of the work, this man shall be blessed in his deed.

The test of true religion.

26If any man among you seem to be religious, and bridleth not his tongue, but deceiveth his own heart, this man's religion is vain.

27Pure religion and undefiled before God and the Father is this, To visit the fatherless and widows in their affliction, and to keep himself unspotted from the world.

CHAPTER 2

The test of brotherly love.

My brethren, have not the faith of our Lord Jesus Christ, the Lord of glory, with respect of persons.

2For is there come unto your assembly a man with a gold ring, in goodly apparel, and there come in also a poor man in vile raiment:

3And ye have respect to him that weareth the gay clothing, and say unto him, Sit thou here in a good place; and say to the poor, Stand thou there, or sit here under my footstool:

4Are ye not then partial in yourselves, and are become judges of evil thoughts?

5Hearken, my beloved brethren, Hath not God chosen the poor of this world rich in faith, and heirs of the kingdom which he hath promised to them that love him?

6But ye have despised the poor. Do not rich men oppress you, and draw you before the judgment seats?

7Do not they blaspheme that worthy name by the which ye are called?

8If ye fulfil the royal law according to the scripture, Thou shalt love thy neighbour as thyself, ye do well:

9But if ye have respect to persons, ye commit sin, and are

convinced of the law as transgressors.

¹⁰For whosoever shall keep the whole law, and yet offend in one point, he is guilty of all.

¹¹For he that said, Do not commit adultery, said also, Do not kill. Now if thou commit no adultery, yet if thou kill, thou art become a transgressor of the law.

¹²So speak ye, and so do, as they that shall be judged by the law of liberty.

¹³For he shall have judgment without mercy, that hath shewed no mercy; and mercy rejoiceth against judgment.

The test of good works.

¹⁴What doth it profit, my brethren, though a man say he hath faith, and have not works? can faith save him?

¹⁵If a brother or sister be naked, and destitute of daily food,

¹⁶And one of you say unto them, Depart in peace, be ye warmed and filled; notwithstanding ye give them not those things which are needful to the body; what doth it profit?

¹⁷Even so faith, if it hath not works, is dead, being alone.

¹⁸Yea, a man may say, Thou hast faith, and I have works: shew me thy faith without thy works, and I will shew thee my faith by my works.

¹⁹Thou believest that there is one God; thou doest well: the devils also believe, and tremble.

²⁰But wilt thou know, O vain man, that faith without works is dead?

The illustration of Abraham.

²¹Was not Abraham our father justified by works, when he had offered Isaac his son upon the altar?

²²Seest thou how faith wrought with his works, and by works was faith made perfect?

²³And the scripture was fulfilled which saith, Abraham believed God, and it was imputed unto him for righteousness: and he was called the Friend of God.

²⁴Ye see then how that by works a man is justified, and not by faith only.

²⁵Likewise also was not Rahab the harlot justified by works, when she had received the messengers, and had sent them out another way?

²⁶For as the body without the spirit is dead, so faith without works is dead also.

CHAPTER 3

Part II. A true faith will control the tongue.

My brethren, be not many masters, knowing that we shall receive the greater condemnation.

²For in many things we offend all. If any man offend not in word, the same is a perfect man, and able also to bridle the whole body.

³Behold, we put bits in the horses' mouths, that they may obey us; and we turn about their whole body.

⁴Behold also the ships, which though they be so great, and are driven of fierce winds, yet are they turned about with a very small helm, withersoever the governor listeth.

⁵Even so the tongue is a little member, and boasteth great things. Behold, how great a matter a little fire kindleth!

⁶And the tongue is a fire, a world of iniquity: so is the tongue among our members, that it defileth the whole body, and setteth on fire the course of nature; and it is set on fire of hell.

⁷For every kind of beasts, and of birds, and of serpents, and of things in the sea, is tamed, and hath been tamed of mankind:

⁸But the tongue can no man tame; it is an unruly evil, full of deadly poison.

⁹Therewith bless we God, even the Father; and therewith curse we men, which are made after the similitude of God.

¹⁰Out of the same mouth proceedeth blessing and cursing. My brethren, these things ought not so to be.

¹¹Doth a fountain send forth at the same place sweet water and bitter?

¹²Can the fig tree, my brethren, bear olive berries? either a vine, figs? so can no fountain both yield salt water and fresh.

¹³Who is a wise man and endued with knowledge among you? let him shew out of a good conversation his works with meekness of wisdom.

¹⁴But if ye have bitter envying and strife in your hearts, glory not, and lie not against the truth.

¹⁵This wisdom descendeth not from above, but is earthly, sensual, devilish.

¹⁶For where envying and strife is, there is confusion and every evil work.

¹⁷But the wisdom that is from above is first pure, then peaceable, gentle, and easy to be intreated, full of mercy and good fruits, without partiality, and without hypocrisy.

¹⁸And the fruit of righteousness is sown in peace of them that make peace.

CHAPTER 4

Part III. The rebuke of worldliness.

From whence come wars and fightings among you? come they not hence, even of your lusts that war in your members?

²Ye lust, and have not: ye kill, and desire to have, and cannot

obtain: ye fight and war, yet ye have not, because ye ask not.

³Ye ask, and receive not, because ye ask amiss, that ye may consume it upon your lusts.

⁴Ye adulterers and adulteresses, know ye not that the friendship of the world is enmity with God? whosoever therefore will be a friend of the world is the enemy of God.

⁵Do ye think that the scripture saith in vain, The spirit that dwelleth in us lusteth to envy?

⁶But he giveth more grace. Wherefore he saith, God resisteth the proud, but giveth grace unto the humble.

⁷Submit yourselves therefore to God. Resist the devil, and he will flee from you.

⁸Draw nigh to God, and he will draw nigh to you. Cleanse your hands, ye sinners; and purify your hearts, ye double minded.

⁹Be afflicted, and mourn, and weep: let your laughter be turned to mourning, and your joy to heaviness.

¹⁰Humble yourselves in the sight of the Lord, and he shall lift you up.

¹¹Speak not evil one of another, brethren. He that speaketh evil of his brother, and judgeth his brother, speaketh evil of the law, and judgeth the law: but if thou judge the law, thou art not a doer of the law, but a judge.

¹²There is one lawgiver, who is able to save and to destroy: who art thou that judgest another?

¹³Go to now, ye that say, To day or to morrow we will go into such a city, and continue there a year, and buy and sell, and get gain:

¹⁴Whereas ye know not what shall be on the morrow, For what is your life? It is even a vapour, that appeareth for a little time, and then vanisheth away.

¹⁵For that ye ought to say, If the Lord will, we shall live, and do this, or that.

¹⁶But now ye rejoice in your boastings: all such rejoicing is evil.

¹⁷Therefore to him that knoweth to do good, and doeth it not, to him it is sin.

CHAPTER 5

Part IV. The rich warned.

Go to now, ye rich men, weep and howl for your miseries that shall come upon you.

²Your riches are corrupted, and your garments are motheaten.

³Your gold and silver is cankered; and the rust of them shall be a witness against you, and shall eat your flesh as it were fire. Ye have heaped treasure together for the last days.

⁴Behold, the hire of the labourers who have reaped down your fields, which is of you kept back by fraud, crieth: and the cries of

them which have reaped are entered into the ears of the Lord of sabaoth.

5Ye have lived in pleasure on the earth, and been wanton; ye have nourished your hearts, as in a day of slaughter.

6Ye have condemned and killed the just; and he doth not resist you.

Part V. Exhortations in view of the coming of the Lord.

7Be patient therefore, brethren, unto the coming of the Lord. Behold, the husbandman waiteth for the precious fruit of the earth, and hath long patience for it, until he receive the early and latter rain.

8Be ye also patient; stablish your hearts: for the coming of the Lord draweth nigh.

9Grudge not one against another, brethren, lest ye be condemned: behold, the judge standeth before the door.

10Take, my brethren, the prophets, who have spoken in the name of the Lord, for an example of suffering affliction, and of patience.

11Behold, we count them happy which endure. Ye have heard of the patience of Job, and have seen the end of the Lord; that the Lord is very pitiful, and of tender mercy.

12But above all things, my brethren, swear not, neither by heaven, neither by the earth, neither by any other oath: but let your yea be yea; and your nay, nay; lest ye fall into condemnation.

13Is any among you afflicted? let him pray. Is any merry? let him sing psalms.

14Is any sick among you? let him call for the elders of the church; and let them pray over him, anointing him with oil in the name of the Lord:

15And the prayer of faith shall save the sick, and the Lord shall raise him up; and if he have committed sins, they shall be forgiven him.

16Confess your faults one to another, and pray one for another, that ye may be healed. The effectual fervent prayer of a righteous man availeth much.

17Elias was a man subject to like passions as we are, and he prayed earnestly that it might not rain: and it rained not on the earth by the space of three years and six months.

18And he prayed again, and the heaven gave rain, and the earth brought forth her fruit.

19Brethren, if any of you do err from the truth, and one convert him;

20Let him know, that he which converteth the sinner from the error of his way shall save a soul from death, and shall hide a multitude of sins.

P.S. We have been trying for some years to write a good presentation of what the Lifesavers way of life is all about—a presentation that brings you right up to date as of today. It turns out that a really good job has recently been done in an interview published in the March 1990 issue of *Sober Times*, a monthly news mag-

azine on the addiction scene. Milt Schwartz, the editor, interviewed Tom P., one of the co-founders of Lifesavers Associates, and Tom P. Jr., the other co-founder. We are running the interview here just as it appeared in *Sober Times*.

An AA Oldtimer Talks About the Early Years

Interview by Milt Schwartz

Hankins, NY—Tom P., 79, is a legend among AA oldtimers. A failed advertising executive, he first came to AA in 1941. AA co-founder Bill Wilson became his sponsor. Tom P. was in and out of AA for five years before taking his last drink on October 10, 1946.

Eight months later, Tom P.—a three-pack-a-day smoker—worked the Twelve Steps on his nicotine addiction and that craving was also removed.

Convinced that the Twelve-Step program would work equally well for non-alcoholics with other addictions and serious mental problems, Tom P. organized a group called All Addicts Anonymous. Commonly known among members as the "Nut Club," they met regularly in Chappaqua, New York.

Tom P. claims to have worked closely with Bill Wilson on the editing of the third edition of the Big Book and says he contributed to the writing of *Twelve Steps and Twelve Traditions* of Alcoholics Anonymous.

An accomplished author, Tom P. has written two books on recovery, and is currently working on a third.

In 1961, Tom P. and a group of recovering people from All Addicts Anonymous purchased land on a prominent ridge overlooking the town of Hankins in the Catskill Mountain range of New York. They subsequently renamed All Addicts Anonymous the "Lifesavers." Eventually, the Lifesavers became legally incorporated as a religion.

The group currently numbers about fifty, including as members a lot of children. Each family has its own home. Together, the members own 300 acres, some of which is used to grow the organic foods they eat. Throughout the last thirty years, they have constructed several new buildings which serve as offices and warehouses for the variety of businesses that they own and operate.

The most impressive building is the auditorium, built as an addition to the main house. This structure boasts a full-sized stage, and serves as a venue for the many theatrical and musical productions that the Lifesavers present throughout the year. Located in the same building is their own private school, with grades from kindergarten through high school.

Recently, *Sober Times* traveled to the tiny hamlet of Hankins, New York, to speak with Tom P. and his son, Tom P., Jr. Hankins is located two hours north of Manhattan in the western foothills of the Catskill Mountains.

Tom P. is a small man with a full white beard and penetrating, sparkling blue eyes. Despite his many years, he is full of energy and enthusiasm, with a gift for gab and a remarkable memory for detail.

His son, Tom P., Jr., is in some ways a young carbon-copy of his father. He is demonstrative, vociferous, lively, and sports the same full beard. Father and son both seem at peace with their world; both men love to laugh.

The following interview was conducted on a cold weekday morning in Tom P.'s comfortable two-story frame house, which sits proudly on a knoll overlooking the land Tom P., his son and his fellow Lifesavers built into a thriving clean and sober community.

SOBER TIMES: *Would you tell us your story?*

TOM P.: I'm an alcoholic. I started drinking in college, at the University of Michigan. I did some messy drinking for a few years. Then I got out in the world to make a living. I started out in the advertising business in Chicago, then on to Detroit, where I got fired. Getting fired in Detroit gave me a terrible shock, because I had no resources.

Anyhow, I got over to Cleveland with a very good job. I began to learn how to drink there. I drank a lot every day but I kept it in order. I mainly stayed out of bad trouble, but...it became a very basic part of my living.

I got into New York with a very big job. By this time my drinking had become basic, like eating. I put away somewhere between a pint and a fifth a day routinely. This was around 1939 and I hit good times. I got a job with Young and Rubicam. My head got so big, I began to work twelve, fourteen, sixteen hours a day. I was a big shot now. [Laughs.]

But I found to work that way I needed not a pint a day but a quart, just to keep going. All of a sudden, the goddamn thing blew up. I went off my rocker and got hauled off to a bughouse. Of course, it was a very ritzy bughouse. There were wall-to-wall psychiatrists.... I really was bonkers.

Did they treat you for alcoholism in the hospital?

No. They called it manic-depressive syndrome. The first night I was very talkative. So they sat me down and gave me a couple of big belts of henbane/scopolomine.... [When] I got out they said, "We don't know what the hell is wrong with you."

They never thought it might be drinking?

Oh, yeah, they said that whatever is going on, you're drinking too damn much and you shouldn't drink anymore. So I stayed sober for about three weeks. Then I thought, "Well, I'll drink a little, but I won't drink much," so I took one drink a day for thirty days.... I started to drink again. And a year later I'm nuts again. So back to the bughouse.

We didn't spend much time talking this time. Instead they gave me twelve shocks. Shock treatment. [It could] send you into convulsions. In those days they used to loosen joints and break legs. It took five guys to hold you. I had three shocks a week. I remember thinking as I was walking around the grounds, "There's gotta be another way to live." That was horrible.

I think the shock did me some good. It made me take life seriously. That was the first step. This was 1941. Then three months later I'm in AA. I got sober, I loved it. I was still an atheist, but I would get up and mumble the Lord's Prayer.

Was Bill Wilson your sponsor?

Yeah, but not in the first year. I went into this meeting and would see this light surrounding Bill. I would get this tremendous sense of power when he was talking. Afterward, I approached him and said, "I want what you got." And he said, "OK, hang around and talk to me afterward." And we went from there.

I stayed sober for eleven months and then decided I would have what they call a slip. I figured, if it doesn't go well, I'll go back and be a success in AA. The problem was, I couldn't get sober again. Instead of going to two meetings a week, I started going to four meetings a week. I did everything on earth to save my soul.

Were you talking to Wilson during that time?
   Oh, all the time.

Was he frustrated with you?
   Once in a while. [Laughs.] He was a marvelous guy. He and I had ferocious fights, like cats and dogs. He got so tired of me that he would put me over to Lois. I was hospitalized nine times. In the last year, I hit a hospital every six weeks. I finally got sober on October 10, 1946.

What kind of sponsor was Bill Wilson?
   He just kept complaining that none of the people he sponsored ever got sober—which is a fact. [Laughs.]

Did you call him in the middle of the night?
   I usually called Lois because he was very cranky about being called. He was a very faithful and good man as a sponsor.

How many people did he sponsor?
   If you added it up, it's gotta be hundreds.

[To Tom P., Jr.] Do you remember that period?

TOM P., JR.: The very, very end of it. I have a vague memory of Dad's last trip to the hospital. Bill Wilson was riding shotgun. At that point I was six years old. My real memories were the sober years, with people coming in doing Twelve-

Step work. My basic memories were the up times and a lot of sane, happy people around.

How fast did AA grow?

TOM P.: They went from 700 members to 2,000 the year I came in, 1941. Wilson worked himself to death. He was on the road all the time trying to cope with this explosion, out talking to these new groups.

Did he travel with Lois?

Not much. In the very early days he did.

The first four or five years were pretty rough and then after that he made a pretty good living. I was always delighted that they got a comfortable home and an income. What kind of a world is this if you can't take some money off your work?

The basic thing that kept you from getting sober was the God business, right?

Right. I couldn't get it down. It's a peculiar thing—after you have a spiritual experience, you see things in a different way. But then, all of the old stuff washes back. Your whole former self is apt to come back. You just get back into an ordinary mind. Then the spiritual experience begins to look like everybody else sees it—a form of sickness or any overwrought thing.

Sometime in 1946 I got through the God thing, and that's where it turned around.

Can you describe the beliefs of your group here today?

What we used to call All Addicts Anonymous we now call the Lifesavers. All of it is based on the Twelve Steps of AA and Four Absolutes of the Oxford Group; absolute honesty, absolute purity, absolute unselfishness, and absolute love. My son and I started it because we were trying to get our families into the program.

Before the Steps were written, the AA program was the Absolutes, plus a word-of-mouth program which amounted to six steps that Ebby T. had passed to Bill Wilson out of his experience with the Oxford Group. You gotta admit you're licked, you gotta get your life turned over to a Higher Power, you gotta confess your faults, you gotta make restitution, you gotta try to help others. These plus the Absolutes were the program before the Steps were written in 1939.

Your idea was that the Twelve Steps could work for anything. When did you come to this realization?

When I used it to break the drug habit. I saw it work for alcohol. Then I was one of the worst tobacco nuts that ever drew the breath of God. I was a three-pack-a-day man. I couldn't think, I couldn't do anything unless I had a cigarette in my hand.

You quit smoking when you were eight months sober. What did Bill Wilson think about that?

He said, "I wish to hell I could do that." But he died of emphysema. He was a tough old bird, but he went through hell. Emphysema is an ugly way to die. Choke to death slowly over a period of years. And then toward the end you don't choke slowly—it's day and night. The last time I saw him he was in the oxygen tent.

So you used the Twelve Steps to quit smoking?

You betcha! That was the start of All Addicts Anonymous, which we now call Lifesavers. We then called it the Nut Club.

TOM P., JR.: Along about when I was graduating from high school and going on to college, I was interested in applying these principles in Alateen, which was just getting started. A couple of guys who were not alcoholic were also interested. There was one guy who was anxiety ridden, another who was depressive, then me who was just a teenage person looking to work the program. We started having meetings once a week that were like AA; it was the Twelve Steps for everybody. That was the Nut Club. We weren't working the Absolutes specifically at this point.

It evolved very slowly because we weren't interested in building a big movement. We were interested in providing a resource for people who weren't alcoholics but who had various addictions and wanted a life change.

When we moved here in 1961 we got this piece of land up in the country. We had this idea that we wanted to live a simple life, close to nature and to practice the AA principles, and to make that available for people who want to come and get some of it.

In September of 1964 we opened the doors of East Ridge, initially as a place for drunks to come and learn the basics of the AA program. It became a community. When we started we let the drunks smoke, and we let them drink coffee, and we let them eat sugar and apple pie for dessert and meatloaf for dinner. The whole nine yards.

How many people do you have here altogether?

TOM P.: About fifty. A couple of times a week we have a program meeting.

At the beginning we had a lot of recovering alcoholics going through here—it was like a drying out place. And then the government got involved and established a lot of standard treatment places, moving from the spiritual model to the medical model. We changed our focus rather than go to the medical model.

You had to conform to these secular norms. That isn't basically what AA was about to us. So we simply changed our incorporation. We were incorporated as an educational facility originally. We became a religion incorporated in the state of New York. We are a religion to this day in the same way that Methodists are, or Episcopalians. We do everything they do. We marry people. We baptize people.

We call it The Queen's Work. We got the name from Father Ed Dowling, who was Bill Wilson's sponsor. When he died, we picked up the name.

What does it mean?

Holy Wisdom. Holy Wisdom is a person, a female. She's the first creature that God made. It's all in the Book of Proverbs.

We also run a number of businesses here. Land development, the type of development that protects the environment. We're involved in organic foods. We grow some, and we're very interested in providing organic fish and organic foods that are not contaminated.

A lot us eat meat, but in a sort of kosher way. We have it in concentrated form like in food supplements. But you won't see people just eating hamburger around here.

There are a lot of requirements to live in this community. If someone lights up a cigarette he's broken a rule of this community.

This is a real community, based on the Twelve Steps and the Four Absolutes. It's worked out quite well. This thing from the beginning was an experiment—AA for everybody, for the children, people living together and putting it into a community and making it a whole life.

APPENDIX C

Alcoholics Anonymous

Freed Slaves of Drink, Now They Free Others

by Jack Alexander

Three men sat around the bed of an alcoholic patient in the psychopathic ward of Philadelphia General Hospital one afternoon a few weeks ago. The man in the bed, who was a complete stranger to them, had the drawn and slightly stupid look that inebriates get while being defogged after a bender. The only thing that was noteworthy about the callers, except for the obvious contrast between their well-groomed appearances and that of the patient, was the fact that each had been through the defogging process many times himself. They were members of Alcoholics Anonymous, a band of ex-problem drinkers who made an avocation of helping other alcoholics to beat the liquor habit.

The man in the bed was a mechanic. His visitors had been educated at Princeton, Yale and Pennsylvania and were, by occupation, a salesman, a lawyer and a publicity man. Less than a year before one had been in shackles in the same ward. One of his companions had been what is known among alcoholics as a sanitarium commuter. He had moved from place to place, bedeviling the staffs of the country's leading institutions for the treatment of alcoholics. The other had spent twenty years of life, all outside institution walls, making life miserable for himself, and his family and his employers, as

(continued on p. 302)

300

"They know what it is to have a hand
so shaky a towel must be used in this
fashion to get a glass to the mouth."

This picture appeared on the first page of the famous
Jack Alexander article on Alcoholics Anonymous
(see facing page) that ran in the *Saturday Evening
Post* on March 1, 1941, and triggered the worldwide
growth of AA.

well as sundry well-meaning relatives who had had the temerity to intervene.

The air of the ward was thick with the aroma of paraldehyde, an unpleasant cocktail smelling like a mixture of alcohol and ether which hospitals sometimes use to taper off the paralyzed drinker and soothe his squirming nerves. The visitors seemed oblivious of this and of the depressing atmosphere that clings to even the nicest of psychopathic wards. They smoked and talked with the patient for twenty minutes or so, then left their personal cards and departed. If the man in the bed felt that he would like to see one of them again, they told him, he had only to put in a telephone call.

They made it plain that if he actually wanted to stop drinking, they would leave their work or get up in the middle of the night to hurry to where he was. If he did not choose to call, that would be the end of it. The members of Alcoholics Anonymous do not pursue or coddle a malingering prospect and they know the strange tricks of the alcoholic as a reformed swindler knows the art of bamboozling.

Herein lies much of the unique strength of a movement which, in the past six years, has brought recovery to around 2000 men and women, a large percentage of whom had been considered medically hopeless. Doctors and clergymen, working separately or together, have always managed to salvage a few cases. In isolated instances, drinkers have found their own methods of quitting. But the inroads into alcoholism have been negligible and it remains one of the great unsolved public-health enigmas.

By nature touchy and suspicious, the alcoholic likes to be left alone to work out his puzzle, and he has a convenient way of ignoring the tragedy which he inflicts meanwhile upon those who are close to him. He holds desperately to a conviction that, although he has not been able to handle alcohol in the past, he will ultimately succeed in becoming a controlled drinker. One of medicine's queerest animals, he is, as often as not, an acutely intelligent person. He fences with professional men and relatives who attempt to aid him and he gets a perverse satisfaction out of tripping them up in argument.

There is no specious excuse for drinking which the trouble shooters of Alcoholics Anonymous have not heard or used themselves. When one of their prospects hands them a rationalization for getting soused, they match it with half a dozen out of their own experiences. This upsets him a little and he gets defensive. He looks at their neat clothing and smoothly shaved faces and charges them with being goody-goodies who don't know what it is to struggle with drink. They reply by relating their own stories—the double Scotches and brandies before breakfast; the vague feeling of discomfort which precedes a drinking bout; the awakening from a spree without being able to account for the actions of several days and the haunting fear that possibly they had run down someone with their automobiles.

They tell of the eight-ounce bottles of gin hidden behind pictures and in caches from cellar to attic; of spending whole days in motion-picture houses to stave off the temptation to drink; of sneaking out of the office for quickies during the day. They talk of losing jobs and stealing money from their wives' purses; of putting pepper into whiskey to give it a tang; of tippling on bitters and sedative tablets, or on mouthwash or hair tonic; of getting into the habit of camping outside the neighborhood tavern ten minutes before opening time. They describe a hand so jittery that it could not lift a pony to the lips without spilling the contents; of drinking liquor from a beer stein because it can be steadied with two hands, although at the risk of chipping a front tooth; of tying an end of a towel about a glass, looping the towel around the back of the neck and drawing the free end with the other hand, pulley fashion, to advance the glass to the mouth; of hands so shaky they feel as if they were about to snap off and fly into space; of sitting on hands for hours to keep them from doing this.

These and other bits of drinking lore usually manage to convince the alcoholic that he is talking to blood brothers. A bridge of confidence is thereby erected, spanning a gap which has baffled the physician, the minister, the priest or the hapless relatives. Over this connection, the trouble shooters convey, bit by bit, the details of a program for living which has worked for them and which, they feel, can work for any other alcoholic. They concede as out of their orbit only those who are psychotic or who are already suffering from the physical impairment known as wet brain. At the same time they see to it that the prospect gets whatever medical attention is needed.

Many doctors and staffs of institutions throughout the country now suggest Alcoholics Anonymous to their drinking patients. In some towns the courts and probation officers cooperate with the local group. In a few city psychopathic divisions the workers of Alcoholics Anonymous are accorded the same visiting privileges as staff members. Philadelphia General is one of these. Dr. John F. Stouffer, the chief psychiatrist, says: "The alcoholics we get here are mostly those who cannot afford private treatment, and this is by far the greatest thing we have ever been able to offer them. Even among those who occasionally land back in here again we observe a profound change in personality. You would hardly recognize them."

The Illinois Medical Journal, in an editorial last December, went farther than Doctor Stouffer, in stating: "It is indeed a miracle when a person who for years has been more or less constantly under the influence of alcohol and in whom his friends have lost all confidence, will sit up all night with a 'drunk' and at stated intervals administer a small amount of liquor in accordance with a doctor's order without taking a drop himself."

This is a reference to a common aspect of the Arabian Nights' adventures to which Alcoholics Anonymous workers dedicate themselves. Often it involves sitting upon, as well as up with, the intoxicated person, as the impulse to jump out a window seems to be an attractive one to many alcoholics when in their cups. Only an alcoholic can squat on another alcoholic's chest for hours with the proper combination of discipline and sympathy.

During a recent trip around the East and Middle West I met and talked with scores of A.A.'s, as they call themselves, and found them to be unusually calm, tolerant people. Somehow they seemed better integrated than the average group of non-alcoholic individuals. Their transformation from cop fighters, canned-heat drinkers and, in some instances, wife beaters, was startling. On one of the most influential newspapers in the country I found that the city editor, the assistant city editor and a nationally known reporter were A.A.'s, and strong in the confidence of their publisher.

In another city I heard a judge parole a drunken driver to an A.A. member. The latter, during his drinking days, had smashed several cars and had had his own operator's license suspended. The judge knew him and was glad to trust him. A brilliant executive of an advertising firm disclosed that two years ago he had been panhandling and sleeping in a doorway under an elevated structure. He had a favorite doorway, which he shared with other vagrants, and every few weeks he goes back and pays them a visit just to assure himself he isn't dreaming.

In Akron, as in other manufacturing centers, the groups include a heavy element of manual workers. In the Cleveland Athletic Club I had luncheon with five lawyers, an accountant, an engineer, three salesmen, an insurance man, a buyer, a bartender, a chain-store manager, a manager of an independent store and a manufacturer's representative. They were members of a central committee which co-ordinates the work of nine neighborhood groups. Cleveland, with more than 450 members, is the biggest of the A.A. centers. The next largest are located in Chicago, Akron, Philadelphia, Los Angeles, Washington, and New York. All told, there are groups in about fifty cities and towns.

In discussing their work, the A.A.'s spoke of their drunk-rescuing as "insurance" for themselves. Experience within the group has shown, they said, that once a recovered drinker slows up in this work he is likely to go back to drinking, himself. There is, they agreed, no such thing as an ex-alcoholic. If one is an alcoholic—that is, a person who is unable to drink normally—one remains an alcoholic until he dies, just as a diabetic remains a diabetic. The best he can hope for is to become an arrested case, with drunksaving as his insulin. At least, the A.A.'s say so, and medical opinion tends to support them. All but a few said that they had lost all desire for alcohol. Most serve liquor in their homes when friends drop in and they still go to bars with companions who drink. The A.A.'s tipple on soft drinks and coffee.

One, a sales manager, acts as bartender at his company's annual jamboree in Atlantic City and spends his nights tucking the celebrators into their beds. Only a few of those who recover fail to lose the feeling that at any minute they may thoughtlessly take one drink and skyrocket off on a disastrous binge. An A.A. who is a clerk in an Eastern city hasn't had a snifter in three and a half years, but says that he still has to walk fast past saloons to circumvent the old impulse; but he is an exception. The only hang-over from the wild days that plagues the A.A. is a recurrent nightmare. In the dream, he finds himself off on a rousing whooper-dooper, frantically trying to conceal his condition from the community. Even this symptom disappears shortly, in most cases. Surprisingly, the rate of employment among these people, who formerly drank themselves out of job after job, is said to be around 90 per cent.

One-hundred-per-cent effectiveness with non-psychotic drinkers who sincerely want to quit is claimed by the workers of Alcoholics Anonymous. The program will not work, they add, with those who only "want to want to quit," or who want to quit because they are afraid of losing their families or their jobs. The effective desire, they state, must be based upon enlightened self-interest; the applicant must want to get away from liquor to head off incarceration or premature death. He must be fed up with the stark social loneliness which engulfs the uncontrolled drinker and he must want to put some order into his bungled life.

As it is impossible to disqualify all borderline applicants, the working percentage of recovery falls below the 100-per-cent mark. According to A.A. estimation, 50 per cent of the alcoholics taken in hand recover almost immediately; 25 per cent get well after suffering a relapse or two, and the rest remain doubtful. This rate of success is exceptionally high. Statistics on traditional medical and religious cures are lacking, but it has been informally estimated that they are no more than 2 or 3 per cent effective on run-of-the-mine cases.

Although it is too early to state that Alcoholics Anonymous is the definitive answer to alcoholism, its brief record is impressive and it is receiving hopeful support. John D. Rockefeller, Jr., helped defray the expense of getting it started and has gone out of his way to get other prominent men interested.

Rockefeller's gift was a small one, in deference to the insistence of the originators that the movement be kept on a voluntary, non-paid basis. There are no salaried organizers, no dues, no officers and no central control. Locally, the rents of assembly halls are met by passing the hat at meetings. In small communities no collections are taken, as the gatherings are held in private homes. A small office in downtown New York acts merely as a clearinghouse for information. There is no name on the door and mail is received anonymously through a post office box. The only income, which is money received from the sale of a book describing the work, is handled by The Alcoholic Foundation, a board composed of three alcoholics and four non-alcoholics.

In Chicago twenty-five doctors work hand in hand with Alcoholics Anonymous, contributing their services and referring their own alcoholic patients to the group, which now numbers around 200. The same co-operation exists in Cleveland and to a lesser degree in other centers. A physician, Dr. W. D. Silkworth, of New York City, gave the movement its first encouragement. However, many doctors remain skeptical. Dr. Foster Kennedy, an eminent New York neurologist, probably had these in mind when he stated at a meeting a year ago: "The aim of those concerned in this effort against alcoholism is high, their success has been considerable and I believe medical men of good will should aid."

The active help of two medical men of good will, Drs. A. Wiese Hammer and C. Dudley Saul, has assisted greatly in making the Philadelphia unit one of the more effective of the younger groups. The movement there had its beginning in an offhand way in February, 1940, when a business man who was an A.A. convert was transferred to Philadelphia from New York. Fearful of backsliding for lack of rescue work, the newcomer rounded up three local bar flies and started to work on them. He got them dry and the quartet began ferreting out other cases. By last December fifteenth, ninety-nine alcoholics had joined up. Of these, eighty-six were now total abstainers—thirty-nine from one to three months, seventeen from three to six months, and twenty-five from six to ten months. Five who had joined the unit after having belonged in other cities had been nondrinkers from one to three years.

At the other end of the time scale, Akron, which cradled the movement, holds the intramural record for sustained abstinence. According to a recent checkup, two members have been riding the A.A. wagon for five and a half years, one for five years, three for four and a half years, one for the same period with one skid, three for three and a half years with one skid each, one for two and a half years and thirteen for two years. Previously, most of the Akronites and Philadelphians had been unable to stay away from liquor for longer than a few weeks.

In the Middle West the work has been almost exclusively among persons who have not arrived at the institutional stage. The New York group, which has a similar nucleus, makes a sideline specialty of committed cases and has achieved striking results. In the summer of 1939 the group began working on the alcoholics confined in Rockland State Hospital, at Orangeburg, a vast mental sanitarium which gets the hopeless alcoholic backwash of the big population centers. With the encouragement of Dr. R. E. Blaisdell, the medical superintendent, a unit was formed within the walls and meetings were held in the recreation hall. New York A.A.'s went to Orangeburg to give talks and on Sunday evenings the patients were brought in state-owned buses to a clubhouse which the Manhattan group rents on the West Side.

Last July first, eleven months later, records kept at the hospital showed that of fifty-four patients released to Alcoholics Anonymous, seventeen had had no relapse and fourteen others had had only one. Of the rest, nine had gone back to drinking in their home communities, twelve had returned to the hospital and two had not been traced. Doctor Blaisdell has written favorably about the work to the State Department of

Mental Hygiene and he praised it officially in his last annual report.

Even better results were obtained in two public institutions in New Jersey, Greystone Park and Overbrook, which attracts patients of better economic and social background than Rockland, because of their nearness to prosperous suburban villages. Of seven patients released from the Greystone Park institution in two years, five have abstained for periods of one to two years, according to A.A. records. Eight of ten released from Overbrook have abstained for about the same length of time. The others have had from one to several relapses.

Why some people become alcoholics is a question on which authorities disagree. Few think that anyone is "born an alcoholic." One may be born, they say, with a hereditary predisposition to alcoholism, just as one may be born with a vulnerability to tuberculosis. The rest seems to depend upon environment and experience, although one theory has it that some people are allergic to alcohol, as hayfever sufferers are to pollens. Only one note is found to be common to all alcoholics—emotional immaturity. Closely related to this is an observation that an unusually large number of alcoholics start out in life as an only child, as a youngest child, as the only boy in a family of girls or the only girl in a family of boys. Many have records of childhood precocity and were what are known as spoiled children.

Frequently the situation is complicated by an off-center home atmosphere in which one parent is unduly cruel, the other overindulgent. Any combination of these factors, plus a divorce or two tends to produce neurotic children who are poorly equipped emotionally to face the ordinary realities of adult life. In seeking escapes, one may immerse himself in his business, working twelve to fifteen hours a day, or in sports or in some artistic side line. Another finds what he thinks is a pleasant escape in drink. It bolsters his opinion of himself and temporarily wipes away any feeling of social inferiority which he may have. Light drinking leads to heavy drinking. Friends and family are alienated and employers become disgusted. The drinker smolders with resentment and wallows in self-pity. He indulges in childish rationalizations to justify his drinking—he has been working hard and he deserves to relax, his throat hurts from an old tonsillectomy and a drink would ease the pain, he has a headache, his wife does not understand him, his nerves are jumpy, everybody is against him, and so on and on. He unconsciously becomes a chronic excuse maker for himself.

All the time he is drinking he tells himself, and those who butt into his affairs, that he can really become a controlled drinker if he wants to. To demonstrate his strength of will, he goes for weeks without taking a drop. He makes a point of calling at his favorite bar at a certain time each day and ostentatiously sipping milk or a carbonated beverage, not realizing that he is indulging in juvenile exhibitionism. Falsely encouraged, he shifts to a routine of one beer a day, and that is the beginning of the end once more. Beer leads inevitably to more beer and then to hard liquor. Hard liquor leads to another first-rate bender. Oddly, the trigger which sets off the explosion is as apt to be a stroke of business success as it is to be a run of bad luck. An alcoholic can stand neither prosperity nor adversity.

The victim is puzzled on coming out of the alcoholic fog. Without his being aware of any change, a habit had gradually become an obsession. After a while, he no longer needs his rationalizations to justify the fatal first drink. All he knows is that he feels swamped by uneasiness or elation, and before he realizes what is happening he is standing at a bar with an empty whiskey pony in front of him and a stimulating sensation in his throat. By some peculiar quirk of his mind, he has been able to draw a curtain over the memory of the intense pain and remorse caused by preceding stemwinders. After many experiences of this kind, the alcoholic begins to realize that he does not understand himself; he wonders whether his power of will, though strong in other fields, isn't defenseless against alcohol. He may go on trying to defeat his obsession and wind up in a sanitarium. He may give up the fight as hopeless and try to kill himself. Or he may seek outside help.

If he applies to Alcoholics Anonymous, he is first brought around to admit that alcohol has him whipped and that his life has become unmanageable. Having achieved this state of intellectual humility, he is given a dose of religion in its broadest sense. He is asked to believe in a Power that is greater than himself, or at least to keep an open mind on that subject while he goes on with the rest of the program. Any concept of the higher Power is acceptable. A skeptic or agnostic may choose to think of his Inner Self, the miracle of growth, a tree, man's wonderment at the physical universe, the structure of the atom or mere mathematical infinity. Whatever form is visualized, the neophyte is taught that he must rely upon it and, in his own way, to pray to the Power for strength.

He next makes a sort of moral inventory of himself with the private aid of another person—one of his A.A. sponsors, a priest, a minister, a psychiatrist, or anyone else he fancies. If it gives him any relief, he may get up at a meeting and recite his misdeeds, but he is not required to do so. He restores what he may have stolen while intoxicated and arranges to pay off old debts and to make good on rubber checks; he makes amends to persons he has abused and, in general, cleans up his past as well as he is able to. It is not uncommon for his sponsors to lend him money to help out in the early stages.

This catharsis is regarded as important because of the compulsion which a feeling of guilt exerts in the alcoholic obsession. As nothing tends to push an alcoholic toward the bottle more than personal resentments, the pupil also makes out a list of his grudges and resolves not to be stirred by them. At this point he is ready to start working on other active alcoholics. By the process of extroversion, which the work entails, he is able to think less of his own troubles.

The more drinkers he succeeds in swinging into Alcoholics Anonymous, the greater his responsibility to the group becomes. He can't get drunk now without injuring the people who have proved themselves his best friends. He is beginning to grow up emotionally and to quit being a leaner. If raised in an orthodox church he usually, but not always, becomes a regular communicant again.

Simultaneously with the making over of the alcoholic goes the process of adjusting his family to his new way of living. The wife or husband of an alcoholic, and the children, too, frequently become neurotics from being exposed to drinking excesses over a period of years. Re-education of the family is an essential part of a follow-up program which has been devised.

Alcoholics Anonymous, which is a synthesis of old ideas rather than a new discovery, owes its existence to the collaboration of a New York stockbroker and an Akron physician. Both alcoholics, they met for the first time a little less than six years ago. In thirty-five years of periodic drinking, Doctor Armstrong, to give the physician a fictitious name, had drunk himself out of most of his practice. Armstrong had tried everything, including the Oxford Group, and had shown no improvement. On Mother's Day, 1935, he staggered home, in typical drunk fashion, lugging an expensive potted plant, which he placed in his wife's lap. Then he went upstairs and passed out.

At that moment, nervously pacing the lobby of an Akron hotel, was the broker from New York, whom we shall arbitrarily call Griffith. Griffith was in a jam. In an attempt to obtain control of a company and rebuild his financial fences,

he had come out to Akron and engaged in a fight for prox-
ies. He had lost the fight. His hotel bill was unpaid. He was
almost flat broke. Griffith wanted a drink.

During his career in Wall Street, Griffith had turned some
sizeable deals and had prospered, but, through ill-timed
drinking bouts, had lost out on his main chances. Five months
before coming to Akron he had gone on the water wagon,
through the ministrations of the Oxford Group in New York.
Fascinated by the problem of alcoholism, he had many times
gone back as a visitor to a Central Park West detoxicating
hospital, where he had been a patient, and talked to the in-
mates. He effected no recoveries, but found that by working
on other alcoholics he could stave off his own craving.

A stranger in Akron, Griffith knew no alcoholics with whom
he could wrestle. A church directory, which hung in the lobby
opposite the bar, gave him an idea. He telephoned one of the
clergymen listed and through him got in touch with a member of the local Oxford Group. This person was a friend of
Doctor Armstrong's and was able to introduce the physician
and the broker at dinner. In this matter Doctor Armstrong became Griffith's first real disciple. He was a shaky one, at first.
After a few weeks of abstinence, he went East to a medical
convention and came home in a liquid state. Griffith, who
had stayed in Akron to iron out some legal tangles arising
from the proxy battle, talked him back to sobriety. That was
on June 10, 1935. The nips the physician took from a bottle
proffered by Griffith on that day were the last drinks he ever
took.

Griffith's lawsuits dragged on, holding him over in Akron
for six months. He moved his baggage to the Armstrong
home, and together the pair struggled with other alcoholics.
Before Griffith went back to New York, two more Akron converts had been obtained. Meanwhile, both Griffith and Doctor
Armstrong had withdrawn from the Oxford Group, because

they felt that its aggressive evangelism and some of its other methods were hindrances in working with alcoholics. They put their own technique on a strict take-it-or-leave-it basis and kept it there.

Progress was slow. After Griffith had returned East, Doctor Armstrong and his wife, a Wellesley graduate, converted their home into a free refuge for alcoholics and an experimental laboratory for the study of the guests' behavior. One of the guests, who, unknown to his hosts, was a manic depressive as well as an alcoholic, ran wild one night with a kitchen knife. He was overcome before he had stabbed anyone. After a year and a half, a total of ten persons had responded to the program and were abstaining. What was left of the family savings had gone into the work. The physician's new sobriety caused a revival in his practice, but not enough of one to carry the extra expense. The Armstrongs, nevertheless, carried on, on borrowed money. Griffith, who had a Spartan wife, too, turned his Brooklyn home into a duplicate of the Akron ménage. Mrs. Griffith, a member of an old Brooklyn family, took a job in a department store and in her spare time played nurse to inebriates. The Griffiths also borrowed, and Griffith managed to make odd bits of money around the brokerage houses. By the spring of 1939 the Armstrongs and the Griffiths had between them cozened about one hundred alcoholics into sobriety.

In a book which they published at that time the recovered drinkers described the cure program and related their personal stories. The title was Alcoholics Anonymous. It was adopted as a name for the movement itself, which up to then had none. As the book got into circulation, the movement spread rapidly.

Today, Doctor Armstrong is still struggling to patch up his practice. The going is hard. He is in debt because of his contributions to the movement and the time he devotes gratis to alcoholics. Being a pivotal man in the group, he is unable to turn down the requests for help which flood his office.

Griffith is even deeper in the hole. For the past two years he and his wife have had no home in the ordinary sense of the word. In a manner reminiscent of the primitive Christians they have moved about, finding shelter in the homes of A.A. colleagues and sometimes wearing borrowed clothing.

Having got something started, both the prime movers want to retire to the fringe of their movement and spend more time getting back on their feet financially. They feel that the way the thing is set up it is virtually self-operating and self-multiplying. Because of the absence of figureheads and the fact that there is no formal body of belief to promote, they have no fears that Alcoholics Anonymous will degenerate into a cult.

The self-starting nature of the movement is apparent from letters in the files of the New York office. Many persons have written in saying that they stopped drinking as soon as they read the book, and made their homes meeting places for small local chapters. Even a fairly large unit, in Little Rock, got started in this way. An Akron civil engineer and his wife, in gratitude for his cure four years ago, have been steadily taking alcoholics into their home. Out of thirty-five such wards, thirty-one have recovered.

Twenty pilgrims from Cleveland caught the idea in Akron and returned home to start a group of their own. From Cleveland, by various means, the movement has spread to Chicago, Detroit, St. Louis, Los Angeles, Indianapolis, Atlanta, San Francisco, Evansville and other cities. An alcoholic Cleveland newspaperman with a surgically collapsed lung moved to Houston for his health. He got a job on a Houston paper and through a series of articles which he wrote for it started an A.A. unit which now has thirty-five members. One Houston member has moved to Miami and is now laboring to snare some of the more eminent winter-colony lushes. A Cleveland traveling salesman is responsible for starting small units in many different parts of the country. Fewer than half of the A.A. members have ever seen Griffith or Doctor Armstrong.

To an outsider who is mystified, as most of us are, by the antics of problem drinking friends, the results which have been achieved are amazing. This is especially true of the more virulent cases, a few of which are herewith sketched under names that are not their own.

Sarah Martin was a product of the F. Scott Fitzgerald era. Born of wealthy parents in a Western city, she went to Eastern boarding schools and "finished" in France. After making her debut she married. Sarah spent her nights drinking and dancing until daylight. She was known as a girl who could carry a lot of liquor. Her husband had a weak stomach and she became disgusted with him. They were quickly divorced. After her father's fortune had been erased in 1929, Sarah got a job in New York and supported herself. In 1932, seeking adventure, she went to Paris to live and set up a business of her own, which was successful. She continued to drink heavily and stayed drunk longer than usual. After a spree in 1933 she was informed that she had tried to throw herself out a window. During another bout she did jump, or fall—she doesn't remember which—out of a first-floor window. She landed face first on the sidewalk and was laid up for six months of bonesetting, dental work and plastic surgery.

In 1936 Sarah Martin decided that if she changed her environment by returning to the United States, she would be able to drink normally. This childish faith in geographical change is a classic delusion which all alcoholics get at one time or another. She was drunk all the way home on the boat. New York frightened her and she drank to escape it. Her money ran out and she borrowed from friends. When the friends cut her, she hung around Third Avenue bars cadging drinks from strangers. Up to this point, she had diagnosed her trouble as a nervous breakdown. Not until she had committed herself to several sanitariums did she realize, through reading, that she was an alcoholic. On advice of a staff doctor, she got in touch with an Alcoholics Anonymous group. Today she has another good job and spends many of her nights sitting on hysterical women drinkers to prevent them from diving out of windows. In her late thirties Sarah Martin is an attractively serene woman. The Paris surgeons did handsomely by her.

Watkins is a shipping clerk in a factory. Injured in an elevator mishap in 1927, he was furloughed with pay by a company which was thankful that he did not sue for damages. Having nothing to do during a long convalescence, Watkins loafed in speak-easies. Formerly a moderate drinker, he started to go on drunks lasting several months. His furniture went for debt and his wife fled, taking their three children. In eleven years, Watkins was arrested twelve times and served eight workhouse sentences. Once, in an attack of delirium tremens, he circulated a rumor among the prisoners that the county was poisoning the food in order to reduce the workhouse population and save expenses. A mess-hall riot resulted. In another fit of D.T.'s, during which he thought the man in the cell above was trying to pour hot lead on him, Watkins slashed his own wrists and throat with a razor blade. While recuperating in an outside hospital, with eighty-six stitches, he swore never to drink again. He was drunk before the final bandages were removed. Two years ago a former drinking companion got him into Alcoholics Anonymous and he hasn't touched liquor since. His wife and children have returned and the home has new furniture. Back at work, Watkins has paid off the major part of $2000 in debts and petty alcoholic thefts and has his eye on a new automobile.

At twenty-two, Tracy, a precocious son of well-to-do parents, was a credit manager for an investment-banking firm whose name has become a symbol of the money-mad 20's. After the firm's collapse during the stockmarket crash, he went into advertising and worked up to a post which paid him $23,000 a year. On the day his son was born Tracy was fired. Instead of appearing in Boston to close a big advertising contract, he had gone on a spree and had wound up in Chicago, losing out on the contract. Always a heavy drinker, Tracy became a bum. He tippled on canned heat and hair tonic and begged from cops, who are always easy touches for amounts up to a dime. On one sleety night Tracy sold his shoes to buy a drink, putting on a pair of rubbers he had found in a doorway and stuffing them with paper to keep his feet warm.

He started committing himself to sanitariums, more to get in out of the cold than anything else. In one institution, a physician got him interested in the A.A. program. As part of it, Tracy, a Catholic, made a general confession and returned to the church, which he had long since abandoned. He skidded back to alcohol a few times, but after a relapse in February, 1939, Tracy took no more drinks. He has since then beat his way up again to $18,000 a year in advertising.

Victor Hugo would have delighted in Brewster, a heavy-thewed adventurer who took life the hard way. Brewster was a lumberjack, cow hand and wartime aviator. During the post-war era he took up flask-toting and was soon doing a Cook's tour of the sanitariums. In one of them, after hearing about shock cures, he bribed the Negro attendant in the morgue, with gifts of cigarettes, to permit him to drop in each afternoon and meditate over a cadaver. The plan worked well until one day he came upon a dead man who, by a freak of facial contortion, wore what looked like a grin. Brewster met up with the A.A.'s in December 1938, and after achieving abstinence got a sales job which involved much walking. Meanwhile, he had got cataracts on both eyes. One was removed, giving him distance sight with the aid of thick-lens spectacles. He used the other eye for close-up vision, keeping it dilated with an eye-drop solution in order to avoid being run down in traffic. Then he developed a swollen, or milk, leg. With these disabilities, Brewster tramped the streets for six months before he caught up with his drawing account. Today at fifty, and still hampered by his physical handicaps, he is making his calls and is earning around $400 a month.

For the Brewsters, the Martins, the Watkinses, the Tracys and the other reformed alcoholics, congenial company is now available wherever they happen to be. In the larger cities A.A.'s meet one another daily at lunch in favored restaurants. The Cleveland groups give big parties on New Year's and other holidays at which gallons of coffee and soft drinks are consumed. Chicago holds open house on Friday, Saturday and Sunday—alternately, on the North, West and South Sides—so that no lonesome A.A. need revert to liquor over the weekend for lack of companionship. Some play cribbage or bridge, the winner of each hand contributing to a kitty for paying off entertainment expenses. The others listen to the radio, dance, eat or just talk. All alcoholics, drunk or sober, like to gab. They are among the most society-loving people in the world, which may help to explain why they got to be alcoholics in the first place.

Notes

1n. The question has long been debated whether the freedom from alcohol addiction which occurs for example in Alcoholics Anonymous is really a cure, since the person must abstain from alcohol in order to maintain his recovery, and whether such an event had not better be called an "arrest" of the disease. The view of your present authors is that *cure* is a perfectly good word for what happens to anyone who is successful in AA. If a man who once had stomach ulcers is now totally free of them, and free of all signs and symptoms of them, but has to abstain from pepper and vinegar in order to stay well, we say that that man has been cured of his stomach ulcers, and that the recovered alcohol addict is in exactly the same case.

2n. If you are an early-stage addict, or a genteel and well-bred addict, or perhaps a refined lady addict, who resents being addressed as an addict—greetings! Several of your authors were "cultured" or "high-class" or "unusual" addicts who wasted precious years hiding behind that kind of garbage while their addictions steadily dragged them deeper and deeper into the swamp. If you know you are an addict —nay, if you even faintly suspect it—the very first step toward deliverance is to get down off your high horse, start calling your trouble by its right name, and get used to the crude manners and forthright speech of your fellow addicts. For it is among them that you will find your salvation—nowhere else.

3n. *Fermented* alcoholic beverages—wines, beers, ales, meads, etc.— have been generally and liberally used by almost every human culture on earth from the earliest times right on through to the present. They contain from 3 to 15 percent alcohol. Beers average around 5 percent, wines around 12. You can certainly get drunk on these beverages, but it takes a lot of guzzling to do so. To get drunk and stay drunk, or to keep yourself half-swacked most of the time, the way a modern alcoholic does, is much more easily done with a higher concentration of alcohol in the beverage, and this is precisely what *distilled spirits* provide. Distilled liquors—whiskey, brandy, gin, etc. —contain from 35 to 50 percent alcohol, averaging around 40 percent. You can *maintain* states of inebriety for long periods of time with these liquors without overloading the stomach, thus greatly facilitating the development of addiction. A modern man can become alcoholic on wine or beer, but almost none of the earlier peoples seem to have done so. Most of our winos drink "fortified" wines, that is, wines that have been laced with spirits to increase alcohol content to between 16 and 23 percent. And a *very* large majority of modern alcoholics are high-proof boozers: users of distilled spirits.

4n. This statement of the origin of distilled spirits is based on Berton Roueché's researches, but there is wide disagreement on the point among various authorities. A ninth-century Arabian origin of distillation has been challenged on grounds that the equipment of the time probably would have been unable to produce condensation of ethyl alcohol. An eleventh-century Italian origin of alcohol distilled from wine has been suggested instead. (The distillation of ethyl alcohol unadulterated by water is later still: 1796.) Some authorities point to primitive distillation in the Orient of liquors based on rice or millet. One thing is certain: there was no large-scale production of distilled spirits until modern times.

5n. It was not until a hundred years after the discovery of America that opium smoking, the vice of the Far East, initially came upon the human scene. The use of the poppy goes back to time immemorial, but the vice of opium smoking, the addiction, does not make its debut until the 1600s, first emerging as a terrible problem in China sometime after the middle of the seventeenth century. It is a historical fact that narcotics addiction was forced upon the Oriental world by pressure of Western nations who stood to profit from the drug traffic. Originating in Java, opium smoking was brought to the Chinese mainland, where it spread rapidly. The danger to the nation was recognized by the Chinese authorities, who tried to meet it by banning the sale of opium and the opening of opium-smoking houses. These prohibitions, however, were generally ignored, and as the eighteenth century progressed foreign traders discovered in China a booming and highly profitable market for the drug. In 1799 the alarmed Chinese government reacted with more urgent measures, prohibiting the native cultivation of the opium poppy and all import of opium. The result was a very weird historical situation. Efforts to enforce the import restrictions on opium brought the Chinese government into direct conflict with the British government, leading to the first Opium War of 1839–42. After being put down in that fight, the Chinese still refused to legalize the opium trade until, after further war, they were *compelled* to do so in 1858.

6n. The National Council on Alcoholism is the principal privately funded information organization in the alcoholism field. NCA is characterized by one outstanding peculiarity: while proclaiming that alcoholism is a disease, the council is very careful never to make any negative statements concerning alcohol as a beverage. This is as if the American Cancer Society were to express no opinion on nicotine or the American Heart Association no opinion on cholesterol. NCA's literature on alcoholism expounds at length on social costs and "modes of treatment," but it is mute on the harmful aspects of alcohol as a social beverage.

Governor Shafer's National Commission of Marijuana and Drug Abuse,[25] which reported to the president in March 1973, made the kind of relevant and needed statement which NCA has never made in its thirty-year history. The Commission called for *public acknowledgement by the liquor industry* that "compulsive use of alcohol is the most destructive drug-use pattern in this nation," and called also for research by the liquor industry into the relation between drinking and traffic accidents, violent crime, and domestic discord.

It made some sense for Alcoholics Anonymous as an organization to stay out of controversy about the use and abuse of alcohol and to concentrate on the recovery of alcoholics, but it made no sense at all for NCA to set up in business as an *information* agency and then sedulously fail to supply any information on the negative aspects of alcohol as a social beverage. With AA and NCA—the two most directly concerned organized groups in the country—devoted to a policy of silence, the liquor industry has been free for forty years since the end of Prohibition to promote the joys of drinking as if alcohol were nectar ambrosia. Among the industry's recent moves along this line is the massive use of television for the introduction and hard-sell of new, sweet, fortified wines to the youth market, now said to be turning from other drugs back to alcohol.

NCA has often been criticized by professionals in the alcoholism field for being a sort of handmaiden of Alcoholics Anonymous. (It was founded by AAs in the first place.) As a result, NCA officials have bent over backwards to prove that their purpose was *not* to promote AA to the general public. They have gone so far that their literature hardly mentions Alcoholics Anonymous. It would seem a much fairer criticism of NCA today to say that it is a sort of hand-maiden of the liquor industry. That industry (around $24 billion in annual sales) certainly is benefited by having it widely believed that alcohol abuse is mainly a disease from which a relatively few unfortunates suffer and which no one else need worry about—and by having it widely believed that this disease is "treatable," so that even the unfortunates will shortly get well.

The fact is that at least 10 percent of all drinkers become compulsive drinkers, that is, alcoholics. And the number of dependent drinkers (incipient alcoholics) has been estimated by some authorities to run as high as *one out of every four drinkers.* The fact is that the more drinkers we have, the more alcoholics we will have; the fewer drinkers, the fewer alcoholics. There is solid reason and urgent need for reducing the number of drinkers.

In the light of these facts, it seems irresponsible of the National Council not to assign itself a primary job of cutting down on *all* use of alcohol by everybody, not just alcoholics. As obvious first moves NCA should be pressing (1) for "hazardous to health" labels on all alcoholic beverage containers, and (2) for a total elimination of alcohol advertising in all media. Governor Shafer's commission established that the two worst drug problems in this country are alcohol and heroin, and that alcohol is much the worse of the two.

It makes less sense to advertise alcohol than to advertise heroin.

7n. An exception to the rule is this: the Secretary of Health, Education, and Welfare makes the statement that alcoholism *can* be treated successfully (Special Report to the Congress, 1971).[28] The secretary and his writers have been careful to bury it well back in the book (page 82)—which is a very strange place indeed for a claim of this magnitude—but there it is. Up ahead of it, they give reviews of a variety of current treatments which, while dealing with the physical and psychical complications, do not produce recovery from the addiction itself in any considerable numbers. So how can they get away with this "successful treatment" claim? They get away with it by the false device of including Alcoholics Anonymous among "treatments" for alcoholism. It is the old "multidisciplinary" gambit. (See page 136.) It is false because Alcoholics Anonymous is not, and on anybody's reckoning *cannot* be, a "treatment."

8n. From the *Medical Tribune,* September 8, 1968: " 'The cure rate for alcoholic doctors is far below that for other alcoholics,' a physician member of International Doctors in Alcoholics Anonymous stated at the group's annual session here. . . . 'about 75 percent of alcoholics who voluntarily come to AA for help are successful in stopping drinking,' he told *Medical Tribune.* 'But with doctors this drops to less than 50 percent'. . . . the physician estimated that in the United States there are from 5,000 to 10,000 problem drinkers in the medical profession."

9n. Howard and Martha Lewis report: "Addiction to narcotics is an occupational disease of physicians. One percent of all M.D.s, more than 2,500 physicians, are addicted to the use of drugs. Medicine's addiction rate is from 30 to 100 times greater than that of the population at large. About 15 percent of all the nation's known narcotic addicts are physicians. Moreover, Dr. Solomon Garb, of the Cornell University Medical College, has concluded that the rate of addiction among doctors is on the rise. At most major facilities for addict rehabilitation, there are generally enough physicians present as patients to constitute a sizable medical sub-community. . . . Much of the disciplinary activity of medical societies and state licensing boards deals with addicted doctors. In some areas, addiction poses the profession's largest single disciplinary problem."[16]

10n. The physical complications of alcoholism, as indicated by the U.S. Department of Health, Education, and Welfare,[27] comprise a very wide spectrum of alcohol-related illnesses, including the following. *Gastrointestinal:* esophagitis, esophageal carcinoma, gastritis, malabsorption, chronic diarrhea, pancreatitis, fatty liver, alcoholic hepatitis, cirrhosis (may lead to cancer of liver). *Cardiac:* alcoholic cardiomyopathy, beriberi. *Skin:* rosacea, telangiectasia, rhinophyma, cutaneous ulcers. *Neurologic and psychiatric:* peripheral neuropathy, convulsive disorders, alcoholic hallucinosis, delirium tremens, Wernicke's syndrome, Korsakoff's psychosis, Marchiafava's syndrome. *Muscle:* alcoholic myopathy. *Hematologic:* megaloblastic anemia. *Vitamin deficiency disease:* beriberi, pellagra, scurvy. *Metabolic:* alcoholic hypoglycemia, alcoholic hyperlipemia.

11n. Again quoting H. and M. Lewis: " 'Our biggest problem is in dealing with physicians who are mental cases.' So one state medical society has reported to the A.M.A. Medical Disciplinary Committee. From its investigation, the committee has concluded that mental illness among physicians is a widespread disciplinary problem. Among the terms used by disciplinary officials to describe the individual physicians who are currently in practice: 'mentally unbalanced,' 'severely disturbed,' 'deranged,' 'irrational,' 'alcoholic,' 'senile,' 'psychotic.' Studies show that physicians have the highest suicide rate of perhaps any occupational group, a barometer of mental illness. More than one in every fifty male doctors takes his own life, nearly two hundred times the rate for the general population."[16]

12n. Note that this definition would include most forms of psychiatry and psychoanalysis as well as the so-called eclectic methods within the meaning of psychotherapy. The key factor is the presence of the professional. The definition clearly excludes all forms of nonprofessional help—self-help, mutual help, group help—and the spiritual, religious, and psychological kinds of help that a person might receive for example in Alcoholics Anonymous, therapeutic communities, or Teen Challenge. These latter resources produce high rates of recovery, remarkably higher than psychotherapy, but evidently they do not come within the purview of the U.S. Department of Health, Education, and Welfare. The Department does give a brief reference to Alcoholics Anonymous but seems excessively nervous that AA may be a threat to the professionals. "Many physicians," the department concludes, "emphasize that, valuable and widely accessible as it is, AA should not be considered a complete form of treatment for all alcoholics, but should be viewed for most as an adjunct to and not a substitute for various forms of professional therapy."[27] Since the recovery rate in Alcoholics Anonymous is incomparably higher than that of any and all forms of medical or psychotherapeutic treatment, the people who wrote the HEW booklet in this instance seem to be more interested in protecting professional interests than in the recovery of alcoholics. A very small tail wants to wag a very big dog.

13n. Dr. Eysenck is professor of psychology in the University of London, director of the psychological laboratories at the Institute of Psychiatry, Maudsley and Bethlem Royal Hospitals. A leader in behavior and conditioning therapy, he has traveled and lectured extensively throughout the world and has spent considerable time in the United States as visiting professor at the University of Pennsylvania and the University of California. Eysenck is an outstanding figure in experimental research in the field of personality, and his interest and competence extend over a very broad area, including the testing of intelligence, selection procedures in schools and universities, vocational guidance and occupational selection, psychotherapy and its effects, national differences, racial intolerance, public opinion surveys, industrial productivity, and many others. Dr. Eysenck has been an advocate of scientific rigor in the design of psychological experiments and has been critical of much loose thinking current at present under the label of "psychology." He has demanded that psychological findings be submitted to a searching criticism and that clear distinctions be made between the proper applications of psychology where enough is known to support social action and those aspects of psychology wherein personal opinions rather than experimentally demonstrated facts seem to be involved. Eysenck is editor in chief of the journal *Behaviour Research and Therapy*, has written and/or edited a dozen books, and has written some three hundred articles in the technical journals.

14n. The Washingtonian Movement (see pp. 8–9) in mid-nineteenth century did indeed produce large numbers of recoveries from alcoholism, but it was not a treatment, for the same reasons that AA is not a treatment, and since the motive power both in the Washingtonians and in Alcoholics Anonymous is clearly acknowledged to be God, the work of one may well be said to be an extension of the work of the other. The resemblance between the two movements, both in principles and in practices, is remarkable. On important points, the operations were identical.

15n. This figure is a projection based on the actual membership totals reported by AA groups around the world, calculated according to a special survey to correct for the not inconsiderable number of nonreporting groups and the number of members who are not affiliated with any group.

16n. The Shafer Commission,[24] reporting to the president early in 1973, gave the total drinking population of the United States as 74,080,000 adults 18 years and over and 5,977,000 youths of ages 12 through 17. The combined United States total of the adult and youth drinking population is slightly more than 80 million. Of this number, the Shafer Commission finds that approximately 10 percent engages in what it calls "intensive and compulsive use" of alcohol; in other words, 10 percent of all drinkers are addicted. So that means 8 million alcoholics in the U.S.

Another critically important figure needs to be observed here: How many alcoholics, at any given time, are ready to accept help? It is well known that the vast majority are *not.* No statistics are available, but a recent survey among knowledgeable people in the field gave combined estimates as certainly not over 10 percent. Out of 8 million alcoholics, not more than 800,000 are available to be aided, influenced, or affected in any way with a view to recovery.

17n. *So Fair a House,* by Daniel Casriel, M.D.[3] *Synanon: The Tunnel Back,* by Lewis Yablonsky[29] *Synanon,* by Guy Endore[6]. Endore's book is the most recent, comprehensive, and readable of the three. Yablonsky, a sociologist, has his eye on fellow professionals and their interest in technical explanations for Synanon's success. Casriel was the first psychiatrist to become an enthusiast for Synanon. His experiences there permanently altered his therapeutic approach.

18n. It is hard to overestimate the importance of Emerson's influence on Dederich. "Trust thyself: every heart vibrates to that iron string," Emerson wrote. Dederich, in his profound Santa Barbara conversion experience, grasped at God as sheer psychic immanence, God-with-in-every-man. And he has never let go.

Emerson's essay, "Self-Reliance," is a glowing, numinous invitation to all men to seek this real Self, the inner divine presence. Once locked onto that, then, he said, "Do your thing." The phrase—Emerson's own—has swept our culture. More than half the time it is misunderstood as: do what you please—any old thing. Early on in Synanon, Dederich seemed to be working out the possibilities of this ultra-permissive reading. Later, with heavy responsibilities thrust on him for the care of hundreds and then thousands, he moved nearer to the traditional reading: God is indeed within, but we hear him imperfectly if at all. It is arrogance to assume that everything we think of is God's will. First ask, Does it satisfy all the requirements of reason in the situation?

Dederich moved Synanon steadily in its first decade toward reasonableness and a conservative sense of individual and social responsibility. But Emerson's own greatest weakness is apt to be Synanon's: a tendency to go it alone, to ignore the wisdom of tradition, and finally to imagine that strengths that come only from God are somehow the product of one's own mere personality—the classic error of subjectivism.

References

1. American Medical Association 1967. *Manual on Alcoholism.*

2. Brecher, Edward M. and the Editors of Consumer Reports 1972. *Licit and Illicit Drugs: The Consumers Union Report on Narcotics, Stimulants, Depressants, Inhalants, Hallucinogens, and Marijuana—including Caffeine, Nicotine, and Alcohol.* Boston: Little Brown and Company.

3. Casriel, D. 1963. *So Fair a House: The Story of Synanon.* Englewood Cliffs, N.J.: Prentice-Hall.

4. Chafetz, M., Cumming, E., Glasscote, R., Hammersley, D., O'Neill, F., and Plaut, T. 1967. *The Treatment of Alcoholism, A Study of Programs and Problems.* A publication of the Joint Information Service of the American Psychiatric Association and the National Association for Mental Health.

5. Cohen, S. 1969. *The Drug Dilemma.* New York: McGraw Hill.

6. Endore, G. 1968. *Synanon.* Garden City, N.Y.: Doubleday.

7. Eysenck, H. J. 1952. The Effects of Psychotherapy: An Evaluation. *J. Consult. Psychol.* 16: 319–24.

8. _____ 1960. The Effects of Psychotherapy, in *Handbook of Abnormal Psychology.* Ed. H. J. Eysenck. London: Pitmans.

9. _____ 1966. *The Effects of Psychotherapy.* New York: International Science Press.

10. _____ 1964. The Outcome Problem in Psychotherapy: A Reply. *Psychotherapy* 1: 97–100.

11. ———— 1959. Learning Theory and Behaviour Therapy. *J. Men. Sci.* 105: 61–75.

12. Hill, M. and Blane, H. 1967. Evaluation of Psychotherapy with Alcoholics. *Quart. J. Stud. Alc.* 28: 76–104.

13. Keller, M. 1970. The Great Jewish Drink Mystery. *Brit. J. Addict.* 64: 287–296.

14. Lehrman, N. S. 1961. The Potency of Psychotherapy. *The Journal of Clinical and Experimental Psychopathology and Quarterly Review of Psychiatry and Neurology* 22: 106–111.

15. Leonard, H., Epstein, L., Rosenthal, M. 1972. The Methadone Illusion. *Science* 176: 881–884.

16. Lewis, H. and M. 1970. *The Medical Offenders.* New York: Simon and Schuster.

17. Loeb, E.M. 1943. Primitive Intoxicants. *Quart. J. Stud. Alc.* 4: 387–398.

18. McDonnell, Kilian 1968. The Pentecostals and Drug Addiction. *America,* March 30.

19. McKinlay, A. P. 1953. New Light on the Question of Homeric Temperance. *Quart. J. Stud. Alc.* 14: 78–93.

20. Malan, D. H. 1963. *A Brief Study of Psychotherapy.* London: Travistock Publications.

21. Rachman, S. 1971. *The Effects of Psychotherapy.* New York: Pergamon Press.

22. Ravi Varma, L. A. 1950. Alcoholism in Ayurveda. *Quart. J. Stud. Alc.* 11: 484–491.

23. Roueché, B. 1960. *Alcohol, Its History, Folklore, Effect on the Human Body.* New York: Grove Press.

24. Sanford, W. 1953. Psychotherapy. *Am. Rev. Psychol.* 4: 317–42.

25. Shafer, R. P., Chmn. 1973. *Drug Abuse in America: Problem in Per-*

spective: The Second Report of the National Commission on Marihuana and Drug Abuse. Washington, D.C.: U.S. Government Printing Office.

26. Sorokin, P. A. 1957. *The Crisis of Our Age.* New York: Dutton.

27. U.S. Department of Health, Education, and Welfare 1967, 1972. *Alcohol and Alcoholism.*

28. U.S. Department of Health, Education, and Welfare, the Secretary 1971. *First Special Report to the U.S. Congress on Alcohol and Health.* Rockville, Maryland: U.S. Department of Health, Education, and Welfare.

29. Yablonsky, L. 1965. *Synanon: The Tunnel Back.* New York: The Macmillan Company.